The Folk-Lore Society

FOR COLLECTING AND PRINTING

RELICS OF POPULAR ANTIQUITIES, &c.

ESTABLISHED IN
THE YEAR MDCCCLXXVIII

PUBLICATIONS
OF
THE FOLK-LORE SOCIETY
[CII]

BRITISH CALENDAR CUSTOMS

ENGLAND
VOL. II: FIXED FESTIVALS
JANUARY–MAY, INCLUSIVE

BY

A. R. WRIGHT, F.S.A.
PRESIDENT OF THE FOLK-LORE SOCIETY IN 1927-1928

EDITED BY

T. E. LONES, M.A., LL.D., B.Sc.

Reprinted by permission of the
Folk-Lore Society
KRAUS REPRINT LIMITED
Nendeln/Liechtenstein
1968

Printed in Germany

Lessing-Druckerei – Wiesbaden

EDITOR'S PREFACE TO VOL. II

THIS volume continues the carrying out of the Author's chief object, viz.: the collection and utilization of first-hand records of observances of popular calendar customs, as and for the purposes mentioned in the Introduction to Volume I.

The results obtained from the separation of fixed-date from movable-date festivals, which constitute the subject-matter of Volume I, have been very satisfactory.

The most valuable parts of the Volume are the selected records, the results of extensive searches initiated by Arthur Robinson Wright, nearly half a century ago. These records, whether long or short, are followed immediately by full references to their authorities. Wherever possible, each long record has been given in one long paragraph so as to avoid any misreading of the ambit of the authority; the gain in utility outweighs the loss of literary style.

The records themselves are especially numerous and, in some cases, are given at great length, thus necessitating careful abridgment before use in the Volume. This may be exemplified by means of the records of the customs of letting-in the New Year; wassailing the apple trees in January; the Haxey custom of throwing the hood, on the Epiphany; the Plough Monday procession; the Valentine customs; the St. Mark's Eve divinations, especially the church-porch watch; the old May Fair, near Piccadilly; and the wearing of the oak on the 29th of May.

The records of the remarkable Walsall custom of distributing Moseley's Dole are fully dealt with; a detailed analysis of that old custom has been long overdue.

Most of the fixed-date customs are of an eminently popular and hilarious nature. They present less of that dignified, sometimes solemn, controlling influence of the Church which, although favouring the enjoyment of the people, viewed with displeasure any wilful neglect of its services.

The Volume gives selected records for every county and their numbers vary in a manner such as a general knowledge of English folklore would lead us to expect. Thus, the numbers suggest that Yorkshire, Devonshire, Lincolnshire, Cornwall, Norfolk, Worcestershire, Herefordshire, Derbyshire, Gloucestershire, Northumberland, Staffordshire, Suffolk, Lancashire, Northamptonshire, and Cheshire, should be placed in the higher part of the scale and that Kent, Surrey, Warwickshire, Wiltshire, Cambridgeshire, Rutland, and Essex, should be arranged in the lower part of the scale, the remaining counties being arranged in the intervening part of the scale. It should be understood that the marginal county references are necessarily incomplete and that they are not intended to be a subsidiary scheme of classification.

Attention may be conveniently directed here to a few corrections for Volume I. These are as follows :

P. 5, lines 10-11 and 23, " Budestown " should be replaced by " near Okehampton."

P. 76, line 24, " Mothersole " should be substituted for " Nethersole."

P. 79, line 7 from the foot of the page, " [*Devonshire*] " should be " [*Cornwall*]."

P. 145, 2nd line from the foot of the page, " [*Cumberland*] " should be " [*Westmorland*]."

A consolidated Index will form part of Volume III.

T. EAST LONES

CONTENTS

	PAGE
Editor's Preface to Volume II	vii
New Year's Day	1
Twelfth Night	50
Twelfth Day	78
St. Distaff's Day	91
Plough Monday	93
Straw Bear Tuesday	103
All Souls' Mallard Day	104
St. Wulfstan's Day	105
St. Agnes' Eve and Day	106
St. Paul's Eve	111
St. Paul's Day	112
January	115
St. Bride's Day	117
Candlemas	118
St. Blase's Day	130
St. Valentine's Eve and Day	136
February	157
St. David's Day	158
St. Chad's Day	160
St. Winwaloe's Day	161
St. Piran's Day	162
St. Constantine's Day	163
St. Gregory's Day	164
St. Benedict's Day	165
Lady Day	166

Contents

	PAGE
MARCH	168
ALL FOOLS' DAY	171
ST. RICHARD'S DAY	176
CUCKOOS AND THE CALENDAR	177
ST. GEORGE'S DAY	178
ST. MARK'S EVE	183
ST. MARK'S DAY	192
APRIL	194
MAY-DAY EVE	195
MAY DAY	200
2ND MAY	245
DAY OF THE INVENTION OF THE HOLY CROSS	246
8TH MAY. HELSTON FURRY DANCE	247
13TH MAY	251
14th MAY	252
ST. FRANKIN'S DAYS	253
OAK-APPLE DAY	254
MAY	271

LIST OF PLATES

I. FIG. 1. A "BUSH" BURNT ON NEW YEAR'S MORNING *facing* p. 22
   FIG. 2. A CALLENIG, OR APPLE-GIFT *facing* p. 22
II. THE KING OF THE BEAN *facing* p. 52
III. CARRYING THE "HOLLY TREE" AT BROUGH, WESTMORLAND *facing* p. 68
IV. HAXEY HOOD GAME, 1932 *facing* p. 88
V. PLOUGH JAGS, BURRINGHAM, 1934 *facing* p. 94
VI. DISTRIBUTION OF LOAVES AT WOODBRIDGE, CANDLEMAS DAY, 1937 *facing* p. 124
VII. VALENTINE Sent by the Fourth Duke of Portland to a Miss Betsy Keates, 1847 *facing* p. 142
VIII. MAY REVELS AT ICKWELL, BEDFORDSHIRE, 1936 *facing* p. 218
IX. THE PADSTOW HOBBY HORSE, WITH THE TEAZER *facing* p. 232
X. THE MINEHEAD HOBBY HORSE *facing* p. 236

FIXED-DATE FESTIVALS

New Year's Day
1st January

In olden times, the advent of a new year was signalized by the ringing of church bells and by dancing, singing, music, horn-blowing, and many other merry proceedings in the streets. Many people, however, awaited and welcomed the advent of a new year in their homes, where the custom of letting-in the new year and exchanging new year's greetings was celebrated. For centuries, this was the procedure and, taken as a whole, it constituted a popular custom which retained a permanence of form and a continuity of observance, year by year.

In the eighteenth century, the " watch meeting," a monthly midnight service, was initiated by the Wesleyan Methodists and, later, the name " watch-night service " was given to the impressive service held in order to await and welcome the advent of a new year. The bell-ringing so closely associated with the service, as conducted by the Church, has long excited public interest, year by year, and will be considered later ; see p. 18.

During recent years, there has been an increasing tendency for people not to celebrate the new year's custom in their own homes but to go to hotels, boarding-houses, and other places of refreshment and amusement, in seaside and inland towns, in order to take part in the new year's festivities of those places.

Taking a general view, the custom of celebrating the advent of a new year presents a complex combination of ceremonies beginning late on old year's night and terminating after the last of the new year's merry peals. The essential part, however, of the celebration of the advent of a new year is performed during the few minutes, solemn and impressive, when the old year is tolled out and the hour of midnight is struck.

LETTING-IN THE NEW YEAR

[*Durham, etc.*] In the old, homely form of this custom, no inmate of the house should leave it, after midnight of the last day of the old year, until the new year has been let-in by a man or boy who visits the house for that purpose. This man or boy is called a " first-foot " and, in some counties, *e.g.* Durham and Yorkshire, a " lucky bird."

[*Gloucestershire, etc.*] Letting-in a new year is a northern rather than a southern custom, but forms of it, less ceremonial than the full-dress northern custom, used to be celebrated generally, in Gloucestershire, Herefordshire, Leicestershire, Monmouthshire, Norfolk, Somerset, Staffordshire, Warwickshire, and Worcestershire. Further, a belief that the characteristics of the first person to enter or call at a house, on new year's morning, influenced the luck of the household during the ensuing twelve months, was widespread and extended to the south of England.

[*Yorkshire, etc.*] There were marked variations in the methods of celebrating the custom, especially in respect of the complexion, dark or light, of the first-foot. Richmond, for instance, preferred a dark first-foot and Bradford a light one; Marshland preferred a light and most of the rest of Lincolnshire a dark first-foot; Blackburn favoured a dark and Preston a light first-foot.

THE FULL-DRESS NORTHERN CUSTOM

[*Cheshire, etc.*] The letting-in custom, as it was practised in many parts of the north of England, Cheshire, and Derbyshire, presented special features. The first-foot was dark-complexioned, preferably tall and black-haired; if he squinted or was flat-footed, or if his eyebrows met, he was not favoured. It was customary for the first-foot to set out with bread, whisky, and some combustible substance, usually coal. He knocked at the door of the house he had decided to visit and was admitted. Silence was maintained by all while he entered and placed the coal or other combustible substance on the fire and the bread on the table. Then wine and cake were given to him, whereupon he wished all present a happy new year.

COUNTY RECORDS OF THE CUSTOM

The following records relating to the observance of the letting-in custom show how events, even the most trivial, have been believed to affect the fortunes, good and bad, of the new year, or to foreshadow their nature.

[*Cheshire*] In Cheshire, a dark-complexioned person was encouraged to act as first-foot, for it was believed that a light-complexioned or red-haired one would bring ill-luck, others say death, during the year.—Good Luck and Bad, Singular Village Customs in Cheshire, by Delta. (*Chester Courant, n.d.*)

In this record, " person " is probably intended to refer to a man or boy; in Cheshire, as in the County of Stafford and the Teme Valley counties, Herefordshire, Shropshire, and Worcestershire, the belief that a female first-foot was unlucky, was very strong.

[*Cornwall, etc.*] In rural districts, a female is considered to be unlucky as a first-foot. I knew a lady who sent a cabman before her into her house, after promising him a glass of whisky. To guard against the possibility of a woman being the first-foot, boys were encouraged to sand the door-steps and passages of a house early on new year's day. (*Popular Romances of the West of England*, Robert Hunt, 1881, p. 382.)

[*Cumberland*] In Cumberland, the custom of first-footing by dark men has declined a good deal in popularity, except at Carlisle and in parts of the county near the Scottish border. (*Folk-Lore*, vol. 40, 1929, p. 283.)

[*Derbyshire*] At Castleton and Bradwell, a man or boy having black or, at least, dark hair takes in the new year directly after midnight. A certain parish clerk of Castleton had jet-black hair and used to take-in the new year at some houses in the parish. Dark-haired boys, it is said, used to obtain a great deal of money for taking-in the new year. It is customary to give the first-foot cake and wine. Black or dark hair is obligatory in the High Peak but the term " first-foot " is not known there. Miss Barber of Castleton, aged 76, said that the black-haired man ought to be a stranger and not a member of the family visited. At Bradwell, they have what they call " lucky bags," into which they put things for good luck. (*Memorials of Old Derbyshire*, J. Charles Cox, Editor, 1907, p. 365.)

[*Durham*] Many of the customs and superstitions observed in the county of Durham are sinking into disuse, though there are some which still retain their ground. It is the practice for friends to visit each others' houses, on a new year's day, in the morning, to be the first-foot and to wish a happy new year, and the influence of this first visitor is often believed to affect the nature of the events of the succeeding twelve months. It is considered to be very unlucky for a female to be a first-foot, or for any person to enter a house, on such an occasion, without taking in bread or spirits. (*An Historical, etc., View of the County Palatine of Durham*, E. Mackenzie and M. Ross, 2 vols., vol. 1, Newcastle-upon-Tyne, 1834, p. cxviii.)

The landlady of the Three Tuns, at Durham, always told my brother, on 31st December, that if he was going out he was to come in before midnight as he was far too fair in complexion and hair to be her first-foot. A man with black hair was the luckiest first-foot and he should bring in a piece of coal. My brother had to go to Durham every year, on 31st December, to be ready for the Sessions next morning. (F. M. Marwood, 1902.)

A relative who spent the new year's days of 1872, 1873 and 1874 at Croxdale, County Durham, tells me that he was employed on each occasion to act as first-foot in the house. He was sent out of the house, late on new year's eve, to return just after midnight and perform the ceremony. The first-foot must bring in a piece of coal, a piece of iron, and a bottle of whisky. He gives everyone a glass of whisky and every woman a kiss.—C. S. Burne. (*Folk-Lore Journal*, vol. 3, 1885, p. 282.)

" Lucky bird " is the first man or boy who enters a house, on new year's morning. He must be dark or, at least, not red-haired and must leave something behind him.—Gainford. (*Folk-Lore*, vol. 20, 1909, p. 73.)

[*Gloucestershire*] The first-foot, either on Christmas or New Year's Day, should be a man, for luck's sake.—St. Briavels. (*Folk-Lore*, vol. 13, 1902, p. 174.)

At Minchinhampton, it was considered lucky for the first person who came to the door, on 1st January, to be dark-haired. Either sex was equally lucky. I think this is now obsolete. (Miss J. B. Partridge.) [1]

My gardener tells me that, as a boy, he frequently earned twelve to fourteen shillings on a new year's morning, by going as a first-foot. It was done early in the morning. The practice was to go in at one door, wish the inmates of the house a happy new year, and then go out of the house by another door, if there was one. He says that he never heard of any preference, in this part of the world, for a dark or a light man.—E. Sidney Hartland, Gloucester. (*Folk-Lore*, vol. 7, 1896, p. 90.)

The door is opened, at midnight, to let-in the new year and hear the bells, if possible. A man, preferably a dark one, is encouraged to be the first to step over the threshold and wish all a happy new year. Some people would give a man a glass of beer, or pence, to step over the threshold. (Emily Hodges, Chedworth.)

[*Herefordshire*] As the clock struck twelve, it was customary to open the back door to let the old year out and then the front door was opened to let-in the new year, at Ledbury. A funeral service [2] was held on the old year, or " Old Tom," at Bromyard. It was and is considered very unlucky for a woman to enter a house first on new year's day and it has been said that, on new year's day, a woman would not enter a house without first inquiring whether a man had been there that day. (*The Folk-Lore of Herefordshire*, Ella Mary Leather, Hereford, 1912, p. 90.)

[*Hertfordshire*] As usual, a number of Berkhamsted residents welcomed the new year by forming a ring in the High Street and singing Auld Lang Syne, after midnight had been tolled. Several Berkhamsted residents have not missed this informal ceremony since childhood. New year's greetings are exchanged

[1] Available evidence suggests that the date of this record was earlier than 1916.

[2] This was a jovial performance, chiefly by youths. On the last night of the year, it was customary, in Guernsey, for boys to have a mock funeral of a grotesque figure representing *Le vieux bout de l'an*. (*Guernsey Folk Lore*, Sir E. MacCulloch, 1903, p. 36.)

under the shelter of the famous yew tree in the churchyard. This tree is believed to be almost as old as the church itself, viz. 715 years. (*West Herts and Watford Observer*, Friday, 8th January, 1937, p. 10, *g*.)

[*Lancashire*] In Blackburn, Burnley, and other places in Lancashire, it was generally believed that a man or boy with black or dark hair should let-in the new year and that, if let-in by one of light complexion and especially one with red hair, bad luck for inmates of the house would follow. The record next given, however, shows that a light-complexioned man or boy was sometimes encouraged to act as a first-foot.

For years past, an old lady, a friend of mine, has regularly reminded me to pay her an early visit, on new year's day; in short, to be her first caller and to let-in the new year. I have done this for years, except on one occasion. When I, who am of a fair complexion, have been her first visitor, she has enjoyed happy and prosperous years but, on the occasion I missed, some dark-complexioned, black-haired gentleman called and sickness, trouble, and commercial disasters followed.—Prestonensis. (*N. and Q.* ii, 2, 1856, pp. 325-6.)

A friend of mine, a professional man, asked me if I, being dark, would bring him in the new year, two or three years ago. At that time, I was not acquainted with the custom, having lately removed from Derbyshire to Lancashire but, after having the custom explained to me, I promised to comply with my friend's wish. On new year's eve, I had supper at my friend's house, at his request, and spent a pleasant evening, until near midnight, when I went out of the house and then the door was securely fastened. When the church bells began to ring-in the new year, I knocked at the door and was asked from within, "Who's there?" I gave a satisfactory reply, was admitted, and let-in the new year. During the past year, my friend was informed of a custom of taking in a loaf or a piece of bread as a symbol of plenty and so, at his request, the next year was let-in with this additional ceremony but small biscuits were used instead of bread. This same friend, who is light complexioned, has told me the results of letting-in a new year for his sister. The consequence was, he said, that his sister and her husband moved, shortly afterwards, from Lancashire into Cumberland, thence to Westmorland, Ireland, and Yorkshire and, finally, to Blackburn. From there they have not moved since, because they have taken care always to get a dark-complexioned man to let-in the new year.—Ben Bryan, Blackburn. (*Long Ago, A Journal of Popular Antiquities*, Alex. Andrews, Editor, vol. 1, 1873, pp. 42-4.)

Should a dark-complexioned person be the first to enter a house on new year's morning, the household looked forward with confidence to a prosperous new year but, if the first to enter happened to be light complexioned, more especially if he had red hair, the omen was considered to be bad. (*History of the Fylde of Lancashire*, John Porter, Fleetwood and Blackpool, 1876, p. 108.) The person referred to above would be a man or boy, not a female.

My sister and I were staying with relations in Lancashire, on New Year's Day, 1900, and about 5 a.m. a heavy step came up into the upper hall, off which the bedrooms opened, and a man's voice called out, " Good New Year to you ! " We found that this was a very old Lancashire custom, called " First foot in the house." The man who entered the house we were in has been the first to enter it for eleven years and he always gets ten shillings in gold. He must be a man with dark hair and not flat feet and he must come in at the hall door, go up through the halls and call out " Good New Year to you ! " three times, and go out at the back door.—E. Skeffington Thompson. (*Folk-Lore*, vol. ii, 1900, p. 220.)

[*Leicestershire*] In Leicestershire, it is believed that, if the first-foot is a dark man, good luck will follow. Mrs. Billson, a native of the Bagworth district, said that she remembered vividly her mother and grandmother preventing anyone from crossing the threshold, until a dark man had entered the house. She added, " We reckoned this back as far as 130 years."—Miss S. A. Squires. (*County F.L.*, vol. 1 (3), *Leicestershire and Rutland*, Charles James Billson, 1895, p. 70.)

[*Lincolnshire*] In many parts of Lincolnshire, the new year was let-in by a dark-complexioned man and it was considered to be unlucky for a light-complexioned man or for any woman to be a first-foot. In Marshland, there were many who preferred to have the new year let-in by a light-complexioned man. Great care was taken to insure that something green and not dead should be taken into the house, soon after the advent of the new year and before anything had been taken out. (*County F.L.*, vol. 5, *Lincolnshire*, Mrs. Gutch and Mabel Peacock, 1908, pp. 168-9; *Bygone Lincolnshire*, William Andrews, Editor, 2 vols., vol. 2, Hull, 1891, p. 94.)

An old farmer and his niece always took care to be the first to leave the house on new year's day and return with an egg, a flower, or a piece of holly. (*The Antiquary*, vol. 14, 1886, p. 12.)

There is still [1899] many a house in Marshland where much is thought of the first foot which crosses the threshold, on a new year's morning, and I have often thought it an unconscious tribute from the conquered race to their fair-haired Norse conquerors, that the first-foot must be a light-haired, fair-complexioned man. First-foot must bring something in with him and, on no account, may anything be taken out of the house till something has been brought in, for the popular saying is: "Take out, then take in, bad luck will begin; Take in, then take out, good luck comes about."—The Rev. R. M. Heanley in a Paper entitled: "The Vikings: Traces of their Folk-Lore in Marshland." (*The Saga Book of the Viking Club*, vol. 3, 1902, p. 41.)

[*Isle of Man*] On New Year's Day, in the Isle of Man, an old custom, called the Quaaltagh, was observed. In almost every parish in the Island, a party of young men used to go from house to house, singing a song whose words expressed a wish for a happy new year to everyone. The young men were invited in and were given the best that the house could provide. One of them, of dark complexion, entered the house first. Two lines of the song, given as they are translated from the Manx, by Joseph Train, are the following:

> " May they of potatoes and herrings have plenty,
> With butter and cheese and each other dainty."

The actors do not dress up like the mummers of England nor the guisards of Scotland. (*An Historical and Statistical Account of the Isle of Man*, Joseph Train, 2 vols., vol. 1, Douglas, 1845, pp. 114-5.)

[*Norfolk*] On the last day of the old year, my landlady's husband goes out at a quarter to twelve and then comes home to let-in the new year. Nobody but the husband must let it in. They were angry when I called it a superstition. Once, my landlady allowed some friend in first and all that year nothing save bad luck and sickness came to that house.—Charles Roper on Witchcraft Superstition in Norfolk. (*Harper's Monthly Magazine* for October, 1893, vol. 26, European edition, p. 793.)

In other counties, Staffordshire and Warwickshire are examples, the new year was let-in sometimes in a manner similar to that described above for Norfolk.

In Norfolk, it is lucky to see a man or a boy for the first person on new year's day. (Miss Matthews' Oral Collection, *n.d.*)

[*Northumberland, etc.*] In the North, much importance is attached to the first-foot that crosses the threshold. That of a fair man is luckier than that of a dark man,[1] but a woman's is very unlucky. In some districts, special weight is attached to the first-foot being a person with a high instep, a foot that " water runs under." A flat-footed person would bring great ill-luck for the coming year. (*Notes on the Folk-Lore of the Northern Counties of England and the Borders*, William Henderson, 1879, p. 74.)

From New Year's Eve until the following morning, at Berwick-upon-Tweed, bands of youths wander all night about the streets and hurry to their friends' houses in order to be what they term the " first-foot." A woman is considered to be unlucky as a first-foot. An old carter once admitted, as his first-foot, a woman who squinted very much and, after entering, asked to be allowed to light her pipe. In the following April he broke his arm. To go to a house empty-handed, as a first-foot, is considered to be unlucky. The first-foots are regaled with cake, cheese, and spirits. If possible, the house door is kept closed until some friend or acquaintance arrives with a bottle of Glenlivet. (*The*

[1] In Newcastle, a dark-complexioned man was generally preferred.

History of Berwick-upon-Tweed, Frederick Sheldon, Edinburgh, 1849, pp. 335-6.) Glenlivet is a brand of whisky, popular in the West Midlands in the second half of the nineteenth century.

I have always heard that a flat-footed person was unlucky. My mother's family, all living in Belford, believe this; they prefer the first-foot to be dark, but if a woman then she should be fair, though at the best a woman was not thought to bring good luck. The first-foot had to carry something into the house, such as a loaf or a piece of coal.—Miss L., Belford. (*County F.L.*, vol. 4, *Northumberland*, M. C. Balfour and Northcote W. Thomas, 1904, p. 64.)

On new year's day, to meet, as first-foot, a person whose eyebrows met, was considered unlucky. (*Denham Tracts*, vol. 2, 1895, p. 340.)

At Stamfordham, in Northumberland, the first-foot must be a bachelor. He generally brings in a shovelful of coals, but whisky is coming into fashion as an offering. One inhabitant of the village was considered to be a lucky first-foot and always went as such to the blacksmith's house hard by. One year, by accident, some one else was first-foot. This was considered an ill omen and, during the next hay harvest, the house was broken into and half a sovereign stolen. (*Notes on the Folk-Lore of the Northern Counties of England and the Borders*, William Henderson, 1879, p. 74.)

[*Nottinghamshire*] It was customary, in Nottinghamshire, to sit up on old year's night till the church clock struck at midnight, when only a dark-complexioned first-foot was admitted. A gold piece put out near the door and taken in, in the morning, was believed to be a sure sign that the family would not want money during the year. (*Nottinghamshire Facts and Fictions*, collected and edited by John Potter Briscoe, Principal Librarian, Nottingham Free Library, 1876, p. 19.)

[*Shropshire*] In the Stretton Valley, it is unlucky if a woman goes to a house before noon on a new year's day, no matter how many men may have preceded her. A dark-haired man is generally believed to be the most lucky first visitor. About Clun, if a woman were to call at a house on new year's day without having ascertained that some man had been there before her, she would be thought to have a spite against the inmates. To provide against such a mischance, old-fashioned people engage some man or boy to pay them an early visit on new year's day. About Clun, old-fashioned families used to sit up till midnight and then let a man come in at the back door and go out at the front door, to bring in the new year, wishing a happy one to all the inmates. Members of an old-fashioned family, at Shrewsbury, are equally careful that the first comer shall enter at the front door and go out at the back. The first who comes in is rewarded with a silver coin, a mince-pie, and mulled elderberry wine; the next comer gets a copper coin, and the others have mulled beer. " This was always done at home," writes the young daughter of a farmer, in 1878. It seems that parties of young men are in the habit of going about on purpose to offer their good wishes in this way.

Edgmond boys go in parties round the village and neighbourhood, on new year's day (or used to do so), with the cry, shrilly recited on two notes, " Please to let the new year in, please to let the new year in." Sometimes they only shouted, " We wish you a merry Christmas and a happy New Year," but in any case they expected coppers.

At Burford, Church Stretton, and Worthen, the boys sing:

" I wish you a merry Christmas, a happy New Year,
A pocket full of money and a cellar full of beer;
A good fat pig to last you all the year.
Please to give me a new year's gift."

An old man who, more than forty years ago, used to let the new year in at a farm-house, at Longnor, always entered without knocking or speaking and silently stirred the fire, before he offered any greeting to the family. This procedure, very suggestive of midwinter fire-worship, is the only trace which I have anywhere met with of any ceremony in bringing in the new year, though the custom, under one name or another, First-foot or Lucky bird, is observed throughout the northern counties of

England, in Scotland, and also in Pembrokeshire. (*Shropshire Folk-Lore,* Charlotte Sophia Burne, 1883, pp. 314-7.)

The first-foot must be a dark man or boy. A light- or sandy-haired person is considered unlucky as a first-foot. (MS. note, *n.d.*, R. F. T., Wellington, Shropshire.)

[*Somerset*] In Somerset, the first-foot must be a married man and the doors must not be opened till he has come in. (Mrs. Braine, from C. T. MS. note, *n.d.*)

[*Staffordshire*] The custom of letting-in a new year, in South Staffordshire, was popular until about the year 1880. Every new year's morning, during the period 1850 to 1880, commencing about 6 a.m., parties of boys went from house to house in their own districts. They sang a few short carols and then called out:

" Please let the new year in,
The old year out, the new year in."

In many cases, they sang lines exactly like those sung at Burford, Church Stretton, and Worthen, see p. 11, except that the two lines given above were sometimes substituted for the fourth line of the Shropshire version. The boys were occasionally invited to enter the house visited. A female was not at all encouraged to let-in a new year, the term " first-foot " was rarely used, and no discrimination was made in respect of complexion, whether dark or light. In north Staffordshire, the custom of letting-in a new year was celebrated with more ceremony than in the south of the county, a dark-complexioned man being generally preferred as a first-foot. Still, the record given below, purporting to be for Eccleshall, which is about six miles farther north than Stafford, would pass without comment, if it were a record of the custom as celebrated in the south of the county.

Joseph Austin, Eccleshall, born in 1875, used to go with other boys to let-in the new year. He never heard the question of complexion mentioned; he himself is dark to swarthiness.—22nd March, 1892. (*Folk-Lore,* vol. 20, 1909, p. 222.)

It has always been our custom to have the sweep, he being the darkest man obtainable, to let-in the new year. After the hall clock has struck twelve, he comes in at the front door, shakes hands with us all, wishing us a happy new year, and is taken out at the back door. He always brings his brush with him and wears a top hat. This is at Stafford. (MS. note, Nora R. Wright.) See also p. 14 for an account of an old Teme Valley custom.

New year's day is ushered in with the merry pealing of bells, whilst in some houses the wassail bowl is still passed round; each one drinking must express some seasonable sentiment. The first person to enter the house, the first-foot, must be a male and dark; should a female or a male with light or red hair be a first-foot, ill-luck will follow.—Stone, Staffordshire. (*Notes on the Folk-Lore of North Staffordshire*, [W.] Wells Bladen . . . p. 17.)

[*Suffolk*] It is thought lucky, on first going out on a new year's day, to meet a big man, a man big in height and breadth, a well-proportioned man. (*The East Anglian, etc.*, vol. 4, Lowestoft, 1869, pp. 113-4.)

[*Westmorland*] Squint-eyed and red-haired persons must not enter the house, on new year's day, or a year of bad luck will follow.—Mr. T. Thompson. (*The Kendalian, n.d.*)

[*Worcestershire*] The custom of letting-in a new year is observed, in Worcestershire, on a very small scale compared with the frequency of its observance during the nineteenth century. Seventy years ago, boys and men, singly or in groups, used to visit private houses and farms where it was likely that money, mince-pies, and apples would be obtained for letting-in the new year. It was not customary to take anything into the house visited and no question was raised about the complexion of the first-foot, whether dark or light, but no woman was encouraged to act as a first-foot. In these respects, the custom was like that of the county of Stafford, south of Lichfield. The custom was celebrated in different ways in different parts of the county of Worcester, but it was usual for a boy or man to call at a house, early on new year's morning, sing a carol, and knock at the door, which the householder would open and, at the same time, exchange friendly greetings with his visitor; in some cases, he directed him through his premises, entering at the front door and leaving by the back door, or *vice versa*. At Evesham, Kidderminster, Stourbridge, and Dudley, boys obtained substantial sums of money for letting-in the new year and, in Dudley, the boys often booked orders the day before, from householders, for letting-in the new year.

On New Year's Day, 1855, a farmer was particularly careful to direct a boy throughout his premises,[1] entering at the back door and leaving by the front door. (*Pictures of Nature in the Silurian Region around the Malvern Hills, etc.*, Edwin Lees, Malvern, 1856, pp. 294-5.)

On New Year's Day, 1857, at a farm-house in the county,[2] the inmates rose before it was light to admit the first carol-singer and conduct him all through the house, entering at the front door and leaving by the back door.—Cuthbert Bede. (*N. and Q.*, ii, 3, 1857, p. 343.)

[*Worcestershire, etc.*] I may mention that letting-in the new year is still considered unlucky in most of the villages in the Teme Valley, Worcestershire and Herefordshire, unless it be accomplished by a man or boy. In the old climbing-boy days, chimneys in that district used to be swept on new year's morning so that one of the right sex should be the first to enter. The young urchins of the neighbourhood went the round of the houses before daylight, singing songs, when one of their number would be admitted into the kitchen for good luck all the year. This is still practised and, at some of the farm-houses, should washing-day chance to fall on new year's day, it is either put off or, to make sure before the women come, the waggoner's lad is called up early so that he may be let out and let in again. I lived in that district for many years and the boys of the village used to come to me overnight to know beforehand if I should want the new year let-in. I do not think the custom is confined to that locality.—S. A. (Unnamed and undated newspaper cutting in Mr. T. F. Thistleton Dyer's own copy of his *British Popular Customs*, 1876.)

[*Yorkshire*] In Yorkshire, it is considered to be very lucky for a

[1] Probably near Malvern or Worcester.
[2] Probably near Leigh, four miles west of Worcester.

New Year's Day

dark man to be the first-foot in the new year. After the clock strikes twelve, any dark man knocks and enters a house, carrying with him a bunch of holly and a lump of coal, for good luck and plenty throughout the year. He places the coal on any fire there may still be burning and then wishes every one a happy New Year. He is then given silver, wine, cheese, and cake for refreshment. (MS. note signed " Yorkshire Maid of Miss Canziani.")

Near Sheffield, the man who lets in the new year carries in a mince-pie, a piece of coal, and whisky, to insure good luck to the household. (*Memorials of Old Derbyshire*, J. Charles Cox, Editor, 1907, p. 365, footnote.)

The first person who entered a house on the first day of January, not being a member of that household, was always supposed to have taken in the new year. A person with black hair was always considered lucky, but woe to the one with red hair who presumed to let-in the new year. (Papers, Reports, etc., read before *The Halifax Antiquarian Society*, 1904-5, Halifax, 1905, p. 3.)

The man or boy who is the first to enter a house for the purpose of letting-in a new year, generally called a first-foot, is also called a " lucky bird," in the West Riding. If he be fair, especially if he has red hair, he is supposed to bring luck ; if he be dark, it is unlucky. This was so much observed in the Bradford and Huddersfield district that a red-haired man was sometimes hired to come round. On the other hand, a record for the North Riding (Easingwold) states that John White, a carrier, when a boy, used to go round as a lucky bird ; his hair was a dark brown. He started as early as 3 a.m. and received a shilling, a sixpence, or not less than a fourpenny piece, at each house. He was not allowed in the house, unless he carried a piece of holly or something else that was green. (*Folk-Lore*, vol. 5, 1894, p. 341.)

In the North Riding, the advent of the new year is made known by the ringing of the church bells and the loud knocking at your door by the first-foot or lucky bird. This happens immediately on the last stroke of twelve. The first-foot to cross your threshold, for none must go out until the first-foot has come in, must be a man or boy with dark hair. Such only can bring luck to the household, for should he have light hair he could only bring dire and disastrous results. (*County F.L.*, vol. 2, *North Riding of Yorkshire, York, and the Ainsty*, Mrs. Gutch, 1901, p. 230.)

In East Yorkshire, great importance is attached to the person who enters the house first in the new year, the first-foot or lucky bird. This person must be dark and a male. (*Folk-Lore of East Yorkshire*, John Nicholson, Driffield, 1890, p. 20.)

The first-foot, who must be a dark man, brings a bottle of whisky and a piece of coal. He puts the coal on the fire; then you will have plenty of fuel throughout the year. The mistress of the house opens the door to him.—Richmond, Yorkshire. (Miss J. B. Partridge. From Mrs. Day, born and bred in Swaledale. MS. note, *n.d.* but probably not later than 1916.)

A note in *Folk-Lore*, vol. 2, 1900, p. 220, states that the Rev. E. W. Clarke records that, at Hull, the first-foot should have dark hair and a high instep.

LONDON'S NEW YEAR CELEBRATIONS

[*London, etc.*] During recent years, on New Year's Eve, people have assembled, in numbers increasing year by year, on the steps of St. Paul's. The numbers were small originally and consisted mainly of Scots in London, bent on seeing the old year out in the Scottish manner. The assembly having become so large and mixed, the Dean and Chapter decided to arrange for organized community singing, on New Year's Eve, 1935. (*The Times*, 18th November, 1935, p. 15, *d*.)

Later, a communication by the Dean to *The Times* stated that the community singing, conducted from the steps of the Western Entrance, would continue until 11.45 p.m., when the service in the Cathedral would begin and be amplified to the assembly outside and broadcast throughout the country.—W. R. Matthews, Dean of St. Paul's. (*The Times*, 19th November, 1935, p. 15, *d*.)

In London, therefore, the advent of the New Year, 1936, was awaited and welcomed in a manner never to be forgotten. The top of the dome of St. Paul's was illuminated and the cross surmounting it stood isolated against a starless sky. Within the porch, the giant Christmas trees still stood covered with coloured lights. When community singing began, at about 11.15 p.m., all available space before the west front had been occupied by many thousands of people. The lower parts of Ludgate Hill were occupied by revellers who amused themselves by singing, dancing, and horn-blowing. The community singing, directed by Canon Sheppard, was accompanied by the Wood Green Excelsior Band, and, at about 11.45 p.m., the assembly sang " Abide with me." An address by the Dean followed and, some minutes later, the first stroke of midnight was heard. On the last stroke of midnight the crowd started to sing " Auld Lang Syne " and soon afterwards began to move homewards. Another year had passed and the community singing had been a success. (*The Times*, 1st January, 1936, p. 12, *f*.)

Listeners-in were entertained by a broadcast entitled " Chimes at Midnight," which enabled them to form mental pictures of the New Year's activities of many cities and towns. Later, they listened-in to the singing and music of St. Paul's and soon after midnight to the ringing of the bells of Berwick-upon-Tweed, Edinburgh, and other places.

Concurrently with the ceremonies at St. Paul's, there were festivities at the theatres, hotels, inns, and restaurants, and revels in the streets. The internal decorations for Christmas were still to be seen at many places of entertainment and refreshment, so that there was a bright display of colour and artistic effect for the New Year. Many of the decorations recalled the pretty decorations of the 'seventies and 'eighties but with the important difference that up-to-date electric bulbs were used instead of candles and gas. There were many novelties at the hotels and theatres; at the Savoy Hotel, Strand, a very large suspended hour-glass was used to indicate the approach and advent of the New Year.

In London, the year 1937 dawned amid the cheers and laughter of jostling thousands in Piccadilly, Shaftesbury Avenue, and St. Paul's Churchyard. It is estimated that not less than 100,000 people rallied to the inducements offered by hotel and restaurant proprietors to see the New Year in at their establishments. In the streets, the crowds were very large, and enterprising street sellers did a brisk trade in whistles, squeakers, masks, balloons, and paper hats. The crowds, which had been singing, cheering, and dancing and, incidentally, showing that the old phrase, " A happy New Year " has not yet been forgotten, joined heartily in " Auld Lang Syne," as midnight struck. At St. Paul's, the usual watch-night service was held but last year's successful experiment of organized community singing was not repeated; Canon Sheppard, who directed the singing last year, was ill at Cannes. The assembled thousands, however, took part in community singing of their own. (*The Times*, 1st January, 1937. p. 11, *c*.)

CHURCH-BELL RINGING CUSTOMS

[*Staffordshire*] The proceedings for bidding farewell to the old and welcoming the new year vary at different churches. Usually, the old year is tolled out by a muffled peal, the leather or other caps being removed from the bell clappers, a few minutes before midnight, in readiness for the ringing-in of the new year. In some cases, the old year is tolled out slowly by unmuffled bells. This slow tolling favours the production of an echo, rendering the tolling more impressive. An echo of this kind could be heard, about sixty years ago, in the Sedgley part of the Silurian ridge extending from Dudley towards Wolverhampton. At one church, probably Christ Church, Coseley, the bells were tolled once in succession; this was followed by a rather long pause when, from another direction, came a distinct echo giving the impression of a solemn muffled peal from another church; then the operations were repeated.

NEW YEAR'S RINGING RECORDS

[*Bedfordshire*] The old year is rung out and the new year rung in at Arlesey, Blunham, Cardington, Leighton Buzzard, Woburn, and other places in Bedfordshire. At Meppershall, a muffled peal is rung for half an hour, ceasing a few minutes before twelve o'clock to allow removal of the mufflers. At midnight the number twelve is struck on the tenor bell and then an open peal is

New Year's Day

rung for half an hour. (*The Church Bells of Bedfordshire*, Thomas North, Leek, 1883, p. 109).

In the Parish of Henlow, the method is to muffle the bells, leaving one side of the tenor clapper uncovered. The muffled peal is then rung for a short time before midnight, the half-muffled tenor giving the effect of a tolling of the passing bell. Just before twelve o'clock the mufflers are removed while the tenor continues to toll slowly. Then, as midnight finishes striking, all the bells ring-in the new year.—The Rev. J. G. Williams, Henlow. (*The Times*, 2nd January, 1936, p. 6, *e*.)

[*Buckinghamshire*] At the Church of St. Peter and St. Paul, Wingrave, the New Year, 1937, was rung-in. (*The Bucks Herald*, 8th January, 1937, p. 4, *g*.)

[*Derbyshire*] At Chapel-en-le-Frith, where bell-ringing customs were well kept up, it was and may still be customary to ring the old year out and ring the new one in.

[*Devonshire*] At All Saints' Church, East Budleigh, each bell clapper has one of its sides muffled, so that a subdued tone alternates with a full one, during the peal, and thus the old year is rung out; then, on the advent of the new year, the mufflers having been removed, a full peal is rung. (*Trans. Devon. Assoc.*, vol. 24, Plymouth, 1892, p. 301.)

At Honiton Clist, the old year is rung out by a muffled peal and the new year welcomed by an open one. (*English Bells and Bell Lore*, Thomas North, Leek, 1888, pp. 144-5.)

[*Essex*] At Rayleigh Parish Church, a half-muffled peal was rung in the evening, for forty-five minutes, to mark the approaching end of the year 1936, and, at midnight, the advent of the year 1937 was welcomed by a period of change-ringing on the bells. The bells of St. Clement's Church, Leigh, and those of St. Mary's Parish Church, at Langdon Hills, contrary to past practice, were silent when the New Year, 1937, arrived. (*The Southend Standard*, 7th January, 1937, p. 19, *b*, and p. 13, *g*.)

[*Hertfordshire*] At the Church of St. Paul, Hoddesdon, and the Church of St. Peter and St. Paul, Kimpton, the advent of the year 1937 was welcomed by open peals. (*The Hertfordshire Mercury*, 8th January, 1937, p. 15, *c*, and p. 7, *e*.)

The year 1937 was rung-in at the Church of St. Nicholas, Harpenden. (*The Herts Advertiser*, 8th January, 1937, p. 6, *a*.)

With bells half-muffled, at St. Lawrence's Church, Abbots Langley, the Old Year 1936 was bidden farewell, and the year 1937 was welcomed by a merry peal. At St. Mary's, the Parish Church of Rickmansworth, the year 1936 was rung out by a muffled peal and the year 1937 was welcomed by a full peal. (*The West Herts and Watford Observer*, 8th January, 1937, p. 18, *g*, and p. 5, *d*.)

Much Hadham, Abbots Langley, and Kings Langley have observed church-bell ringing customs for many years and, at St. Paul's, Langleybury, near Kings Langley, the old year has been tolled out for many years and the new year welcomed by open peals.

[*Lincolnshire*] In the Churchwardens' Accounts of Kirton-in-Lindsey is the record :

" 1632. Item to the ringing of the new year's day morninge ... 12d." (*A Book about Bells*, Rev. George S. Tyack, [1898], p. 174.)

Ringing the old year out and the new year in is heard in many towns and villages in Lincolnshire and the ringing is very varied. At Hollbeach All Saints', at midnight, the bells are fired, three times three. At Stainby and Waltham, the old year is rung out by a muffled peal. At South Kelsey, the new year's peal is rung at 5 a.m., on new year's day. (*English Bells and Bell Lore*, Thomas North, Leek, 1888, pp. 144-5.)

[*Northamptonshire*] At St. Sepulchre's Church, Northampton, and at Weston Favell, the old year is rung out by a muffled peal and the new year rung in by a merry, open peal. (*The Church Bells of Northamptonshire*, Thomas North, Leicester, 1878, p. 150.)

[*Rutland*] The new year's ringing-in ceremony is performed at Oakham, Langham, and other places in Rutland. The custom is a very old one. (*The Church Bells of Rutland*, Thomas North, Leicester, 1880, p. 104.)

[*Yorkshire*] On New Year's Eve, the bells ring merrily until near midnight, when a muffled peal is rung. The silence is broken by the striking of 12 midnight, eagerly listened for at open windows and doors and in the streets. When the last stroke of the hour is over, the bells ring so merrily that the old church tower rocks again. (*Folk-Lore of East Yorkshire*, John Nicholson, Driffield, 1890, p. 20.)

CREAM, CROP, OR FLOWER OF THE WELL

[*Herefordshire*] It was formerly the custom, in Herefordshire farm-houses, for the servants to sit up to see the new year in and, at midnight, to rush for the " cream of the well," the first water drawn in the new year, which was thought to be beautifying and lucky. The maid who succeeded in getting it would present it to her mistress, who would give a present for it. (*The Folk-Lore of Herefordshire*, Ella Mary Leather, Hereford, 1912, p. 91.)

[*Monmouthshire*] The Rev. T. A. Davies, Llanishen, Monmouthshire, says that less than thirty years ago he had seen an old well, near a small larch wood not far from " The Cross," Llanishen, dressed with sprigs of box by an old man of 80 years of age. This was on new year's eve and, at 12 midnight, the old man and another old neighbour used to race to the well to see who would be first in getting what they called the " crop of the well," with which to make tea. (*South Wales Argus*, 10th March, 1928.)

[*Northumberland*] Early on new year's day, the Croft-foot Well of Birtley and the Old Kirk Well, High Well, and Riverside Well of Wark, used to be visited by the villagers who wished to be the first to drink the water of the well on new year's morn; such water was believed to possess exceptional and even supernatural qualities. The villagers of Wark called this water the " flower of the well " and the one who was first in obtaining it cast an offering of flowers, grass, hay, or straw into the well and thus late comers would learn that their chances of obtaining the first draught from the well had vanished. At Birtley, the villagers of a generation ago visited the well, in the early hours of the new year, like their neighbours at Wark. They believed that the first to fill his flask or bottle with the water would find that the water retained its freshness and purity throughout the year and brought good luck to the house in which it remained. (*County F.L.*, vol. 4, *Northumberland*, M. C. Balfour and Northcote W. Thomas, 1904, pp. 2 and 5.)

MISTLETOE CUSTOMS

On new year's day, a mistletoe bough used to be hung up in farm-houses, private houses, and cottages throughout Herefordshire and in parts of Worcestershire, the mistletoe of the preceding year having been previously burnt. The following description refers to the observance of the custom in private houses and cottages, in the last century; the custom, as celebrated in Herefordshire at many farm-houses is described below and on p. 23.

[*Herefordshire*] There is scarcely a house or cottage in Herefordshire that has not its bunch of mistletoe for new year's day. The ancient custom is still observed aright by all the old true Herefordshire inhabitants and especially by the poorer classes. The mistletoe bough is cut on the eve of the new year and hung up in state as the clock strikes twelve; the old mistletoe bough which has hung throughout the year is, at the same time, taken down and burnt.—The Mistletoe in Herefordshire, Dr. Bull. (*Trans. Woolhope Naturalists' Field Club for* 1864-5, Hereford, 1865, p. 339.)

BURNING THE BUSH

[*Herefordshire*] Early on new year's morning, annually, it was customary at farms, in Herefordshire, to burn the " Bush," the hawthorn or blackthorn bush which, with the mistletoe bough, had hung in the farm-house kitchen since the preceding new year's day. During the burning of the bush, a new one was made and, together with a new mistletoe bough, was hung up in the kitchen, to remain there till the next new year's day and then to be duly burned. The mistletoe, therefore, was not taken into the house before new year's day; to do so was considered unlucky. The method of making a new bush (see Plate I, Fig. 1) varied at different farms but, by one method, a thorn branch with four stout twigs branching out in four directions, at right angles, was held over a flame to make the twigs pliable and scorch their

PLATE I

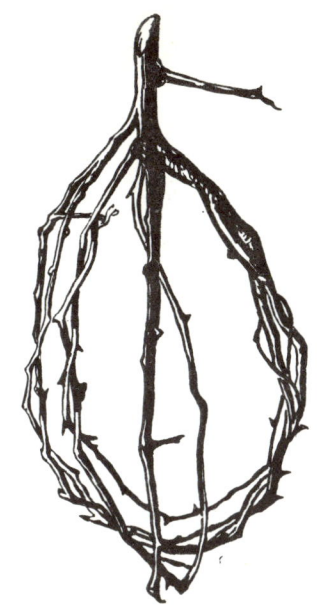

Fig. 1.—A "BUSH" BURNT ON NEW YEAR'S MORNING

6½ in high
Fig. 2.—A CALLENIG, OR APPLE-GIFT

extremities, the twigs being then plaited together so as to form two arches, one within the other and in planes at right angles.

The " Burning," as described to me by Mr. Lilwall of Logaston, who took part in the ceremony last new year's day, consists in scorching the thorn either before or after the four branches have been plaited into the form of two rings, one within the other, and takes place in the field of wheat first sown. After " Old Ci-der " has been repeated several times and the health of the farmer on whose land the burning takes place has been drunk, the company go to the farm-house, where they are served with further supplies of cider and plum cake.—J. W. Lloyd. (*Trans. Woolhope Naturalists' Field Club for* 1900-1, Hereford, 1901, pp. 104-5.)

The custom was generally kept up all over Herefordshire, until about forty years ago, and survives here and there in the Leominster and Kington districts. At Brinsop, the old bush was filled with straw and carried burning over the ridges ; it was said that evil spirits could be caught in it and thus destroyed, between 12 p.m., 31st December, and 6 a.m., 1st January. Formerly, it was believed that without this ceremony there would be no crops. (*The Folk-Lore of Herefordshire*, Ella Mary Leather, Hereford, 1912, pp. 91-3.)

ALLENDALE NEW YEAR CUSTOM

[*Northumberland*] The custom of men celebrating the new year, by carrying pans of blazing tar on their heads, is still kept up at Allendale, Northumberland, and was observed in the year 1936. (Letter, dated 19th July, 1936, from Miss Violet Alford, Bath.)

In some counties, *e.g.* Northumberland, Westmorland, and Cumberland, tar and tar barrels have long been utilized in celebrating some of their popular customs. A cutting from a newspaper gives a photo of young men celebrating the Allendale custom and describes it as follows : " Dancing under fire. Young men celebrating New Year at Allendale, Northumberland, by carrying wooden pans of blazing tar on their heads. At midnight, they throw their blazing headgear into a bonfire and dance round it." The cutting is marked carefully in ink, 1936, and corroborative evidence shows that this is correct.

Relative measurements made on the photo show that the pans are about one foot nine inches in diameter and six inches deep.

NEW YEAR'S GIFTS

The custom of presenting gifts on new year's day was of ancient origin and records of its celebration are numerous. The customary gifts ranged from expensive articles of jewellery and substantial sums of money to books, gloves, small sums of money, capons, eggs dyed in various colours, cakes, and apples or oranges studded with cloves. These more homely gifts were in use among members of the general public; the expensive gifts were commonly presented to royalty by nobles and courtiers. The chronicler, Matthew Paris, mentions what seem to have been known as new year's gifts in his time and records that, in 1249, on the Day of Circumcision, 1st January, Henry III shamelessly exacted such gifts from wealthy London citizens. (*Matthew Paris, Chron.*, H. R. Luard, Editor, vol. 5, 1880, p. 47.) The usual custom, particularly as observed during the reigns of Henry VIII, Edward VI, and Elizabeth, was for the monarch to receive presents and give presents in return.

At a meeting of the Society of Antiquaries, Chancery Lane, 16th December, 1756, Charles Lyttleton, Dean of Exeter, showed a large parchment roll giving a list of new year's gifts presented to Queen Elizabeth on the 1st January, 1584-5. From this list, it appears that all the bishops, most of the peers and peeresses of the realm, and officers of state, and several servants of the royal household presented new year's gifts to the Queen. The Archbishop of Canterbury gave £40, the temporal lords from £10 to £30, and the peeresses usually gave gowns, mantles, doublets, bracelets, and caskets studded with precious stones. The Queen's physician gave a box of foreign sweetmeats; another physician gave a pot of green ginger and a pot of orange flowers; the apothecary gave a box of lozenges and a pot of preserved fruits; and the master cook gave a marchpayne, a macaroon in fashion at the time. The sum total of the money presents was £828 7s. od.; no valuation was made of the other presents. The roll was signed by Queen Elizabeth and by John Astley, master and treasurer of the jewels. On the back of the roll was a list of presents, duly weighed, of gilt plate. The weight assigned to the Lord Chamberlain was 400 oz., that for the Earl of Leicester was 130 oz., and so on; the smallest gilt plate present weighed 2 oz. (*Archæologia*, vol. 1, 1770, pp. 9-11.)

On New Year's Day, 1589, Sir Francis Drake presented to the Queen a costly feather fan, having a handle of gold and ornamented with diamonds and pearls. (*Time's Telescope* for 1830, p. 13.)

A similar custom was celebrated during the reign of James I, but the presents were less valuable and the customary presents of purses containing gold were given less freely. Little information is available about the custom during the unsettled and anxious period preceding the Restoration but, according to Pepys's Diary, the custom was kept up in 1660-1. He says: "I had been early this morning" [Jan. 4, 1660-1] " at Whitehall, at the Jewell Office, to choose a piece of gilt plate for my Lord[1] in return of his offering to the King (which it seems is usual at this time of year and an Earle gives twenty pieces of gold in a purse to the King). I chose a gilt tankard, weighing 31 ounces and a half, and he is allowed 30 oz.; so I paid 12s. for the ounce and half over what he is allowed; but strange it was for me to see what a company of small fees I was called upon by a great many to pay there, which, I perceive, is the manner that courtiers do get their estates." (*Memoirs of Samuel Pepys*, Richard Griffith Neville, Baron Braybrooke, Editor, 5 vols., vol. 1, 1828, p. 167).

Courtiers continued to present purses containing gold to the king, on new year's day, but this custom ceased about the end of the eighteenth century. After that time, until early in the nineteenth century, the only new year's presents at Court are said to have been given, in accordance with custom, to the two chaplains in waiting, a crown piece being put under the plate of each chaplain.

[1] Earl of Sandwich.

In a MS. book of accounts of the household expenses of Sir John Francklyn, 1624, are recorded the following items relating to new year's gifts :

"Item to the musicians on New Year's Day in the morning - - - - - - - 1s. 6d."
"Item to the woman which brought the apple stuck with nuts - - - - - - - 1s. 0d."
"Item to the boy who brought two capons - 1s. 0d."
"Item paid for the (wassail) cup - - - 1s. 6d."

(*Archæologia*, vol. 15, 1806, p. 159.)

Capons were customary gifts from tenants to their landlords. In addition to books, gloves, capons, cakes, confections, and oranges and apples stuck with cloves, customary new year's gifts included nutmegs, plain and gilded, nuts, and pins. In olden times, pins used merely for fastening pieces of fabric together were comparatively costly and many housewives used wooden, fish-bone, and thorn substitutes. It is only during the last hundred years that pins, stamped at one operation from a metal wire, have been made at a trivial cost.

Verses, complimentary and congratulatory, used to be sent in large numbers for new year's day. This custom has lost much of its former popularity, but of the millions of Christmas cards that are sent out for Christmas Day many are worded so as to convey good wishes for Christmas and the New Year.

[*Channel Islands*] The first day of the year is strictly observed as a holiday. Presents are given to friends, servants, and children. Visits to relatives and friends are many and the new year's greetings are kindly and sincere. Currant cake is in great favour on this day. (*Guernsey Folk-Lore*, Sir Edgar MacCulloch, 1903, pp. 38-9.)

[*Nottinghamshire*] On the first day of the year, new year's gifts were, and I believe are still, general. In some parts of the county, parties of little children might be seen, a few years since, each with an apple or orange stuck with cloves or rosemary, for presentation to their friends.—On Ancient Customs and Sports of the County of Nottingham, Llewellynn Jewitt.

(*The Journal of the British Archæol. Assoc.*, vol. 8, 1853, pp. 230-1.)

[*Sussex*] At Hastings, apples, nuts, oranges, and money, are thrown out from the windows to be scrambled for by the fisher boys and men. I am told that formerly it was customary to go to the tradesmen's shops to induce them to give away their surplus Christmas stock of fruit and other commodities, on new year's day. Those who made this request shouted " Throw out ! Turn out." (*Sussex Archæol. Society's Collections*, vol. 33, Lewes, 1883, p. 238.)

[*Westmorland*] At Kirkby Stephen, it is the custom for children to beg their new year's gifts on the eve of this day. (*Denham Tracts*, vol. 2, 1895, pp. 33-4.)

[*Yorkshire*] New year's day was regarded, especially in Cleveland, as the time for making presents. It was customary for widows to go from house to house, to obtain gifts. A similar custom is said to be practised in the West Riding, where widows ask for and usually obtain a small measure of wheat at the farmhouses. (*Yorkshire in Olden Times*, William Andrews, Hull, 1890, p. 133.)

On new year's day, the youngsters keep up the old custom of asking for gifts and wishing their neighbours " A happy new year." Rising early, they go in companies from shop to shop and demand loudly " A new year's gift." The gifts are generally of small value. (*The History and Antiquities of Morley*, William Smith, 1876, p. 90.) Sheets of pins were the most usual presents received and were used chiefly in playing games.

On new year's day it is customary at Driffield for the boys of the town to assemble in the main street, to go in disorderly rout to the shops of the chief tradesmen and, standing in the road before each shop, sing out :

> " Here we are at oor toon end
> A shoulder o' mutton an a crown to spend ;
> Hip ! hip ! hooray ! "

until some of the stock of the tradesman is thrown to them.

The rhyme sung by the Flamborough children in their form of the custom is :

> " Here we are at oor toon end,
> A bottle o' gin and a croon to spend.
> If you hain't a penny, a hawp'ny 'll do ;
> If you hain't a hawp'ny, God bless you ! "

(*Folk-Lore of East Yorkshire*, John Nicholson, Driffield, 1890, p. 21.)

The Cleveland new year's greeting is :

> " I wish you a merry Christmas
> And a happy new year,
> A pantry full of roast beef
> And a barrel full of beer."

You may constantly hear the lads of that district calling it through their neighbours' keyholes, on new year's morning. It is also recited by the children of the West Riding when they make their rounds, soliciting new year's gifts. (*Notes on the Folk-Lore of the Northern Counties of England and the Borders*, William Henderson, 1879, p. 75.)

COVENTRY GOD-CAKES

[*Warwickshire*] Referring to a custom, at Coventry, of sending god-cakes as presents on the first day of the year, it is said that the cakes were used by all classes and varied in price from a halfpenny upwards ; the highest price mentioned is a pound. The cakes were triangular in plan, about an inch thick, and filled with a kind of mincemeat. So general was the use of them, on new year's day, that the cheaper sorts were hawked about the streets, as hot cross-buns were in London, on Good Friday. (*N. and Q.*, ii, 2, 1856, p. 229.)

God-cake, a particular kind of cake which it is customary, on new year's day, for sponsors to send to their god-children. The custom seems to be peculiar to Coventry. (*A Warwickshire Word Book*, G. F. Northall, 1896, p. 94.)

The "Coventry," a pastry containing jam, so well-known, especially in the Midlands, is the modern representative of the god-cake.

ST. ALBANS CAKES OR BUNS

[*Hertfordshire*] On returning from the country, I happened to sleep at St. Albans on the night of the 31st December last [1819] and was awakened early the next morning by a confused noise of boys and girls in the street, crying for sale " Popladys! Popladys!" Inquiring at breakfast time the meaning of those words, I was informed that it was an ancient practice in the town to cry and sell in the streets and in the bakers' shops, on new year's day, a species of cake or bun called " Poplady," one of which was brought to me. It was a plain cake, like the cross-buns sold on Good Friday but, instead of being circular, was long and narrow, rudely resembling the human figure, with two dried raisins or currants to represent eyes and another for the mouth, the lower part being formed rather like the outer case of an Egyptian mummy. (*Gentleman's Magazine*, vol. 90, 1820, p. 15.)

I enclose two pope ladies; they are buns made rudely in the shape of a woman and sold at St. Albans, on new year's morning. (*N. and Q.*, ii, 11, 1861, p. 244.)

Pop or pope ladies. In St. Albans and, I believe, in other towns in Hertfordshire, certain cakes are made and sold under this name, on the first day of each year. They have the rude outline of a female figure and two currants serve for eyes. There is a tradition that they have some relation to the myth of Pope Joan, but nothing is known of their origin.—Ridgway Lloyd, St. Albans. (*N. and Q.*, iv, 11, 1873, p. 341.)

At St. Albans, pop ladies are cried and sold in the streets, on new year's day. (*Old English Customs extant at the Present Time*, P. H. Ditchfield, 1896, p. 46.)

Pop ladies. My allusion to the Yule dough, last week, has brought me several communications from the North and one from St. Albans, with a sample of this tasty morsel, in the shape of a doll, eyes, mouth, and all made of dough. I hope the kind sender does not wish me to eat it, but he says they are known at St. Albans as Pop ladies and are sold there on new year's day, just as cross-buns are sold on Good Friday. The demand for them is said to be dying out.—Peter Lombard in Varia. (*Church Times*, 10th January, 1896.)

Cakes of the Poplady type, *i.e.* of crude human form with currants to represent eyes, have been made and sold regardless of dates, but the above five records, consistent and reliable, prove that it was a custom, at St. Albans, to make and sell Popladies on new year's day. Records inconsistent with this conclusion have been rejected. The custom had lost its popularity thirty-five years ago and, from inquiries made locally, is nearly forgotten.[1]

DERBYSHIRE WASSIL CAKES

[*Derbyshire*] These are made on new year's day. They are composed of flour, milk, and the first egg laid by a goose. (*Household Tales*, Sidney Oldhall Addy, 1895, p. 103.)

SUNDERLAND CAKE CUSTOM

[*Durham*] Everyone buys a cake for new year's day. The streets are crowded until after midnight, watching-in the new year. No other night is so busy. (Seen by me, J. B. Partridge, in 1904.)

NEW YEAR'S APPLE GIFTING

[*Gloucestershire*] There is a very pretty custom, now dying out, of presenting on new year's day what is called " The gift." This is an apple set on three wooden legs and having a sprig of box, hung with hazel nuts, stuck into it, the whole looking like a miniature Christmas tree; see Plate I, Fig. 2.[2]—St. Briavels, L. M. Eyre. (*Folk-Lore*, vol. 13, 1902, p. 174.)

[*Herefordshire*] In Herefordshire, the peasantry send about, on

---

[1] See *The Year Book*, William Hone, 1866, p. 807, for an account of a custom celebrated at Cambridge on 1st January, 1832, of crying uncrossed buns in the streets.

[2] From a drawing of a callenig or apple-gift, 6½ inches high, carried about by Welsh children, on new year's day, on p. 452 of *The International Folk-Lore Congress, Papers and Transactions*, Joseph Jacobs and Alfred Nutt, Editors, 1892.

new year's day, a small pyramid made of leaves, apples, nuts, etc., gilt. (*Gentleman's Magazine*, vol. 92, 1822, p. 222.)

There is no trace of this custom at the present time, except that the oldest people remember carrying round apples, or turnips, stuck with oats and then floured. These decorated apples were used to adorn the houses and were carried round when carol singing or, as it is called, " New year's giftin," and they were supposed to bring luck. (*The Folk-Lore of Herefordshire*, Ella Mary Leather, Hereford, 1912, p. 90.)

[*Worcestershire*] A custom resembling that described above, in which apples stuck with oats and floured were used, was celebrated in Worcestershire in the nineteenth century, especially during the Catherning season.

Mr. Jabez Allies, recalling that he saw, during his boyhood, apples roasting on strings before the kitchen fire at a farm-house in Leigh Parish, near Worcester, said that they were thickly studded with oats, instead of cloves, and some of the apples so studded were not roasted but were affixed on wooden skewers and dredged all over with flour so as to resemble, in a manner, a dandelion in full seed. (*Report of the Proceedings of the British Archæol. Assoc. at the General Meeting held, during August, 1848, in Worcester*, 1851, p. 155.)

The following is a description of a Glamorganshire custom which resembles those customs of the decorated apple type described above for the counties of Hereford and Worcester.

There is, in Glamorganshire, a new year's custom of great antiquity and large present observance, called the apple gift or new year's gift. In every town and village you will meet children, on or about new year's day, going from door to door of shops and houses, carrying an apple or an orange curiously decorated. Three sticks in the form of a tripod are thrust into it to serve as a rest ; its sides are smeared with flour or meal and stuck over with oats or wheat grains. A skewer is inserted on one side to serve as a handle. The top of the apple is covered with thyme or other sweet evergreen. The Christian symbolism of this custom is supposed to relate to the offerings of the Wise Men. The older interpretation, however, takes the custom back to the Druidic days. (*British Goblins, etc.*, William Wirt Sykes, United States Consul for Wales, 1880, pp. 252-5.)[1]

WASSAILING CUSTOMS

[*Hampshire*] A custom, not common in other parts of the country, is still observed at Yarmouth, Isle of Wight. On new year's day, children go to houses in the district and sing :

> " Wassail, wassail, to our town !
>   The cup is white and the ale is brown.
>   The cup is made of the ashen tree,
>   And so is the ale of good barley.
>   Little maid, little maid, turn the pin,
>   Open the door and let me in.
>   God be here and God be there,
>   I wish you all a happy new year."

(*The History of Portsmouth, etc.*, Lake Allen, 1817, p. 251.)

[*Lancashire*] At Oldham, on new year's day, the wassailers still come round with their bunches of evergreens hung with oranges, apples, and coloured ribbons, They sing :

> " Here we come a-wassailing
>   Among the leaves so green," etc.

(*Old English Customs Extant at the Present Time*, P. H. Ditchfield, 1896, pp. 43-4.)

[*Yorkshire*] In nearly all parts of Yorkshire, the week after Christmas, children go about with a box containing two dolls, one to represent the Virgin and the other to represent the Child. The box is furnished with various ornaments. The children sing :

> " Here we come a-wassailing
>   Among the leaves so green," etc.,

and, on receiving a coin, uncover the box for display. This old Wassailers' Carol was formerly sung on new year's day only and chiefly by girls who carried a holly-bush decorated with dolls, ribbons, and oranges suspended from the branches. Like the mummers, they see the disadvantage of coming last for the

[1] A very good drawing of an apple gift on p. 254 of Mr. Sykes' book.

New Year's Day

money and have recently begun on Christmas day and, by the new year, have had a week's carolling, and the decorated hollybush has degenerated into a decorated herring-box. (*Yorkshire Folk-Lore*, part of *Yorkshire Notes and Queries*, vol. 1, Bingley, 1888, pp. 28-31.)

THE OLD WASSAILING CAROL

[*Yorkshire*] This carol, already mentioned, seems to be almost forgotten and, in order that it may be recorded in an easily accessible form, is copied here from *Yorkshire Folk-Lore*, part of *Yorkshire Notes and Queries*, vol. 1, Bingley, 1888, pp. 28-9.

> Here we come a-wassailing
> Among the leaves so green,
> Here we come a-wassailing
> So far to be seen.

> *Chorus*
> Love and joy come to you
> And to your wassail too,
> And God send you a happy new year,
> A new year,
> And God send you a happy new year.
> Our wassail cup is made of the rosemary tree,
> So is your beer of the best barley.

We are not daily beggars
That beg from door to door,
But we are neighbours' children
Whom you have seen before.

Call up the butler of this house,
Put on his golden ring,
Bid him bring up a glass of beer,
The better that we sing.

We have got a little purse
Made of shining leather skin;
We want a little of your money
To line it well within.

> Bring us out a table
> And spread the table cloth;
> Bring us out a mouldy cheese
> And some of your Christmas loaf.
>
> God bless the master of this house,
> Likewise the mistress too,
> And all the little children
> That round the table go.
>
> Good master and mistress,
> While you're sitting by the fire,
> Pray think of us poor children
> Who are wandering in the mire.

BLESSING THE APPLE TREES

[*Gloucestershire*] A custom once prevailed at Upton St. Leonard, Gloucestershire, of singing to the trees on new year's day:

> " Blawe, blawe, bear well,
> Spring well in April,
> Every sprig and every spray
> Bear a bushel of apples against
> Next new year's day."

The idea was that high winds were good for the trees by moving the roots. (*Folk-Lore*, vol. 22, 1911, p. 237.)

[*Sussex, etc.*] In Sussex and Devonshire, it was the custom to wassail the orchards; a party of boys visited the orchards and, encircling the apple trees, sang:

> " Stand fast, bear well top,
> Pray God send us a howling crop;
> Every twig, apples big;
> Every bough, apples enow,
> Hats full, caps full,
> Full quarter sacks full."

Then the boys shouted in chorus, and rapped the trees with their sticks. (*Old English Sports*, P. H. Ditchfield, 1891, p. 4.)

[*Worcestershire*] At Castle Morton, boys and girls go early on new year's morning to the farm-houses and sing, all in one breath:

> " Bud well, bear well
> God send you fare well;
> Every sprig and every spray
> A bushel of apples next new year's day.
> A happy new year
> A pocket full of money
> A cellar full of beer.
> Please give me a new year's gift."

(*Guide to Worcestershire*, John Noake, 1868, p. 261.) A similar custom used to be observed at Evesham and Longdon.

MUMMING AND SWORD DANCING

[*Northern Counties*] Many sword dances are still performed in the North of England, about new year's day, and mummers' plays are still acted either at that time or at Christmas. (Miss Violet Alford, Bath, in letter dated 19th July, 1936.)

FADGING

[*Northumberland*] There is much visiting at this season, throughout the North of England, and much hospitality in the matter of rich cake and wine, but the name given to this practice, in Northumberland, is singular. They call it " fadging," or " eating fadge." (*Notes on the Folk-Lore of the Northern Counties of England and the Borders*, William Henderson, 1879, p. 75.)

At Warkworth, at the season of the new year, there is provided a rich cake with its usual accompaniment of wine. Great interchange of visiting takes place. The custom is called " fadging " or " eating fadge." Fadging really means eating the bread of brotherly concord and union. (*Northumberland Words*, R. Oliver Heslop, 2 vols., vol. 1, 1892, p. 271.)

STANGING

[*Cumberland, etc.*] This custom, sometimes called " lifting " or " heaving," was observed until the early years of the twentieth century in Cumberland and Westmorland.

Early in the morning of new year's day, men and youths assembled together carrying stangs and baskets. Any man or woman, in the streets, was liable to be seized by members of the band and enforced to pay sixpence or more before being liberated. Assuming that such payment was refused, the arrested person, if a man, was mounted on a pole or stang ; if the arrested person was a woman, she was put in a basket. In either case, the result was an enforced visit to the nearest inn, where payment of sixpence resulted in release. No respect is paid to any person ; the parson gets mounted like many of his flock, and one of the porters boasts and prides himself for having just before got the Squire across the pole. Nobody, however anxious to do so, is allowed to work on this day. (*Gentleman's Magazine*, vol. 61, 1791, pp. 1169-70.)

On new year's day, stanging is the only peculiar custom I have seen, unwary persons having been seized and forced into an arm-chair, formerly upon a stang or pole, and carried shoulder-high to the nearest inn, where they were set free on payment of a small sum.—Ancient Customs and Superstitions in Cumberland. (*Trans. Historic Soc. Lancashire and Cheshire*, vol. 10, 1858, p. 104.)

In many villages in Cumberland, stanging is a very common custom on new year's day. A party of roughs assembled in the morning and continued to celebrate the custom throughout the day. Old Customs and Usages in the Lake District. (*Trans. Cumb. Assoc.*, Keswick, 1876, p. 116.)

[*Westmorland*] In Westmorland, the ancient custom of stanging is still observed in many towns and villages, on new year's day.—The men lift the women upon a ladder or pole and, occasionally, in a chair or swill, *i.e.* a large basket for herrings and other fish, and, in accordance with the custom, carry them to the nearest inn, where the terms of release are settled. (*Denham Tracts*, vol. 2, 1895, p. 31.)

THE BUSHEL CUSTOM

[*Sussex*] In celebrating this custom, on new year's day, a bushel corn measure is decorated and filled with ale, which is served out free to all comers at the Red Lion Inn, Old Shoreham. It is recorded, in *The Sussex Daily News* of 5th January, 1883, that the custom was observed on New Year's Day, 1883. A new corn measure was decorated with flowers and green paper, and filled with ale which, frothing up and surrounded by the paper decorations, presented the appearance of a large cauliflower. Many were present and the bushel was filled twice, first by Messrs. Vallance, Catt and Company, the brewers, and next by some of the company. There was a regular chairman and a baler who had the privilege of drinking from the measure; the ale was ladled out with a pint mug and drunk from glasses. On inquiry, I found that the custom had been kept for eighty years. —Frederick E. Sawyer. (*Folk-Lore Journal*, vol. 1, 1883, pp. 192-3.)

CHALKING THE DATE OF THE YEAR

[*Yorkshire*] At Skipsea, in Holderness, the youths assemble at twelve o'clock on new year's eve and, after blackening their faces and otherwise disguising themselves, they pass through the village and mark the gates, doors, shutters, and waggons with the date of the new year. No attempt is made to interfere; the inhabitants consider it lucky to have their houses and waggons so dated. (*Old English Customs Extant at the Present Time*, P. H. Ditchfield, 1896, p. 42.)

MANORIAL CUSTOMS

[*Staffordshire*] A goose tenure custom was observed by the lord of Essington Manor, tenant of the lord of Hilton Manor, about five miles north-east of Wolverhampton. The following account of the custom is based on Dr. Plot's description, written in the seventeenth century.

On new year's day, annually, the lord of Essington, or his deputy, was bound to take a goose to Hilton and drive it round the fire in the Hall, at least three times, while Jack of Hilton was blowing the fire. Then the lord of Essington, or his deputy was bound to carry the goose into the kitchen of Hilton Hall and deliver it to the cook. Then the goose was killed, dressed, and cooked. The lord of Essington, or his deputy, then carried the goose to the lord of Hilton's table and received from him a portion of the goose for his own dinner. This service was performed about 50 years since [apparently reckoned from 1680 or 1686] by Sir Gilbert Wakering, the Lady Townsend being lady of the Manor of Hilton. Thomas A. Stokes and John A. Stokes, brothers, both living 1680, were present.

Jack of Hilton is a hollow brass image, about 12 inches high, representing a man kneeling upon his left knee. It has a little hole in the place of the mouth, about the size of a large pin head, and another in the back about ⅜ inch diameter, at which last-named hole it is filled with water, in quantity four and a quarter pints. Set in a strong fire the water evaporates, as in an Æolipile, and issues from the smaller hole in a constant blast of steam, blowing the fire so strongly as to be very audible and to make an impression in that part of the fire where the blast impinges, as I found by experience on 26th May, 1680. (*Natural History of Staffordshire*, Robert Plot, Oxford, 1686, pp. 443-4.)

There are many later records of this tenure custom, but few give additional information concerning it; one of these, abridged to avoid repetition, is the following.

For a century and a half, the lord of Essington observed the custom, which ceased automatically when the Vernons of Hilton became owners of Essington manor. (*N. and Q.*, iii, 4, 1863, p. 461.)

The dates given by Dr. Plot show that the custom was observed during the Stuart period.

During the blowing operation, the inlet or back aperture was probably plugged.

[*Yorkshire*] The following is an account of an old manorial custom the observance of which was regulated by many peculiar conditions. The occupiers of messuages and cottages within the towns of Hutton-Conyers, Melmerby, Baldersby, Rainton, Dishforth, and Hewick had right of estray for their sheep to certain boundaries on a large common near Hutton-Conyers, a few miles from Ripon, and called Hutton-Conyers Moor. Each township aforesaid had a shepherd. The lord's shepherd had the right to tend the lord's sheep anywhere on the common and the towns' shepherds had to give way to him. There was a large coney-warren on the common belonging to the lord of the manor.

On new year's day, annually, the lord of the manor held his court, where, to preserve the right of estray, each town's shepherd brought a large apple-pie and a twopenny sweet cake, except the shepherd of Hewick, who paid a sum of sixteen pence and a wooden spoon. In the pie brought by the shepherd of Rainton, an inner one was made filled with prunes. The pies were measured by the bailiff and, if of the required size, were cut into an aliquot number of parts and distributed among the steward, the bailiff, the tenant of the coney-warren and the towns' shepherds; if a pie were too small, the bailiff might return it and fine the town. The cakes were divided in the same manner. The bailiff gave to each shepherd a slice of cheese and a penny roll, and provided a mixture of furmety and mustard, which was put into an earthen pot placed in a hole in the ground. The bailiff provided wooden spoons for the steward, the tenant of the coney-warren, and himself; the shepherds provided their own wooden spoons. The steward took a large spoonful of the mixture and the others followed in due order; then a glass of ale, paid for by the sixteen pence brought by the shepherd of Hewick, was served to each. Finally, all adjourned to the bailiff's house and the further business of the court was transacted. (Thomas Blount's *Ancient Tenures of Land, etc.* An edition enlarged by I. Beckwith, with considerable additions by H. M. Beckwith, 1815, pp. 555-7.)

DIVINATIONS

The methods employed in order to obtain information about the future include two which used to be very popular. One of these depends on the use of a Bible, on new year's day, and the other on an appeal to the first new moon of the year.

DIPPING IN THE BIBLE

In the usual way of operating this divination, the head of the household places a Bible on the table, on new year's morning, and opens it at random, with eyes closed; then, still with eyes closed, he touches with his forefinger any chapter displayed on the open pages. The chapter thus selected, entirely by chance, is read aloud and its subject-matter is believed to foretell the fortune of the new year. In consequence of its being a purely domestic custom, it would be difficult to ascertain to what extent this divination is practised now, but it is significant that recent known observances have been by aged people, *e.g.* by an old lady who lived near Woodstock and died in 1935, at the age of about 96 years. Again, most of the available records, specific as regards date, belong to a period before 1880.

RECORDS OF THE CUSTOM

[*East Anglia*] Divination by dipping in the Bible is still in common use and much credit is attached to it. The custom is usually celebrated with some little ceremony, on the morning of new year's day before breakfast, as the ceremony must be performed fasting. Little argument is required to show that these modes of divination have descended to us from our Puritan ancestors. (*Vocabulary of East Anglia, etc.*, Robert Forby, 1830, pp. 400-1.)

[*Midland Counties*] In many homes of the Midland Counties, it is customary to try *Sortes sanctorum* before noon, on new year's day. (*N. and Q.*, ii, 3, 1857, p. 5.)

[*Lincolnshire*] Many people are most particular to open a Bible first of all, saying that the verse the eye first rests on (or thumb touches) foretells what the new year will be. A piece of green is also to be brought in and placed in the Bible. (*County F.L.*, vol. 5, *Lincolnshire*, Mrs. Gutch and Mabel Peacock, 1908, p. 169.)

[*Oxfordshire*] About eight years ago, I was staying in a little village in Oxfordshire, on the first day of the year, and happening to pass by a cottage where an old woman lived whom I knew well, I stepped in and wished her a happy new year. She was perturbed and said, " New Year's Day! and I have never dipped." Later, she explained that it was customary to dip in the Bible before 12 o'clock on new year's day and added, " Last year I dipped and opened on Job and have had nothing but trouble since.—S. L. (*N. and Q.*, ii, 12, 1861, p. 303.)

[*Somerset*] Opening a Bible on new year's day in order to obtain a forecast of good and bad luck for the year is a practice still in use in some parts of Somerset. (*The Customs, Superstitions, and Legends of the County of Somerset*, Charles Henry Poole, 1877, pp. 8-9.)

[*Suffolk*] Persons will take the Bible to bed with them on New Year's Eve and, as soon as they awake after twelve o'clock, they open it at random in the dark, mark a verse with their thumb or stick a pin through a verse, turn down a corner of the page, and replace the book under the pillow. That verse is supposed to be a prophecy of destiny, good or bad, during the coming year.— *The New Suffolk Garland*, 1866, p. 179. (*County F.L.*, vol. 1, (2), *Suffolk*, The Lady Eveline Camilla Gurdon, 1893, p. 137.)

A COW AND CAKE DIVINATION

[*Herefordshire*] A custom still in use is to take a particular kind of cake and, on new year's morning, to bring a cow into the farmyard and place the cake on her head. The cow walks forward, tosses her head, the cake falls, and the prosperity of the new year is foretold from the direction of its fall.—*Daily Graphic*, 1st January, 1898. (*Folk-Lore*, vol. 12, 1901, p. 350.)

[*Monmouthshire*] I once saw a flat cake, with a hole in the middle, put on one of the horns of the leading cow of the herd and the family servants standing around and singing :

" Here's a health to thee, Brownie, and to thy white horn,
God send thy master a good crop of corn.
Thee eat thy cake and I'll drink my beer,
God send thy master a happy new year."

But the cow did not eat the cake ; she tossed it by throwing up her head and it depended on where the cake fell, in front or behind her, whether the year would be good or bad for her master.

(*Folk-Lore*, vol. 15, 1904, p. 221.) These two records, one for Herefordshire and the other for Monmouthshire, two contiguous counties having many popular calendar customs in common, are mutually explanatory. Except for details, the customs to which they relate are the same and are very suggestive of the customs observed on Twelfth Night (5th January) and described on pp. 57-60.

FIRST NEW MOON OF THE YEAR DIVINATIONS

Those anxious to know their future fortunes in marriage, especially whom they will marry and within what time, sometimes appeal to the first new moon of the year, with much confidence. According to custom, many divinations require that those practising such divinations should maintain secrecy about their proceedings. This is especially important in connection with divinations relating to love and marriage, and if this requirement of secrecy be disregarded the " spell " is believed to be broken, *ipso facto*.

COUNTY RECORDS

[*Herefordshire*] The first new moon in the year was formerly greeted by curious maidens in this fashion :

> " All hail to thee, moon, all hail to thee,
> I prithee kind moon, reveal to me,
> Him who is my life partner to be."

The girl must retire to bed in silence and will dream of her future husband. (*The Folk-Lore of Herefordshire*, Ella Mary Leather, 1912, p. 64.)

[*Lincolnshire*] The first new moon of the year is consulted in love divinations. A girl who wishes to learn when she will marry should tie a new silk handkerchief over her eyes and look at the moon through it, when, it is believed, she will see as many moons as years that will elapse before she marries. (*County F.L.*, vol. 5, *Lincolnshire*, Mrs. Gutch and Mabel Peacock, 1908, pp. 13-4.)

[*Sussex*] Should a girl wish to know what will be the personal appearance of her future husband she must sit across a gate or style and look steadfastly at the first new moon that rises after new year's day. She must go alone and must not have confided her intention to any one. I know no recent instance of this charm being tried, but I hear that the new January moon is still watched by our Sussex maidens who hope to see a likeness of the future husband.—Mrs. Latham. (*Folk-Lore Record*, vol. 1, 1878, p. 30.)

[*Worcestershire*] When the first new moon of the year appears, a girl may go to the garden and, looking steadily at the moon, say :

" New moon, new moon, tell unto me
Which of these three is my husband to be,"

mentioning the names of three young men and curtseying at the naming of each one. When next she sees them, let her notice whether they have their faces or backs towards her ; any one of them who has his back towards her will not be her husband. (*Notes and Queries for Worcestershire*, John Noake, 1856, p. 191.)

[*Yorkshire*] Look at the first new moon of the year through a silk handkerchief which has never been washed. As many moons as you see through the handkerchief, so many years will pass before you are married.—Leeds. (*Notes on the Folk-Lore of the Northern Counties of England and the Borders*, William Henderson, 1879, p. 114.)

When the first new moon of the year is shining, take out of the house something that you have never stood on before, *e.g.* a stool ; stand on it out of doors and bow nine times to the moon. Do all this in silence and you will dream that night of your future husband. It was actually done, less than twenty years ago, by a Swaledale girl.—Richmond. (Mrs. Day, Minchinhampton, native of Swaledale. J. B. Partridge.)

When the first moon of the year is shining, place a bucket of water in the moonlight and bow nine times to the reflection. You will see your future husband's face in the water. All must be done in silence. This seems to be considered a daring and dangerous thing to do, for Mrs. Day says that she and her girl friends never dared to carry it out, though she didn't know why. This would be about 1894-1904. (Miss J. B. Partridge from

Mrs. Day, Minchinhampton, native of Swaledale.) The nature of the expected effect would not be attractive to every girl.

The Yorkshire lass, when appealing to the first new moon of the year, knelt on a ground-fast stone, according to Aubrey, and soon after her appeal retired to rest; he adds that he knew two ladies who did thus, when they were young, and they dreamed of those who married them.—Aubrey's Miscellanies, p. 138. (*Denham Tracts*, vol. 2, 1895, p. 281.)

A ground-fast stone signifies a stone fixed by natural agencies, a stone *in situ*.

DIVINATION BY MOLTEN LEAD

On new year's day, unmarried girls melt lead and pour it into a bucket of water. The lead assumes various shapes, such as, for example, a hammer, and from these shapes they guess the trades or occupations of their future husbands. (*Household Tales*, Sidney Oldhall Addy, 1895, p. 80.)

WEATHER DIVINATIONS

Commencing on new year's day, farmers used to note carefully the weather on every one of the first twelve days of the month of January. Then, associating each day with a month of the year, *e.g.* 3rd January with March, it was believed that the weather of each day would indicate the nature of the weather of the corresponding month.

CORN PRICES' DIVINATION

In earlier times, the most ordinary events happening on a new year's day were carefully observed and made to suit the purposes of a divination. The following is a quaint account of the carrying out of a divination, commencing on a new year's day : " Now if you will know whether corne shall be cheape or deare, take twelve principall graynes of wheate out of the eare, upon the first day of January, and when the hearth of your chimney is most hot, sweepe it cleane, then make a stranger lay one of those graynes on the hot hearth, then marke it well, and if it leape a little, corne shall be reasonably cheape, but if it leape much then corne shall be exceeding cheape, but if it lye still and move not, then the price of corne shall stand and continue still for that month ; and thus you shall use your twelve graynes, the first day of every month, one after another." (*The Second Booke of the English Husbandman*, Gervase Markham, 1615, pp. 8-9.)

DISTRIBUTION OF GIFTS AND BEQUESTS

[*London*] To-day, as on every new year's day, the Will of Mr. Henry Cloker, dated 1573, was read before the Master, Wardens, and Liverymen of the Coopers' Company, in the Church of St. Magnus, near London Bridge. The Will established a charity administered by the Company. (*The Evening News*, 1st January, 1935.)

POPULAR SAYINGS AND BELIEFS

The nature of the sentiments created by the passing from the old to the new year is reflected in the new year's day sayings and beliefs, which relate mainly to luck, good and bad.

[*Cheshire*] Farm servants always entered their new places on the day after, or the day but one after, new year's day. To enter service on new year's day would have been considered very unlucky. (*Cheshire Notes and Queries*, Stockport, 1886, p. 8.)

[*Cornwall*] " To pay money on the first day of January is very unlucky, as it insures a continuance of disbursements throughout the year." (*The History of Cornwall*, Fortescue Hitchins, 2 vols., vol. 1, Helston, 1824, p. 713.)

" On no account, allow anything to be carried out of the house but as much as possible to be brought in." I have known even the dust of the floor swept inwards and money, purposely deposited on the window-sill overnight, brought in on the morning of the new year.—Blisland. (T. Q. Couch in *Western Antiquary*, vol. 3, Plymouth, 1884, p. 91.)

Steps of doors were formerly sanded, on new year's day, for good luck because, I suppose, people coming into the house were sure to bring some of it in with them sticking to their feet. (*Folk-Lore Journal*, vol. 4, 1886, p. 123.) *See also* Sussex, p. 48.

[*Derbyshire*] At Great Hucklow, they say that if you put clothes out on a new year's day, there will be a death in the family before the end of the year. (*Memorials of Old Derbyshire*, J. Charles Cox, Editor, 1907, p. 361.)

[*Devonshire*] " If you wash on new year's day,
You will wash a friend away."
(*Folk Rhymes of Devon*, W. Crossing, 1911, p. 135.)

A washerwoman at Budleigh Salterton would not, on any account, wash clothes on new year's day, because it was certain to wash someone out of the house who would never come back again. (*Trans. Devon. Assoc.*, vol. 33, Plymouth, 1901, p. 128.) This belief was held also at Plymouth.

" A Christmas handsel must be given to the bees, on new year's day."—North Devon. (*Trans. Devon. Assoc.*, vol. 2, Plymouth, 1867, p. 40.) This handsel would be a supply of honey or sugar.

" It is lucky to pay money on the first of January, as it insures the blessing of ready cash for all payments throughout the year." (*Nummits and Crummits*, Sarah Hewett, 1900, p. 50.)

[*Durham, etc.*] " Nothing should be taken out of the house on new year's day, but anything might be taken in." I remember accompanying the mistress of a farm-house, in the county of Durham, to her kitchen on new year's eve. She called her servants together and warned them, subject to dismissal, not to allow anything to be carried out of the house on new year's day. In accordance with this direction, all ashes, dish-washing water, potato parings, etc., were kept in the house until after new year's day, but coal, potatoes, and bread were taken in as usual. (*Notes on the Folk-Lore of the Northern Counties of England and the Borders*, William Henderson, 1879, p. 74.)

[*Gloucestershire*] The first new moon of the year is most important and you should always make a point of seeing it. You curtsey to it nine times, throw it nine kisses, turn the money in your pocket, and say " Good luck." My charwoman sometimes goes up the garden to see the moon ; sometimes she curtseys to it as she stands at her door. When we met early in 1915, she asked eagerly if I had seen the new moon and, in 1916, she called me out of the house to see the first moon of that year.—Minchinhampton. (Miss J. B. Partridge.)

New Year's Day

[*Herefordshire*] It was and still is held very unlucky to gear or harness the horses on new year's day. A resident in the parish of Monkland tried, a few years ago, to hire a horse and cart but could not do so ; the first farmer to whom he applied said that he would not put a horse in a cart on that day for anything. No work was done on new year's day, and if a man were found working he would be placed on a ladder and carried round the parish by the holiday makers, who would call with their burden at the farm-houses, where cider would be given to them. (*The Folk-Lore of Herefordshire*, Ella Mary Leather, Hereford, 1912, p. 91.)

[*Lancashire, etc.*] " To give away a light from the house, on new year's day, is unlucky." It may be asserted, with good reason, that this saying and belief is or has been current in most English counties. Among the counties for which the belief is specifically recorded Lancashire, Lincolnshire, Northumberland, Worcestershire, Yorkshire, Derbyshire, Durham, and Nottinghamshire may be mentioned.

[*Lincolnshire*] " It is unlucky if nothing green (and not dead) be taken into the house on new year's day." (*Bygone Lincolnshire*, William Andrews, Editor, vol. 2, Hull, 1891, p. 94.)

If the first person who enters a house on new year's day should bring bad news, it is a sign of bad luck for the whole year. If anything green is taken in there will be a supply of bread throughout the year. Bad luck follows if, on new year's day, anything is taken out of the house before anything has been taken in, for

" Take out and then take in,
Bad luck will begin ;
Take in and then take out,
Good luck comes about."

(*County F.L.*, vol. 5, *Lincolnshire*, Mrs. Gutch and Mabel Peacock, 1908, p. 169.

[*Isle of Man*] " To eat millet and herring on new year's day insures easy circumstances for the year." " Good luck would be swept away, if the one who swept first, on new year's day, were to sweep towards the door instead of towards the hearth." (*An*

Historical, etc., Account of the Isle of Man, Joseph Train, 2 vols., vol. 1, Douglas, 1845, p. 115.)

[*Norfolk*] " It is very unlucky to meet a cross-eyed or wooden-legged woman when going out on the first day of the week, especially so on the first of January." (*Eastern Daily Press*, 28th March, 1895.)

[*Northumberland*] To spill salt is at all times unlucky, but it is especially so on new year's day." (*Denham Tracts*, vol. 2, 1895, p. 340.)

" It is unlucky to sweep dirt or ashes out of the house, to throw out dirty water, or to leave dirty clothes unwashed, on new year's day." (*Denham Tracts*, vol. 2, 1895, p. 340.)

[*Shropshire*] The correct West Shropshire tradition is that the mistletoe should not be set up till new year's day and some persons even say it is unlucky to bring it into the house before then, exactly coinciding with the popular belief about marsh marigolds of May Day. (*Shropshire Folk-Lore*, Charlotte Sophia Burne, 1883, p. 246.)

The last clause of this record is explained in Miss Burne's *Shropshire Folk-Lore*, 1883, p. 253, where it is stated that May flowers (marsh marigolds, in Shropshire) are very unlucky, if brought into the house before the 1st of May.

On new year's day, annually, an old Shropshire man, who passed away many years ago, used to cut a withy stick and at once put it into his pocket, taking great care not to let it fall to the ground and thus break the charm. I believe that he carried it about with him all the year round. Referring to this custom, a correspondent, T. Caswell of All Stretton, stated that it was common enough throughout Shropshire, sixty years ago.—10th May, 1911. (*Bye-Gones relating to Wales and the Border Counties*, new series, vol. 12, Oswestry and Wrexham, 1911-12, pp. 55 and 96.)

[*Sussex*] In Sussex, it is considered to be lucky to bring mud into the house in January and the mud of this month is called " January butter." (*Sussex Archæol. Society's Collections*, Lewes, 1883, p. 238.) *See also* p. 45.

[*Worcestershire*] " To bring luck, a fresh bunch of mistletoe is

New Year's Day

hung up on new year's day, a small piece of the preceding year's bunch being always kept till then." (*Glossary of West Worcestershire Words*, E. L. Chamberlain, 1882, p. x.)

A Worcestershire farmer used to take down the mistletoe and give it to the cow that calved first after new year's day, to insure good luck for the whole dairy. (*N. and Q.*, ii, 3, 1857, p. 343.)

[*Yorkshire*] To insure good luck to your dairy, give your bunch of mistletoe to the first cow that calves after new year's day.—Leeds. (*Notes on the Folk-Lore of the Northern Counties of England and the Borders*, William Henderson, 1879, p. 114.)

" It is unlucky to throw out the ashes or sweep out the dust, on new year's day."—North Yorkshire. (*County F.L.*, vol. 2, *North Riding, York, and the Ainsty*, Mrs. Gutch, 1901, p. 277.) This was also a popular belief in Whitby.

" To allow a light to leave the house on new year's day was a sign of bad luck." Many years ago, before the introduction of lucifer matches, a man living at a house called " The Pasture," near Heptonstall, and so called " Johnny o' the Pasture," entered an old woman's cottage, one new year's morning, to light his pipe. She allowed him to do so and, soon after he left, a lighted candle fell upon her loom and the whole of her work was destroyed. (Papers, Reports, etc., read before *The Halifax Antiquarian Society*, 1904-5, Halifax, 1905, pp. 3-4.) This belief was strongly held at Whitby and Swaledale ; *see also* p. 47.

WEATHER OMENS

[*Buckinghamshire*]

" If the Calends of January be smiling and gay,
You'll have wintry weather till the Calends of May."

This couplet was communicated to me by a friend who assures me that it is current in Buckinghamshire. (*Notes on the Folk-Lore of the Northern Counties of England and the Borders*, William Henderson, 1879, p. 75.)

A similar omen but relating to February instead of January, *see* p. 117, is the better form.

[*Devonshire*] " If new year's day happen on a Saturday, the

50 *Calendar Customs*

winter will be mean, the summer hot, and the harvest late."
(*Nummits and Crummits*, Sarah Hewett, 1900, p. 106.)

FAIRS

[*Cheshire, etc.*] In olden, as in recent, times, fairs held on New Year's day were few. At Stockport, Cheshire, and Woburn, Bedfordshire, fairs are still held on the 1st of January.

Twelfth Night
5th January

With few exceptions, the customs of Twelfth Night are no longer celebrated in England. The famous Twelfth Night revels lost a great deal of their popularity after the change in the calendar, in 1752, but continued to be held, on a decreasing scale, until about the middle of the nineteenth century. The once popular custom of wassailing the apple trees, in the hope of obtaining a good crop the next season, survived until the early years of the present century, but the custom of lighting Twelfth Night fires, in Herefordshire and adjacent counties, became a custom of the past about the middle of last century.

There are relics of children's customs of going from house to house, singing a wassailing carol, and of customs associated with the beliefs that certain thorn trees or shrubs blossom, that cows go down on their knees, and that bees come buzzing from their hives, at midnight, on the eve of the anniversary of the real Christmas Day.

Twelfth Night is called also Twelfth-day Eve, Old Christmas Eve, and the Eve of the Epiphany; the Epiphany is called Old Christmas Day and Twelfth Day. Another series of names is also in use, for, after the change from the Old to the New Style, many people in Herefordshire, Somerset, Worcestershire, and other counties continued, as far as possible, to keep their Christmas on the 6th of January, and to wassail their apple trees on the 17th of January, called Old Twelfth Night, or on the 18th of January, called Old Twelfth Day. This multiplicity of dates causes confusion and many records are incorrect or ambiguous in respect of the dates of celebration of popular customs, but such records have been used as far as possible.

When attempting to form a mental picture of the conditions attending the celebration of popular customs, before the year 1752, allowance should be made for the change in the calendar. The equivalent of a May-day ceremony on the village green, say in 1740, would be, to-day, a similar ceremony on the 13th or, according to some, the 12th of May.

TWELFTH NIGHT REVELS

During the twelve days ending on Epiphany, revels were held, and one of the most popular and jovial of these was the revel of Twelfth Night. The preparations for the revel were usually on a large scale and included the making of a large and rich Twelfth Cake and the provision of ample supplies of lamb's wool (roasted apples, sugar, nutmeg, ginger, and wine or ale) for the wassail bowl, and also cakes and sweetmeats.

On the day of the revel, members of the household, relatives, and friends assembled together in the evening and, after the usual introductions and conversations, indulged in a sumptuous repast, during which the Twelfth Cake was cut, this being the preliminary step to the election of a King, a Queen, and other officers of the ceremonies. The usual method of election, especially in the seventeenth century, was that performed by means of "the bean and the pea," inserted in the cake before baking. Each person present was handed a slice of the cake and he whose piece contained the bean was elected King of the Bean (*see* Plate II) and she whose slice contained the pea was elected Queen. They enjoyed regal honours until the end of the revel, but their duties were not strenuous, for it was characteristic of the revel that its jovial proceedings rarely became riotous. Sometimes, coins were used instead of the bean and the pea or the selection was effected by drawing suitably marked slips of paper shaken up in a hat.

The choice of King and Queen of the Twelfth Night ceremonies has been assumed, so far, to have been determined by chance, but this was not always so. It was sometimes advisable to choose a King who could be relied upon to contribute handsomely to the costs of the revel.

The following lines give many details of the custom as observed in the seventeenth century :

> " Now, now the mirth comes
>   With the cake full of plums,
> Where Beane's the King of the sport here ;
>   Besides we must know,
>   The Pea also
> Must revell, as Queene, in the Court here.
>   Begin then to chuse
>   This night as ye use
> Who shall for the present delight here,
>   Be a King by the lot,
>   And who shall not
> Be Twelfe-day Queene for the night here.
>   Which knowne, let us make
>   Joy-sops with the cake,
> And let not a man be seen here,
>   Who unurg'd will not drinke
>   To the base from the brink
> A health to the King and Queene here.
>   Next crowne the bowle full
>   With gentle lamb's woll ;
>   Add sugar, nutmeg, and ginger,
>   With store of ale too ;
>   And this ye must do
> To make the wassail a swinger."

(*Hesperides, Twelfe Night or King and Queene,* Robert Herrick, 1648, ll. 1-24.)

[*Devon*] Another event, not noticed now, was Old Christmas Eve, on the 5th of January, when the confectioners tried to excel one another in their art. The streets were crowded with parents and children visiting the various shops. (*Reminiscences of Exeter Fifty Years Since,* James Cossins, 2nd edition, Exeter, 1878, p. 74.)

PLATE II

THE KING OF THE BEAN

This record tends to show (1877 was the date of the 1st edition) that the custom of the Twelfth Cake and revel died out, in Exeter at least, towards the middle of the nineteenth century.

TWELFTH NIGHT CONVIVIAL CUSTOMS

[*Somerset*] Old Christmas Eve was the customary time of the gatherings in the big farm-houses, where a pleasant evening was spent by the household and those invited. The proceedings were not of the hilarious nature of the later part of the Christmas festive season, but were pleasant conversations, mainly reminiscent, interspersed with the singing of old, quaint carols, handed down from years long past and accompanied by music played on violin, clarionet, and flute, usually by players who had performed in the village church before organs were used. (*Tales of the Blackdown Borderland*, F. W. Matthews, Somerset Folk Series, No. 13, 1923, p. 119.)

[*Yorkshire*] In Yorkshire, the Wassail Eve or Twelfth Night was formerly kept. Everyone took, by means of a spoon, a roasted apple from the bowl and ate it and then drank from the bowl to the health of the company. (*A Selection of Antiquarian and Historical Notes*, R. O. Jenoway, Edinburgh, 1827, p. 204.)

In that part of Yorkshire, near Leeds, where I was born and spent my youth, I remember that, when I was a boy, it was customary for many families, on Old Christmas Eve, to invite their relations, friends, and neighbours to their houses to play at cards and have a supper at which mince-pies were indispensable. After supper, the wassail bowl, a large bowl such as is now used for punch, was brought in; I have seen bowls used for this purpose that held more than a gallon. The ingredients put into the bowl, ale, sugar, nutmeg, and roasted apples, were usually called Lamb's Wool and the night on which it was used was commonly called Wassail Eve. Spiced cake was given to everyone and each, in turn, took a roasted apple from the bowl, by means of a spoon, and then drank to the health of the company. Since the change in Style, the wassail bowl is used so little, in this part of the country, that I have scarcely seen it introduced into company these thirty years.—Josiah Beckwith. (*Gentleman's Magazine*, vol. 54, 1784, pp. 98-9.)

WASSAILING CUSTOMS

In the celebration of these customs, adults and children went from door to door, on Old Christmas Eve, with or without wassail cups, and sang a wassailing carol, in order to obtain money, apples, mince-pies, or other gifts.

[*Cornwall*] Some years ago, on Twelfth Night, we had the visit of poor, old Tommy Climo, dressed in a blanketting coat, such as Cornish tinners wear. Hanging from his neck by a collar of listing was his tin wassail bowl containing a lamb's wool mixture. At night time, through all Christmas-tide, we have visits from boys and even men, who bring an empty wassail bowl and sing the following lines:

" Come Maister and Missus, Was-hael doth begin ;
   Pray open your doors and let us come in,
   For singing Was-hael, Was-hael,
   And joy come to our jolly Was-hael.
The Missus at the door, she cannot be mute,
   For 'tis an old custom you cannot dispute
   For singing Was-hael, Was-hael."

—Bodmin. (T. Q. Couch in *Western Antiquary*, vol. 3, Plymouth, 1884, p. 164.)

[*Wiltshire*] On Old Christmas Eve came the wassailers with their traditional song :

" Wassail, wassail !
   All round the town.
   Your cup is so white,
   And your beer is so brown." [1]

The wassailing serves as a link between the jollities of Christmas and those which cluster round the agricultural festivals, though the custom of wassailing the apple trees which, I believe, survives in Devonshire has disappeared here, at Stourton.—In a

[1] The song, seven verses and chorus, is given in *The Antiquary*, vol. 44, 1908.

Wiltshire Village: Some Old Songs and Customs, E. E. Balch. (*The Antiquary*, vol. 44, 1908, p. 381.)

TWELFTH-TIDE RUSTIC AMUSEMENTS

During Twelfth-tide, performances were often given by parties of mummers, morris, sword, and other dancers. Compared with the numbers of these performances, the number of records of them is small and the following description is correspondingly brief.

[*Worcestershire, etc.*] One type of these performances was that given on any day favourable for making the venture a financial success. Such were the performances given, about the period 1850-70, by boatmen of the Severn who, prevented by severe frost, in January, from following their usual employment, formed themselves into parties of morris dancers and performed in the streets of neighbouring towns. Dressed up with ribbons and carrying short sticks, they performed their dances, striking their sticks together in unison with their movements. Their performances were picturesque and afforded much amusement, especially to the young spectators. In some of the parties were two characters of outstanding interest to the youngsters: one was a big drummer with a big drum, which received effective bangs; the other was the Fool, who played his part well and rarely missed an opportunity of delivering a whack with an inflated bladder tied to the end of a stick. There were other parties of dancers, who used coloured scarfs and sashes in their dances, but whence they came is not known.

[*Gloucestershire*] Another type of Twelfth-tide rustic amusement includes the traditional mumming play transmitted from father to son during a series of generations. A recent and very interesting display of this kind was given at the National Festival of English Folk Dance and Song, at the Royal Albert Hall, Saturday, 4th January, 1936. The play was performed by a company of traditional mummers, the Marshfield Paper Boys, from Marshfield, Gloucestershire. There were eight players: King William, Little Man John, the Doctor, Father Christmas, Saucy Jack, Father Beelzebub, Tenpenny Nit, and the Town

Crier, who, in a graceful speech, introduces the company to its audience. Father Christmas comes in, makes a speech in praise of Christmas, and invites Little Man John to come forward. Little Man John does so and challenges King William to come forward. King William comes in and then Little Man John suffers a harmless kind of extinction and is resuscitated by the Doctor's magic medicine. After speeches by Saucy Jack, Tenpenny Nit, and Father Beelzebub, the play ends with the Mummers' Song.

[*London*] A very early record relates to the staging by courtiers of a Twelfth Night mumming play, purporting to be for the amusement of Henry IV but really to be part of a plot for assassinating the King. The plot was discovered in good time and the performance was cancelled. (*The New Chronicles of England and France*, Robert Fabyan, 1811 edition, pp. 567-8.)

[*Cornwall*] Guise-dancing has found a last resort in St. Ives and this is the only town where the Cornish Christmas revelry is kept up with spirit. The guise-dancing time is the twelve nights after Christmas, from Christmas day to Twelfth day. Performers outnumber the spectators, who stand at the corners of the streets, badly lighted with gas and made more dismal of late years by the closing of the shops after sunset during this season because of the noise and uproar, the town being given up to the crowd. The whole ceremony was a noisy pantomimic display by performers in quaint or fancy dress. Faithless swains are sometimes punished by friends of the discarded one and other misdeeds do not escape notice. The character of the dancing has deteriorated very much during the past twenty years. It was formerly the custom to organize a play. Wassailing was not popular in this neighbourhood. Father Christmas and King George were the favourite characters.—A St. Ives correspondent, 1861. (*Popular Romances of the West of England*, Robert Hunt, 1881, p. 394.)

The ancient custom of guise-dancing is being observed at St. Ives, Cornwall, this week. Inhabitants disguised in a variety of costumes parade the streets of the town for the first fortnight of the new year. Dancing, often to the accompaniment of concertinas or mouth-organs, takes place in the streets. The proceedings this year will culminate to-morrow, when prizes will be offered for the most beautiful costume, the best family heirloom dress, the best comic costume, and the best character or national costume with song, speech, or dance. After the prize-giving, a procession will be formed and the competitors, carrying lanterns made of hollowed-out turnips, and headed by the St. Ives Silver Band, will parade the streets. (An early edition of *The Times*, 8th January, 1930.)

TWELFTH NIGHT FIRES

A very old custom observed on Twelfth Night included the lighting of fires and was intended to insure success for farm, dairy, and orchard.

[*Gloucestershire*] In Pauntley and neighbouring parishes, a custom prevails intended to prevent smut in wheat; it is in some respects like the Scottish Beltein. On Twelfth Night, all the servants of every farmer assemble in one of the fields that has been sown with wheat. At the ends of twelve strips, they make twelve fires of straw, in a row. Around one fire, which they make larger than the rest, they drink a glass of cider to their master's health and success to the next harvest. Returning home, they receive caraway seed cakes and cider, which they claim as a reward for their past labours. (*The History of the County of Gloucester*, etc., Thomas Rudge, Gloucester, 1803, vol. 2, p. 42.)

[*Herefordshire*] A Herefordshire farmer's wife told me that, about the year 1839, it was customary to light twelve small fires and one large one in a wheat field, on Twelfth Night. The procedure was the same as that described by Brand and so also the ceremony of placing the Twelfth Cake on one of the horns of the best ox. She remembered only one of the three or four verses used on the occasion :

" Fill your cups, my merry men all !
For here's the best ox in all the stall.
Oh ! he is the best ox, of that there's no mistake
And so let us crown him with the Twelfth Cake."

The farmer's wife said that the fires represented Christ and the Apostles and that the one for Judas was lighted and later was kicked about and extinguished.—Cuthbert Bede. (*N. and Q.*, ii, 8, 1859, p. 488.)

A few days since, looking over *The General Evening Post*, among some old customs there noticed, as having been observed in the days of Alfred, it informs us that, in Gloucestershire, the custom of having twelve small fires and one large one in honour of Twelfth Day is celebrated in many parishes. As I have some reason to think that this custom is more generally observed with us in Herefordshire and as I have myself been for many years a constant attendant on this festive occasion, I give the particulars of the whole, as it is kept up in most parishes here. It is here observed under the name of Wassailing, in the following manner. On the Eve of Twelfth Day, at the approach of evening, the farmers, their friends, and their servants assemble and, near six o'clock, walk together to a field where wheat is growing. The highest part of the ground is always chosen and there twelve small fires and one large one are lighted. The attendants, headed by the master of the family, pledge the company in old cider. A circle is formed round the large fire, when a general shout and hallooing takes place, which you hear answered from all the villages and fields near; I have counted fifty or sixty fires burning at the same time. This being finished, the company all return to the house, where a good supper is being prepared. A large cake is always provided, with a hole in the middle. After supper, the company all attend the bailiff, or head of the oxen, to the wainhouse, where the master, at the head of his friends, fills the cup with strong ale and stands opposite the first or finest of the oxen and pledges him in a curious toast. The company then follow his example with all the other oxen, addressing each by his name. Then, the large cake is produced and, with much ceremony, placed on one of the horns of the first ox, which, on being tickled, tosses his head. If he throws the cake behind, it belongs to the mistress; if before, in what is called the boosey, the bailiff claims the cake. The company all return to the house, the doors of which are not opened till some joyous songs are sung. On entering, a scene of mirth begins and reigns through the house till an early hour next morning. Cards are introduced and the merry tale goes round. I have often enjoyed the hospitality and friendship I have been witness to on these occasions.—J. W., Hereford, 24th January, 1791. (*Gentleman's Magazine*, vol. 61, 1791, p. 116.)

The above record is important because it describes the Herefordshire custom before it showed signs of decreasing popularity. The following lines indicate the nature of the curious toast referred to in the record:

> " Here's to thee, Brownie, and thy white horn,
>   God send thy master a good crop of corn,
>   Of wheat and barley and all kinds of grain.
>   May the Lord send us a happy new year,
>   So you eat your oats and we'll drink our beer."

[*Worcestershire, etc.*] On the boundary of S.W. Worcestershire, the farmers used to make twelve fires, one larger than the rest, on the head (east side) of one of their wheat fields. The large fire was called " Old Meg " and around it the farm servants, with their families and friends, congregated to drink warm cider with toasted plum cake in it. After wishing success to the crops, they went to the cow-house. A large plum cake, bound round with tape, was stuck on one of the horns of the best cow, and plum cake and buckets of cider were carried in. Those present drank to the health of the cow, in the following words:

> " Here's to thee, Ball, and to thy white horn;
>   Pray God send thy master a good crop of corn,
>   Of wheat, rye, and barley and all sorts of grain
>   And at this time twelve months we meet here again.
>   The leaves they are green,
>   The nuts they are brown,
>   They all hang so high,
>   That they cannot come down.
>   They cannot come down, until the next year,
>   So thee eat thy oats and we'll drink our beer."

Then the cowman caused the cow to shake off the cake when, if it fell forwards it belonged to the cowman and if backwards to the dairy maid. Finally, the company returned to the farm-house and spent an enjoyable evening. A correspondent informs me that he remembers a similar custom being observed near Tenbury and that Neen Sollars, Shropshire, was the last parish in which he witnessed the celebration of the custom. (*Notes and Queries for Worcestershire*, John Noake, 1856, pp. 219-20.)

From some old records for Worcestershire and Herefordshire, it appears that the custom became evanescent in Worcestershire in the early part of the nineteenth century and that, in Herefordshire, a similar stage was reached about the year 1850.

It may serve a useful purpose to point out that a custom of lighting twelve fires, in Herefordshire, is mentioned on p. 110 of the *Gentleman's Magazine*, vol. 89, 1819, Jan. to June, but this was done after the conclusion of the harvest.

WASSAILING THE APPLE TREES

This custom, which was popularly believed to charm the trees to yield an abundant crop of fruit, was observed in Cornwall, Devonshire, Gloucestershire, Herefordshire, Kent, Monmouthshire, Somerset, Surrey, Sussex, Wiltshire, Worcestershire, and other counties. The season for wassailing the apple trees was that from Christmas to Old Twelfth Day, 18th January, but the custom was most commonly celebrated on Twelfth Night, the 5th of January.

[*Cornwall, etc.*] In the observance of the custom in Cornwall and Devon, a bowl of cider, often with toast in it, was taken into the orchard by the farmer and his men, usually on Old Christmas Eve. Fragments of the toast, or of the cakes made for the company, were placed upon the branches of one of the trees and cider was poured over its roots; the following or a variation of it was then sung :

" Here's to thee, old apple tree,
  Whence thou may'st bud and whence thou may'st blow
  And whence thou may'st have apples enow.

> Hats full, caps full,
> Bushel-bushel-sacks full
> And my pockets full too. Huzza ! "

We doubt not that a liberal supply of cider was taken into the orchard. This is as it should have been if the trees were to bear a large crop, for, [quoting Herrick]

> " More or less fruit they will bring
> As you do give them wassailing."

(*Folk Rhymes of Devon*, William Crossing, Exeter, 1911, p. 140.)

[*Devonshire*] In the Southhams of Devonshire, the farmer, followed by his workpeople carrying a large pitcher of cider, goes to the orchard on Twelfth Night. The farmer and his workpeople stand round one of the best trees and drink cider, saying the following lines three times in succession :

> " Here's to thee, old apple tree,
> Whence thou may'st bud
> And whence thou may'st blow,
> And whence thou may'st
> Bear apples enow.
> Bushel, bushel, sacks full
> And my pockets full too. Hurrah ! "

The farmer and his workpeople then returned to the farm-house, the doors of which had been bolted and were not opened until one of the company guessed correctly the name of some tit-bit being roasted before the kitchen fire. The one who guessed correctly was given the tit-bit. Some believe that if the wassailing were neglected, the trees would not bear any apples that year. (*Gentleman's Magazine*, vol. 61, May, 1791, p. 403.)

Whilst walking from Tor to Torquay, about 10 p.m. on 5th January, 1849, I was surprised to hear repeated sounds of firearms in the direction of the hamlet of Upton. On inquiry, I learnt from one who had frequently taken part in it, that the sounds were connected with a ceremony, then annually performed in the neighbourhood, for wassailing the apple trees. The farmer and his labourers assemble in the kitchen and then go to the orchard, taking with them a pitcher of cider, and all their firearms, charged with gunpowder only. On reaching the first apple tree, they drink cider and repeat a few lines of appeal to the tree for a good yield of apples. The firearms are discharged amongst the trees and the company returns to the farm-house, the doors of which had been closed but are opened after one of the company guesses correctly the name of some speciality roasting before the fire. (*Trans. Devon. Assoc.*, vol. 6, 1873, pp. 266-7.)

A celebration of the ceremony of " blessing the apple trees " having taken place, a few years ago, in an orchard near my house, I obtained the following details from one officially taking part in it. After supper, provided by the owner of the orchard, men, women, and children went to the orchard, carrying a supply of bread, cheese, and cider. They assembled under one of the best trees and hoisted up a little boy and seated him on a branch of the tree. He was to represent a tom-tit and sat crying out " Tit-tit, more to eat," when bread, cheese, and cider were handed up to him. The company, with cups filled with cider, sang a toast to the trees and drank all round. Then they fired a salute to the trees with all the pistols, guns, and other means of making a noise that they could collect. They again stood around and, after another cup of cider, sang :

" To your wassail and my wassail,
And joy be to our jolly wassail."

This concluded the ceremony, which was done in dead of winter. —Torquay, Miss Pinchard. (*Trans. Devon. Assoc.*, vol. 8, 1876, pp. 49-50.)

The instalment, on a branch of one of the trees, of a little boy to represent a tom-tit but treated as if he were representative of some rustic deity, has been considered in relation to a custom observed in Japan.

Dr. Aston, at one time British Consul at Seoul, says that it was customary in Japan, where there were fruit trees, for two men to go to an orchard on the last day of the year ; one of the men climbed a fruit tree and the other stood at the foot of the tree, with an axe. Addressing the tree, he asked whether it would bear well next season; if not, it would be cut down. The man in the tree then said " I will bear well."—Henry Gibbon. (*Devon Notes and Queries*, Exeter, vol. 2, 1903, p. 113.)

The two customs have the same end in view but differ in means —offerings in one case and threats in the other. Mr. R. Pearse Chope says that the boy is obviously the personification of the spirit of the tree and the offerings are to propitiate the spirit in order to obtain a good crop in the coming year.

On Old Christmas Eve, it is customary for farmers to pour large quantities of cider on the roots of the primest apple trees in the orchard and to place toast sops on the branches, all the while singing the following :

> " Yer's tü thee, old apple-tree,
> Be zure yü bud, be zure yü blaw
> And bring voth apples güde enough.
> Hats vul ! Caps vul !
> Dree bushel-bags vul
> Pockets vul and awl !
> Urrah ! Urrah !
> Aw'ess, hats vul, caps vul.
> And dree bushel-bags vul
> Urrah ! Urrah ! "

When enough of this serenading has been accomplished, guns are fired into the branches. When asked why this ceremony was gone through, a labourer said to me, " Yü knaw, mum, us be in 'opes ov 'aving a 'bundant cräp ov awples next yer, an' the trees widden güdy a bit ef us didden holly tü 'm." (*The Peasant Speech of Devon*, Sarah Hewett, 1892, pp. 26-7.)

The custom of firing guns under apple trees, on Twelfth Night, prevailed at Cullompton, Devonshire, in 1889. (*Old English Customs extant at the Present Time*, P. H. Ditchfield, 1896, p. 47.)

In charming the orchards, the custom in Devonshire, followed as late as sixty years ago, was for the farmer and his men to go to the orchards, after dark, with guns and a jug of cider with toast or cake in it. No gun was too old if it would only hold the priming and the more noise the better. When under one of the largest trees, one of the party addressed the tree while guns were discharged. They then drank the cider and ate the sop, taking great care to leave a large piece in a fork of the tree for the robins, or the charm would have no effect. Finally, the men adjourned to the farm-house and drank cider and told tales round the fire. This must be done on Old Twelfiyane, *i.e.* on the eve of Old Christmas Day. (*Folk-Lore*, vol. 6, 1895, p. 93.)

The firing at apple trees on the 5th January was very usual in the Ashburton district, during the 'fifties, when I remember the salvoes of fire-arms from the various orchards on that night. How far back the actual wassailing was observed I do not know, but all the old men spoke of it as having been usual in their younger days. The last occasion in which I took part was on 5th January, 1887, when a party of young men proceeded to our orchard and vigorously saluted the trees with volleys from shotted guns, accompanied by cider drinking, shouting " the old charm " : " Here's to thee, old apple tree," etc., and the libation of cider at the roots of the best-bearing trees. It has been suggested that the shock and smoke of the gun-firing detaches insects, the evil spirits of the orchards, from their hiding-places in the moss and bark, and these insects fall to the ground or become an easier prey to small birds. The shot is supposed to tear the bark and quicken the fruiting, similarly to the action of beating a walnut tree. (*Devon Notes and Queries*, vol. 2, 1903, p. 206.)

[*Herefordshire and Worcestershire*] In a paper read on 28th October, 1878, before members of the *Worcestershire Naturalists' Club*, it is stated that the chief observance connected with the orchards used to be that of wassailing the trees. This wassailing was observed by farmers of the previous century and the writer of the paper adds that he had met persons who had been at the celebration of the custom, in rural districts, and had received from them an account of a wassailing custom on the banks of the Teme, some years before. On this occasion, twelve small fires were lighted on an elevated wheat field and a large fire in the centre of the small ones; this large fire was sometimes called

"Old Meg." The wassailing party, forming a circle round the large fire, drank healths, with much hurrahing, and then went to the orchard. Standing round one of the best-bearing trees, they sprinkled the tree with cider, one of the party singing the lines :

> "Here's to thee, old apple tree,
> Whence thou may'st bud
> And whence thou may'st blow,
> And whence thou may'st
> Bear apples enow ;
> Hats full and caps full,
> Bushels full and sacks full,
> And my pockets full too."

Then the party returned to the farm-house where a bountiful supper and a large quantity of cider was served. (*Transactions of the Worcestershire Naturalists' Club*, Worcester, 1897, pp. 269-70.)

The above described celebration is stated to have taken place on the banks of the Teme. It appears, from other available evidence, that the celebration took place close to the county boundary. Edwin Lees says : "I believe this custom is now worn out, as on inquiry I cannot learn that it is practised in the present day." (*Pictures of Nature in the Silurian Region around the Malvern Hills, etc.*, Edwin Lees, Malvern, 1856, p. 300.)

Those owners of apple trees who preferred to adhere to the Old Style, when making arrangements for wassailing the trees, celebrated the custom on Old Twelfth Night or on Old Twelfth Day, *i.e.* on the 17th January, instead of on the 5th of the month, or on the 18th January, instead of the 6th. Such customs were not uncommon in North-east Cornwall, East Devon, and West Somerset.

[*Cornwall*] It was customary to wassail the apple trees in North-east Cornwall, on Old Twelfth Night eve. A Davidstow man of near ninety had heard his father say how, on Old Twelfth Night eve, people would fire off gunpowder under the apple trees to bring good crops.—Miss B. C. Spooner on Fragments that are left in North-east Cornwall. (*Jubilee Congress of the Folk-Lore Society, Papers and Transactions*, 1930, p. 194.)

[*Devon*] " Thicky Twelfth Night is not the hraight day for wassailing of the arpul drees. Her should be done on Old Twelfth Night, not on Old Christmas Day," said an ancient sage of Stockland, in January, 1908.—Sundry Notes from West Somerset and Devon. (*Folk-Lore*, vol. 19, 1908, p. 91.)

[*Somerset*] People sing to the apple trees and fire off guns, on 17th January, to get a good crop the following season. Libations of hot drinks are poured out beneath the trees. The wassail song runs as follows :

> " Apple tree, apple tree, I wassail thee,
>   To blow and to bear
>   Hats full, caps full, three bushel bags full,
>   And my pockets full too."

(*The Parish of Selworthy*, Frederick Hancock, Taunton, 1897, p. 253.)

In the Bridgwater district, wassailing the apple trees is still observed. According to a local resident, on Old Twelfth Eve, 17th January, a small band of farm labourers, sometimes reinforced by the local blacksmith and the carpenter, pay a visit to all the orchards in the neighbourhood to carry out the old custom of wassailing. The tour begins at 7 p.m., when the men have left work. On entering an orchard, they stand round the largest tree and sing the wassail song handed down orally from father to son :

> " Wassail, wassail, all round the town,
>   The zidur cup is white and the zidur is brown."

Formerly, an old musket was fired, after the song. When the singing is finished the farmer sends out a bucket full of hot cider, with toast floating on the top. The toast is placed on the apple trees for the robins. Old men still believe that if the custom is not observed, a poor crop of apples will be the result. (*The English Illustrated Magazine*, vol. 30, 1904, pp. 273-4.)

The following is a record of transition from the types of wassailing customs already described to that of holloing or shouting to the trees.

[*Devonshire*] The custom is still prevalent in Devonshire of holloing to the apple trees on Old Christmas Eve. Toasted bread and sugar is soaked in new cider made hot for the farmer's family and the boys take out some to pour on the oldest tree and sing :

> " Here's to thee, old apple tree ;
> From every bough,
> Give us apples enow,
> Hat fulls, cap fulls,
> Bushel, bushel, boss fulls.
> Hurrah, hurragh."

The village boys go round also for the purpose and get some coppers for their " hollering," as they call it. (*N. and Q.*, i, 5, 1852, p. 148.)

[*Somerset*] The ancient custom of singing to the apple trees on various farms took place at Wiveliscombe, in Somersetshire, on the 17th January, 1882. (*The Antiquary*, vol. 5, 1882, p. 131.) The original authority for this record was the *Somerset County Gazette*, but no date is available.

[*Surrey*] A friend writes from Camberley, Surrey, saying : " The custom you inquire about is still carried on here. Several boys come round in the evening of Old Christmas Eve, 5th January, and repeat these words to make the fruit trees bear well the next season :

> Here stands a good old apple tree.
> Stand fast root,
> Every bough apples enow,
> Every twig apple big.
> Hat-fulls, cap-fulls,
> Four and twenty sack-fulls.
> Hip, hip, hurrah !

They begin in a low, mumbling tone and get louder and louder until they shout so as to be heard half a mile away. Finally, they blow a huge cow's-horn. They go conscientiously to every tree in the garden, varying the words and substituting ' mulberry,' ' nut,' ' fig,' ' currant,' etc., as required. When I told them our fig trees did not bear, they said they would take care it didn't happen again. I believe this is the only village in the district where the custom still remains."—1907. (A. M. Spoer.)

[*Sussex*] The custom of wassailing the apple trees still prevails at Duncton, near Petworth, and the voices of the young villagers sing to the apple trees on Old Christmas Eve, the old " Mistletoe Bough " being a favourite ditty. The oldest inhabitant can recollect that the custom has been kept up for the last fifty years. (*Old English Customs extant at the Present Time*, P. H. Ditchfield, 1896, pp. 46-7.)

HOLLY NIGHT AT BROUGH

[*Westmorland*] On the Eve of the Epiphany, 5th January, there is an annual procession at Brough-under-Stainmore, Westmorland, called the carrying of the Holling or Holly tree. (*Parliamentary Gazette*, vol. 2, 1843, p. 297.)

Holling, the Eve of the Epiphany, so-called at Brough, where there is an annual procession of an ash tree, lighted on the tops of its branches to which combustible material has been tied. The custom commemorates the Star of Bethlehem. (*Dict. of Archaic and Provincial Words and Phrases*, James Orchard Halliwell, 2nd edition, vol. 1, 1850, p. 456.)

At Brough, there are two head inns which provide for the ceremony, alternately. About 8 p.m., the torches attached to the tree are lighted and, accompanied by the town band, the tree is carried, in stately procession, about the town. Rockets and squibs are discharged and many of the people carry lighted torches and branches. (*See* Plate III.) When the tree has burned enough, it is carried to the centre of the town and, amidst cheers, is thrown down, when two contending parties, patrons of the two inns, seize it, each party trying to take the tree to its inn. A holly tree was used at one time but, holly trees being scarce, an ash tree is used instead. (*The Table Book*, William Hone, 1886, pp. 13-14.)

MOSELEY'S DOLE

[*Staffordshire*] During a period of several centuries, until the year 1825, a custom was celebrated annually, on the Eve

PLATE III

CARRYING THE "HOLLY TREE" AT BROUGH, WESTMORLAND

of the Epiphany, of giving a penny to every man, woman, and child in Walsall and certain neighbouring villages, non-residents, and strangers included; this gift was called Moseley's Dole.

There are important seventeenth century records, one by Sir William Dugdale, Garter King-of-Arms, and another by Dr. Plot, Professor of Chemistry in the University of Oxford. Sir William does not mention the Dole but describes the changes of ownership of Bascote Manor, Warwickshire, at one time belonging to a certain Thomas Moseley; Dr. Plot deals with the custom of the Dole.

After a brief history of the tenure of the Manor from the time of Richard I until Thomas Moseley became lord of it, Sir William continues, as follows: " For 6 Sept. 8. H. 6. [1430], the same John Lee did pass to Thomas Molesley [Moseley] and his heirs his whole right therein; unto whom also T. Wyrth relased his interest, so that in 10. H. 6. [1432] the said T. Molesley, who then wrote himself of Mokkushull, in this County, was certified to be Lord thereof. Which Thomas by his deed of feoffment, bearing date on the day of St. Nicholas 30 H. 6. [1452] granted it to William Lyle and Thomas Magot, in trust for the use of the Town of Walshall; but it so fell out, that the Inhabitants, being kept from the profits thereof, in the beginning of H. 8. time, by John Lyle son of Will. Lyle, the surviving feoffee, who denyed any such trust, pretending it to be his own inheritance, came to Moxhull and drove away Mr. Lyle's cattell; of which unjustifiable act he hasted not to take advantage, by reason he was lyable to their action; and so upon cool debate betwixt them, they grew to this conclusion; viz. that Mr. Lyle should suffer a recovery thereof, which was accordingly done in 6 H. 8. [1515] Richard Hurst and John Forde of Walshall, being the persons to whom it was adjudged. Which Richard and John soon after made a new feoffment thereof to some other of the Inhabitants to the use of the Town; and by the like renewing of Feoffments it hath continued to the said uses untill this day." (*Antiquities of Warwickshire*, William Dugdale, 1656, pp. 231-2.)

Dr. Plot's account reads as follows: " At Walshall, in this County, they have also at this day an unusual ('tis true) but a very good custom of distributing, annually, a certain dole of one peny and no more, on Twelfth Eve, to all persons then residing in the Town or Burg of Walshall and in all the Villages and Hamlets belonging thereunto, viz. Walshall Wood, Shellfield, Bloxwich, Bescot, Harding, Goscot, Woodend, Caldmoore, The Pleck, and Birchills, which they call the Forraigne, and not only to the constant inhabitants of these places but to all strangers too then found in Walshall Town, or within any of the aforesaid villages, within the Liberties of it, whether old or young, rich or poor, men, women or children of what quality or condition soever they may be. This dole-penny is also given to all persons then residing in the parish of Rushall, which upon this account is thought to have been formerly part of the Forraigne of Walshall, which general beneficence they call Moseley's dole, being given by one Thomas Moseley, an inhabitant of this Town [the place of residence is explained here] as tradition goes upon this account, viz. That the said Tho. Moseley walking the streets of this Town, on the Eve of the Epiphany, heard a child crying for bread, which raised his charity to such a strain that he presently vowed that no person hereafter, of what condition soever, should want bread in that Town or Liberties on that day again; whereupon he immediately setled his Manor of Bascot, in Warwickshire, upon the Corporation for ever, for the use above mentioned.

" But the truth of the matter seems rather to be that this settlement (which he made by deed of feoffment on St. Nicholas's Day, 30 of Hen. 6., granting it to William Lyle and Thomas Magot for the use of the Town)[1] was for maintenance, in part at lest, of an obit for his soule and the soule of his wife Margaret, to be celebrated in the Parish Church here and in the Abbey of Hales Owen; it appearing by the accounts of Tho. Nowell, 30 Hen. 8. [1539], one of the Masters of the Guild of St. John Baptist (whereof there were three) who received the Rents and kept the Courts at Bascot, but made their accounts to the Mayor,

[1] Dugdale, *Antiq. of Warwickshire*, 1656, p. 231.

that he claimed an allowance of 13s. 4d. upon his account for that dole,[1] paid to Sir John Dudley, possessor of the Ecclesiastical rights of the Monastery of Hales Owen, to procure an Anniversary to be performed by the religious men of that house for the soules of Thomas Moseley and his wife Margaret; and that he claimed allowance of 15s. 4d. for the like Anniversary in the Parish Church of Walshall, which seems to be all was paid out of it, though another paper, *Ex ipsis. Autog. penes Mayorem & Burgens. de Walshall*,[2] also mentions nine marks[3] paid annually to the Abbey of Halesowen, the rest of the Income wholly accruing to the benefit of the Town, which they since converted to the maintenance of this yearly benevolence, there being no such dole given or instituted either by Will or Feoffment, nor any mention made of it till 30 Hen. 8. when £7 10s. 9d. discharged it.

"However, the Corporation, by way of Gratitude, he having indeed given the estate which maintain'd it, called it Moseley's Dole, sending the Bell-man about the Town that day to excite the people to repair to church to pray for the soules of Thomas Moseley and Margaret his wife, upon which account it was quickly after seized by the Crown, as all other lands were, esteemed any way to be put to superstitious uses; where it continued to the 28. Elizabeth [1587], yet was still rented by the Town for the use of the dole, when it was given by the Queen to Sir Jacob Crofts, Comptroller of her household, who sold it to one Shaw and Headock Esq. and they again to the Mayor and Commonalty of Walshall, who possess it to this day and put as much of it to the same use as the number of persons both in the Burg and Forraigne and parish of Rushall require, which commonly now amounts to about two or three and twenty pounds, the whole Manor yielding them a hundred pounds per annum, or

---

[1] This was not necessarily Moseley's Dole but may have been pence given to lay persons at the obit.

[2] From duly attested documents in possession of the Mayor and Townsmen of Walsall.

[3] Like other sums mentioned by Dr. Plot, this was paid out of the income from the estate and, in the fifteenth century, would have been sufficient to pay the Dole.

thereabout." (*The Natural History of Staffordshire*, Robert Plot, Oxford, 1686, pp. 314-5. or §§ 82-4.)

In the Christmas holidays, two persons appointed by the Corporation distribute the dole in accordance with the custom. The money is paid out of the Corporation estates at Bascot, Warwickshire; in the year 1786, it took upwards of £60 to pay the dole. Some years ago, the Corporation withheld payment of the dole, believing that they had a right to do so, but the people, by riots and other means, compelled its continuance.—*The Universal Magazine* for January, 1788, p. 44. (*N. and Q.*, iii, 1, p. 233.)

Walsall. At this place, there is a very old custom of giving a penny loaf, yearly, on Twelfth Eve, to every person belonging to the town and out-hamlets of the parish that will come and fetch it. The origin of this can hardly now be discovered. (*The History and Directory of Walsall, etc.*, Thomas Pearce, Birmingham, 1813, p. 15.)

This record introduces reference to a change in the method of distribution of the Dole. In 1825, a greater change was made; eleven almshouses were substituted for the Dole.

In 1726, a commission for charitable uses being issued out of Chancery for this and other counties, complaint was made against the Walsall Corporation about this dole, but it plainly appeared that the lands belonged to the Corporation and that the dole was only customary. However, once an attempt was made to withhold it, but the populace enforced the continuance of the custom until 1825. (*The Customs, Superstitions, and Legends of the County of Stafford*, Charles Henry Poole, *n.d.*, but about 1875, pp. 47-8.)

The evidence relating to Moseley's Dole is such as to justify a brief analysis. Sir William Dugdale's account of Bascote Manor, given in full above, is a statement of facts and is of interest for what it says and for what it omits. He does not say anything about the Dole and any statement to the contrary and not supported by evidence has been rejected here. His account shows that, in 1452, Thomas Moseley granted his Bascote estate to William Lyle and Thomas Magot, in trust for the use of the Town of Walsall. He does not say for what valuable considerations Thomas Moseley made the grant, nor does he explain the phrase " to the said uses," in the last line of his account. In relation to the custom of Moseley's Dole, it would be of much interest to know why the grant was made.

The popular tradition that Thomas Moseley made the grant because, having heard a child crying for bread on a certain Eve of the Epiphany, in Walsall, he decided to prevent such a thing happening again, is plausible but, in the absence of corroborative evidence, can have weight only because it has been a remarkably consistent tradition believed for centuries.

Dr. Plot's suggestion that Thomas Moseley's grant of his Bascote estate, 6th December, 1452, was made to ensure maintenance of the obits, as already defined, has long been accepted; the suggestion is well supported by documentary evidence and is consistent with the custom of ancient times, in England, of making grants to secure the performance of some of the most solemn services of the Church. Thus, we can accept the conclusion that the maintenance of the obits at Halesowen Abbey and at Walsall Parish Church [1] was one incident of the tenure of Bascote estate and it is probable that the maintenance of Moseley's Dole was another incident of the tenure. This is supported by several considerations. The costs of the obits and of Moseley's Dole were paid from the same source, the income from the Bascote estate. The Corporation of Walsall rented the estate for the use of the Dole during the period of retention by the Crown, so that, even when the obits were not being maintained, payment of the Dole was continued out of the income from the estate; and, after the estate was re-acquired by the Corporation, the Dole was paid until the year 1825. A further consideration is that, from the time when the inhabitants drove off Mr. Lyle's cattle, as stated by Sir William Dugdale, until the year 1825, the people acted as if they had a personal interest in the estate and a legal right to defend it.

There is no valid evidence to support Dr. Plot's assertion that no such Dole was given or instituted by Will or Feoffment. There certainly was a Feoffment, that of 6th December, 1452, and, on the evidence available, the Dole was instituted by that

[1] St. Matthew's Church, Walsall.

Feoffment. Dr. Plot's assertion that the Corporation of Walsall instituted the Dole is not supported by evidence and, apart from any other consideration, the Corporation was not influenced by affection for the custom. This is not surprising for, by the terms of the custom, the Dole was a universal beneficence to be distributed primarily to the inhabitants of Walsall and the villages aforesaid, but available for anyone, from China to Peru, who happened to turn up in Walsall or one of the aforesaid villages, at the time of distribution. This is not the kind of dole favoured by a Corporation.

More than a century has elapsed since payment of the Dole ceased but, in the period 1880-1900, there were, in the district extending from Lichfield to Stourbridge and from Birmingham to Wolverhampton, persons who remembered the custom during the years 1815-1825. None of them had been a recipient of the Dole, but they remembered the popular tradition about the origin of the custom. The obits were not mentioned, but they recalled the strong opposition by the people to any abolition of the custom, and mentioned a Mr. Moseley, of Walsall, who settled an estate for payment of the Dole.

POPULAR SAYINGS AND BELIEFS

" Cows will be found on their knees at midnight on the Eve of the true anniversary of Christ's birth."

In some forms of this saying and belief, sheep and horses, as well as cows, are included. The saying and belief is well-known in many counties among which may be specially mentioned Cornwall, Devon, Somerset, Dorset, Wiltshire, Hampshire, Lancashire, Monmouthshire, Herefordshire, Warwickshire, Worcestershire, and Buckinghamshire.[1]

[*Cornwall*] The tradition of oxen kneeling on Old Christmas day still lives in Cornwall. I had it from an old Davidstow man of near ninety, whose wife believed it. A family that had been working late, he said, on the Eve of Old Christmas day went to

[1] It is generally believed that, just at midnight, on Christmas Eve, all the cattle kneel down. The same belief prevails in Normandy. (*Guernsey Folk Lore*, Sir Edgar MacCulloch, 1903, p. 34.)

Twelfth Night

sleep in the barn over the shippen. Hearing the most extraordinary groans, at midnight, the father of the family looked down into the shippen and behold! the oxen were on their knees.—Miss B. C. Spooner on Fragments that are left in North-east Cornwall. (*Jubilee Congress of the Folk-Lore Society, Papers and Transactions*, 1930, p. 193.)

It was believed that on the Eve of the Epiphany, the cattle in the fields never lay down but, at midnight, turned their faces to the east and fell on their knees.—Miss M. A. Courtney on Cornish Feasts and Feasten Customs. (*Folk-Lore Journal*, vol. 4, 1886, p. 123.)

[*Devonshire*] An old belief, told me by an old shepherd, is that, on Old Christmas Eve, 5th January, at midnight, sheep, horses, and cattle go down on their knees and moan. It was usual to change their diet and keep them in half the day.—Lady Rosalind Northcote. (*Trans. Devon. Assoc.*, vol. 32, Plymouth, 1900, pp. 86-7.)

It is not until midnight on Old Christmas Eve that cows are believed to go down upon their knees, in commemoration of Christ's birth. (*The Dialect of Hartland*, R. Pearse Chope, 1891, p. 17.)

[*Hampshire; Lancashire*] In the north of Hampshire, the old villagers sit up till twelve o'clock on Old Christmas Night and, as soon as they hear the leaves rustling, they go to the nearest cow shed or horse stable to watch the animals stand up and then lie down on their other side. The rustling of the leaves is connected with the tradition that thorn trees burst into bloom at midnight to commemorate the Saviour's birth. The same belief is current in the neighbourhood of Stonyhurst, Lancashire. (*Old English Customs extant at the Present Time*, P. H. Ditchfield, 1896, p. 52.)

[*Monmouthshire*] An old country woman told the Rev. T. A. Davies, of Llanishen, that her grandfather, when he lived at the Graig, Llanishen, one Old Christmas Eve, heard the cattle lowing in their sheds and, peeping in, he saw the ploughing oxen bowing their knees as they lowed. (*South Wales Argus*, 10th March, 1928.)

THE GLASTONBURY THORN

[*Somerset*] The legend of the Glastonbury Thorn is that Joseph of Arimathea, on his way to Glastonbury, arrived at Wearyhall Hill, south of the town, and rested there after having thrust his stick into the earth. The stick took root and, in due course, blossomed annually on the anniversary of the birth of Christ.

In later times, this legend was utilized to show that the anniversary of Christ's birth was the 6th day of January and not the 25th of December. The Glastonbury Thorn, it is said, was flourishing in Queen Elizabeth's reign but was cut down by soldiers during the Civil War. Assuming, however, that all this were true, there were other trees, reputed descendants of the Glastonbury Thorn, which blossomed in the same way. It is not remarkable that, if such trees existed, they should be visited by many people from all parts of the country.

During the autumn of 1755, John Jackson, an enthusiastic inquirer for details relating to the Glastonbury Thorn, travelled on foot from Woodchurch, in the West Riding of Yorkshire, to Glastonbury. After his return, he said: " The noted tree at Glastonbury, I find, is no fiction and its blossoming on Christmas day, I think, is truly supernatural." At Glastonbury, he asked whether the Thorn ever did blossom on the New Christmas Day, 25th December, and was informed angrily that it had not and never would. No service, he said, was held on Old Christmas Day, yet for most of the day the bells rang as hard as they could at St. John's Church. (*Old Yorkshire*, William Smith, Editor, vol. 4, 1883, pp. 174-5.)

The famous Holy Thorn of Glastonbury has representatives in this part, one at Whitestaunton and another at West Buckland. The latter is reputed to have been a very fine shrub or tree and, I am assured, has burst into flower at midnight, precisely, and has so remained until dawn, the dawn of the real Christmas Day. Now, the tree is a wreck so many pieces of it having been torn away. It still flowers very early but is no longer an object of pilgrimage. The older people tolerate the New Christmas Day but, on Old Christmas Day will not work.

Twelfth Night

(*Tales of the Blackdown Borderland*, F. W. Matthews, Somerset Folk Series, No. 13, 1923, p. 118.)

In my neighbourhood, near Bridgwater, the Christmas thorn blossoms on the 6th of January, and on this day only. The villagers in whose gardens it grows and many other persons believe that this proves that this day, 6th January, is the anniversary of the birth of Christ. (*N. and Q.*, i, 3, 1851, p. 367.)

[*Buckinghamshire*] On the night of December 24th, 1753, about two thousand people went to Quainton, with lanterns and candles, to see a certain blackthorn, alleged to have been a slip from the Glastonbury Thorn. They found no appearance of a bud and concluded that 25th December, New Style, could not be the anniversary of the day of Christ's birth and accordingly refused attendance at Church. (*Gentleman's Magazine*, vol. 23, 1753, p. 49.)

[*Herefordshire*] I have heard it said that the Rosemary blossoms on Twelfth Eve, the same as the Holy Thorn and that, at Orcop and Garway, people sat up to see it. (*The Folk-Lore of Herefordshire*, Ella Mary Leather, Hereford, 1912, p. 19.)

[*London*] Paying a visit to the Botanic Gardens in Regent's Park, yesterday, I met Mr. J. L. North, the curator of the Royal Botanic Society, who showed me the Glastonbury thorn which he brought three years ago, from Glastonbury Abbey and planted in the Gardens. Last Christmas, Mr. North assured me, the Botanic Gardens specimen reached the blossoming stage but did not burst into flower; the cold was too intense and the buds died away. (*Daily News*, 29th May, 1929.)

[*Monmouthshire*] The country woman referred to on p. 75 affirmed that, on Christmas Eve, the big rosemary (really the marine or sea rose, says the Rev. T. A. Davies) always blooms at midnight and immediately sheds its bloom. An elderly roadman, on being told this story, said: " Yes, some friends of mine watched the rosemary bloom and something does happen, and two others went down to a beehive near to watch the bees, for, after midnight, the bees come out and hum a tune and then go back." (*South Wales Argus*, 10th March, 1928.) [1]

---

[1] Cutting from the *South Wales Argus*, which had the printed date torn off but bore a torn written date.

78   *Calendar Customs*

[*Worcestershire*] At Redmarley Farm, in the Parish of Acton Beauchamp, was a holy thorn which used to be visited by many people on Old Christmas Eve, in order to see the flowers which were believed to burst forth at that time. About the middle of the eighteenth century, the farmer, annoyed by the visits of so many people, cut down the tree and, shortly afterwards, his arm was broken accidentally and his premises were burnt down. The country people believed that this was a judgment upon the farmer for cutting down the holy thorn. (*Pictures of Nature in the Silurian Region around the Malvern Hills, etc.*, Edwin Lees, Malvern, 1856, pp. 295-6.)

When an account of the legend of the Glastonbury Thorn is read, it is usually assumed that the hawthorn, whitethorn, or may is meant, but the records given above for Buckinghamshire and Monmouthshire, respectively, mention the blackthorn and the rosemary. The phenomena of the early and the late flowering of trees, shrubs, and herbaceous plants, from year to year, are well known. Early flowering is well marked in the hawthorn, which normally flowers about the 12th May, in Hertfordshire, and still more marked in the blackthorn, which normally flowers about the 3rd April; no data are at hand for the rosemary which, being a cultivated exotic shrub, may be more erratic than the indigenous trees and shrubs. In recent times the hawthorn has been nineteen days and the blackthorn twenty-seven days early in flowering.

FAIR

[*Northumberland*] At the Berwick Hiring Fair for stewards and shepherds on Saturday, 5th January, the wages offered and accepted were £2 weekly, with the usual perquisites. (*Daily News and Leader*, Monday, 7th January, 1918, p. 5, *c*.)

Twelfth Day
6th January

On Twelfth Day, social gatherings were arranged at which ceremonies like those of Twelfth Night were performed, the

Twelfth Day

cutting of the Twelfth Cake, the election of a King and Queen of the ceremonies and, in the orchards, the wassailing of the apple trees. Two centuries ago, Twelfth Day seems to have been the most festive day of the twelve, at any rate in the North of England, for it is said that Twelfth Day was one of the greatest of the twelve and of more jovial observance than the others for the visiting of friends and Christmas gambols. (*Antiquities of the Common People*, Henry Bourne, Newcastle, 1725, pp. 151-2.)

[*Lincolnshire, etc.*] The royal Epiphany custom at the Chapel Royal and the Haxey custom of Throwing the Hood, are still celebrated on the 6th January. The popular beliefs on the determination of the true anniversary of the birth of Christ belong to the 5th and the 6th January; they are described under the 5th of January.

ROYAL CUSTOM ON EPIPHANY

It has long been a custom of the Kings of England to attend personally, or by proxy, at the annual Epiphany service at the Chapel Royal and offer gold, frankincense, and myrrh in commemoration of the offering of presents by the Magi.

[*London*] Yesterday being Twelfth day or Epiphany, their Majesties, accompanied by members of the Royal Family and preceded by officers of the Court and knights of the Garter, Thistle, and Bath, went to the Chapel Royal, St. James's, for the service. During the offertory, the King advanced to the altar and offered three purses respectively containing gold, frankincense, and myrrh, in presence of the Bishop of London. (Cutting inserted opposite p. 19 of Joseph Haslewood's copy of Brand, 1813 edition, and dated by him 1736; other cuttings, inserted opposite p. 23, record the celebration of the custom in 1730 (*Morning Post*), 1750, 1753, 1764.)

In the Lady's Magazine for 1760, it is recorded that Sunday, 6th January, being Twelfth Day and a collar and offering day at St. James's, the King, preceded by officers of the Court and knights of the Garter, Thistle, and Bath, in their collars of their respective orders, went to the Chapel Royal, at St. James's, and offered gold, frankincense, and myrrh, in imitation of the Eastern

80   *Calendar Customs*

Magi. The gold, frankincense, and myrrh are still offered; they are presented in silk bags. (*N. and Q.*, ii, 3, 1857, p. 13.)

During the offertory at the Epiphany service, at the Chapel Royal, St. James's, two officers of Her Majesty's household, in royal livery and preceded by the usher, proceed from the royal pew to the altar rails and offer a red bag, edged with gold lace or braid, which is received in an offertory basin and then placed on the altar. The bag contains the Queen's Epiphany offerings. (*Echo*, 7th January, 1869.)

On Twelfth Day, 6th January, 1936, the gifts of gold, frankincense, and myrrh, from the Magi were commemorated at the Epiphany service at the Chapel Royal, St. James's. (*The Evening News*, 6th January, 1936.)

BELL-RINGING ON EPIPHANY

[*Lincolnshire*] The bells were doubtless formerly rung on Epiphany and on Candlemass, but such customs have been wellnigh discontinued. At Swineshead, Lincolnshire, however, the peals are still rung on Epiphany. (*English Bells and Bell Lore*, Thomas North, Leek, 1888, p. 145.)

KEEPING TO THE OLD STYLE

[*Cornwall*] Many elderly people, at the beginning of the nineteenth century, still kept to the Old Style Calendar and held their Christmas day on Epiphany.—Cornwall. (*Folk-Lore Journal*, vol. 4, 1886, p. 123.)

[*Herefordshire, etc.*] Old Christmas, as it is called, is still religiously observed in Herefordshire and the bordering parts of Worcestershire, and service is celebrated, on Old Christmas day, in some parishes. (*Pictures of Nature in the Silurian Region around the Malvern Hills, etc.*, Edwin Lees, Malvern, 1856, p. 296.)

The late Davies Gilbert used to tell, of his own knowledge, how an old gentleman and lady always walked to church in full dress, on Old Christmas day, and after trying in vain to enter, walked back and read the service at home. (*N. and Q.*, ii, 7, 1859, p. 35.)

[*Worcestershire*] Old Christmas is still observed, especially in the western part of the county. (*Notes and Queries for Worcestershire*, John Noake, 1856, p. 222.)

In Worcestershire, Epiphany or Old Christmas is observed in much the same way as Christmas day itself; and during this season, bands of musicians go round and play at the houses in the neighbourhood. (*Old English Customs extant at the Present Time*, P. H. Ditchfield, 1896, pp. 51-2.)

THE FEAST OF THE STAR

[*Cambridgeshire, etc.*] In some churches, *e.g.* St. Mary's Church, Cambridge, and St. Nicholas' Church, Norwich, a ceremony was performed on Epiphany to commemorate and illustrate the visit of the Magi and their guidance by the Star of Bethlehem to the cradle of Christ. In the Churchwardens' Accounts for St. Mary's, Cambridge, are the following items:

" 1557-8. For making of a stare - - - - 20d.
For penting and gelding the same stere - 20d."

In the Accounts for Yarmouth, 1462-1512, there are entries relating to the making of a new star and the mechanical means for moving it.

[*Norfolk*] In a paper read before the *Norfolk and Norwich Archæological Society* by Mr. Leonard G. Bolingbroke, on Pre-Elizabethan Plays and Players in Norfolk, he points out how highly dramatic were some of the ceremonies performed in our cathedrals and churches before the Reformation. In the Feast of the Star, at Epiphany, the Magi, represented by two priests suitably attired, entered by the west door and proceeded up the nave until, approaching the chancel, they perceived a star suspended in mid-air and said, " Behold the star of the east." Then, the star was moved backwards by means of cords and pulleys and led them to the high altar where a curtain was drawn and they saw a living child in a cradle. Simultaneously, three priests dressed as kings and attended by servants carrying offerings met before the altar. Then followed the presentation of the offerings and a service of prayer, until a boy, representing an angel, addressed the priests with the words : " All things which the prophets said are fulfilled," and thus the ceremony was concluded. (*Norfolk Archæology*, vol. 11, Norwich, 1892, pp. 334-5.)

TWELFTH DAY REVELS

The following is an account of the way in which our ancestors disposed of their provisions during these revels.

On this day, 6th January, about the hours of 5, 6, 7, 8, 9, and 10, and till well-nigh midnight, in some places, will be such a massacre of spice-bread that, ere the next day, at noon, a twopenny brown loaf will be a rarity.—*Vox Graculi*, 1623, p. 52. (*Brcnd*, i, p. 32.)

[*London*] A city merchant, Mr. Thomas North, states that, having been invited by a nobleman in the West End to join his party for Wednesday, the 6th of January, or Twelfth Day, he accepted the invitation and went by coach. During his journey across London, he was amused and astonished at what he saw. All the trades in Town seemed to have given place to the single one of the pastry-cooks and no manufactures were thought worthy of attention but those engaged in the preparation of the incredible number of cakes for the night's revels. By means of flags and streamers, the pastry-cooks' shops competed with one another in advertising their cakes, but one shop, near a church in Fleet Street, surpassed the rest. Arrived at the nobleman's house, Mr. North joined a large company, cheerful and without stiffness and ceremony. There was a sumptuous entertainment at which the main topic was about an immense Twelfth Cake, the cutting of which was followed by the election of the King and the Queen of the ceremonies, the former honour falling to himself, while the title of Queen went to a beautiful Lady who sat opposite him. (Abridged from a MS. copy of Mr. North's Letter to *Reads' Weekly Journal*, Saturday, the 9th of January, 1730-1.)

TWELFTH CAKES

The old English Twelfth Cake lost much of its popularity after the change in the calendar, 1752. For Twelfthtide parties, it was large, round, and apparently not deeper, relatively, than the typical Shrewsbury simnel. The pastry-cooks, competing eagerly with one another in the production of attractive cakes, no doubt introduced novelties in form and composition, but the essential ingredients, in olden times, were flour, sugar including icing, honey, ginger, pepper, and probably dried fruit, for Herrick mentions " plums " ; *see* p. 52. The following record relates to a Twelfth Cake of comparatively recent times.

[*Hampshire*] Here is a recipe for an English twelfth cake, which I found in a cookery book over 100 years old. Put 2 lb. of butter in a stewpan in a warm place and work into a smooth cream with the hand, mix it with 2 lb. of sifted loaf sugar and ¼ oz. each of ground allspice, ground cinnamon, mace, ginger, and coriander, also a large nutmeg grated. Break in 18 eggs by degrees and beat for at least twenty minutes, stir in a gill of brandy and then add 2 lb. of sifted flour and work a little. Next add 4 lb. of currants, ¼ lb. chopped blanched almonds, ½ lb. citron, ½ lb. orange peel and lemon peel cut small. Line a baking-tin with double paper and bake in a slow oven for four hours. Then ice with plain sugar icing.—Jane Morse, English Folk Cookery Association, Fareham, Hants. (*The Times*, 15th January, 1937, p. 8 *e.*)

RELICS OF THE CUSTOM

[*London*] For several years past, I have been in the habit of giving a small Twelfth Night party ; at first, I had such difficulty in obtaining a twelfth cake that I nearly gave up the idea. I tried large and old-established firms to small one-man shops in back streets. Most of my inquiries were received with looks of blank incomprehension. At last, I found a small French pastry-cook's shop in Soho, which was well stocked with *Galettes des Rois.*—Miss P. Taves, Lansdowne Road, W. 11. (*The Times*, 11th January, 1937.) The use of the word " Galette " suggests that broad, thin cakes are meant.

The Master of the Parish Clerks' Company, after their audit dinner on Old Christmas Day, cut the Twelfth Night cake and each past Master had a portion which he took home. This ceremony has been carried out annually, except for the period of the

Great War, for more than forty years to the writer's personal knowledge, he having taken part during that time.—Mr. H. McClintock Harris, Father of the Court of Assistants, Silver Street, E.C. (*The Times*, 22nd January, 1937, p. 10, *e*.)

[*Worcestershire*] Twelfth Cakes seem to be unknown in England, but in France there are often parties round about Epiphanytide and the Twelfth cake is a large, flat pastry cake containing a tiny china doll. The cake is cut soon after the guests arrive and the one who gets the doll is crowned king or queen and is master of the revels for the evening. January 6th, being the Feast of the Epiphany and the local Women's Institute party, we revived the old custom with great success.—Mrs. Hodgins, The Rectory, Alvechurch, Worcestershire. (*The Times*, 14th January, 1937, p. 8, *d*.)

Here, in the South of France, where I have lived for the past fifteen years, every one eats the *Gâteau des Rois* [1] at the Epiphany and the patisseries are full of them, large and small. This cake is always a *brioche* in the form of a ring and in it is always to be found a tiny china Infant Christ.—Mrs. M. L. N. Westall, Antibes (A. M.), France. (*The Times*, 20th January, 1937, p. 10, *d*.)

TWELFTH DAY IN THE NORTH

[*Cumberland, etc.*] In Cumberland and other counties of the North of England, on the night finishing the Christmas holidays, the rustics meet in a large room, begin dancing at 7 o'clock, and finish at twelve, when they sit down to Lobsconse or Lobsconce and Ponsondie, the latter being the wassail-bowl containing the well-known Lamb's Wool and the former consisting of beef, potatoes, and onions fried together. All costs are paid for by subscriptions from those present. (*Times' Telescope* for 1825, pp. 11-12.)

In many of the small towns in Cumberland, some kind of game is brought to the table and also field peas scalded in their shells and served with butter. The supper concludes with a tharve cake, a large flat oaten cake, sometimes containing plums.

[1] Gâteau des Rois = Twelfth Cake.

At all their festivals, tar barrels are common and scarcely a town in Cumberland is without them to-night. (*Time's Telescope* for 1829, p. 12.)

TWELFTH DAY FIRES

[*Gloucestershire*] A custom prevailed about Newent and the neighbouring parishes, on Twelfth day or Epiphany; in the evening, the servants of every farmer assembled together in one of the fields that had been sown with wheat. On the border of this field and on the most elevated part, they made twelve fires of straw and around one fire, larger than the rest, they drank a glass of cider to the success of the next harvest. Then, returning to the farm-house, they were served with caraway-seed cake and cider. (Thomas Blount's *Ancient Tenures of Land, etc.*, W. Carew Hazlitt, Editor, 2 vols., vol. 1, 1874, p. 131.)

[*Herefordshire*] In Herefordshire, on Twelfth day, they make twelve fires of straw, one large one to burn the old witch. Without this ceremony they think they would have no crops. They sing, drink, and dance round it. (*Gentleman's Magazine*, vol. 92, 1822, January-June, pp. 14-5.) This is one of the few available records which refer to the burning of the witch, a phrase which probably includes the burning of insect pests.

[*Staffordshire, etc.*] The ancient custom of blazing the wheat was observed on Blaze Night, the 6th of January. In order to scare witches and other enemies from the growing corn, men and lads ran all over the wheat field with lighted torches of straw; these were bundles of straw tied tightly together. The custom was practised at Standon Hall, not long ago. (*Folk Lore: Old Customs and Tales of my Neighbours*, Fletcher Moss, Didsbury and Manchester, March, 1898, pp. 52 and 200.)

WASSAILING THE APPLE TREES

[*Devonshire*] I remember, in my younger days (a long time ago) being told of the custom of firing at apple trees, on the night of Twelfth day, being carried out in several country places in Devonshire. I especially remember an old gentleman, who had resided for many years at Bovey Tracy, informing me that when it was done, a song was sung, a part of which I remember :

> " Bear and blow,
> Apples enow
> Hats full, caps full
> Bushels full. . . . "

(*Trans. Devon. Assoc.*, vol. 37, Plymouth, 1905, p. 117.)

On Old Christmas day, the apples are christened with cider to ensure a fruitful season. On or about this day, the farmer gives a feast to all who assisted him during the preceding harvest.—Hartland, N. Devon. (*The Dialect of Hartland*, R. Pearse Chope, 1891, p. 17.)

[*Somerset*] I never saw the wassailing of the apple trees performed in Devonshire but, in my early days, I lived in Somerset, in the Parish of Wiveliscombe, about four miles over the border from Devonshire, and the custom was regularly kept up there and I believe it is still, and I have seen it. The procedure was as follows : On the evening of Twelfth day, a number of people formed a circle round one of the apple trees ; some had guns, some had old tea kettles or tin trays to be struck with a poker or fire shovel. The leader of the party sang a song, of which I can remember only one verse, which was :

> " There was an old man
> And he had an old cow
> And how to keep her he didn't know how ;
> So he built up a barn
> To keep this cow warm,
> And a little more cider would do us no harm.
> Harm, my boys, harm !
> A little more cider would do us no harm."

The guns were fired and the kettles and trays banged and then all stooped down and then raised themselves ; these movements were repeated three times and then they shouted :

> " Now, now, now,
> Hats full, caps full

Twelfth Day

   Three-bushel bags full
   And a little heap under the stairs.
   Please God send a good crop."

Then this was repeated and was followed by more gun-firing and kettle-banging. Cider was next passed round and a second verse was sung with the same ceremonies. There were several verses which I cannot recollect.—H. C. Adams. (*Devon Notes and Queries*, vol. 3, 1904-5, p. 156.)

  On Old Twelfth day, 18th January, called also Twelfy day, a custom is kept up of going out and shooting at the apple trees. It was and is an Epiphany custom and I find that it was kept up in country places where, even now, the reformed calendar has not taken root. (*West Somerset Word-Book*, Frederick Thomas Elworthy, 1886, p. 782.)

SHOUTING TO THE APPLE TREES

  [*Devonshire*] The custom of shouting to the apple trees used to be celebrated in the Parish of Chudleigh. The boys of the village went round in the evening of the Feast of Epiphany, visiting each orchard and repeating a doggerel rhyme, calling on the tree to be fruitful in the autumn. The farmers used to attach importance to the custom, believing that its omission would be fatal to the fruiting prospects of the apple trees, for the year. (*Western Antiquary*, vol. 9, Plymouth, 1890, p. 164.)

TWELFTH DAY WASSAILING

  [*Worcestershire*] On Old Christmas day, at Offenham, near Evesham, the children go round, singing a wassailing song:

   " Whistle, wastle, through the town,
    The cup is white and the ale is brown;
    The cup is made of the ashen tree;
    Come all good fellows and drink with me.
    The Missis is up and the Master down,
    This is the best house in all the town."

(*The Rambler in Worcestershire*, John Noake, 2 vols., 1851-4, vol. 2, p. 88.)

TWELFTH DAY MORRIS DANCERS

[*Derbyshire*] The morris dancers who go about from village to village, about Twelfth Day, have their Fool, their Maid Marian, generally a man dressed in woman's clothes and called the Fool's wife, and sometimes there is a hobby horse. The dancers are dressed up in ribbons and tinsel, but the bells are usually discarded. (*Journ. British Archæol. Assoc.*, vol. 7, 1852, p. 201.)

THROWING THE HOOD

[*Lincolnshire*] On a certain Old Christmas day, according to local tradition, a Lady Mowbray was out riding when her red hood was blown away by a strong wind. Twelve men working in the fields chased and caught the hood but their efforts afforded her ladyship so much amusement that, when they restored the hood to her, she gave them money and also decided to settle land, in trust, for maintaining an annual celebration, on Old Christmas day, at Haxey, of a sport, to be called " Throwing the Hood " and to be followed by a feast. Accordingly, twelve half-acres and the half-acre on which, it was said, the hood was blown away, were settled as and for the purposes aforesaid. Some, however, believe that the custom is a relic of rites performed in ancient Celtic times.

Old Christmas day is the great day of the year at Haxey, where the Hood is still kept up in the old traditional manner; the day is a general holiday and people invite their friends to come. For the celebration of the custom, there are necessary twelve men, called Boggans, and the Fool. During the week before Old Christmas day, the Fool and his twelve Boggans employ their evenings in going round the district collecting money to keep up the custom. They go dressed in their ceremonial clothes, but the Fool does not colour his face. Their songs are " The Farmer's Boy," " John Barleycorn," and " Drink England dry." At the celebration of the Haxey Hood, in previous years, the procession of the twelve Boggans, headed by the Fool, marched from Wroot to Haxey; watch was kept from Haxey Church tower and, as soon as the first glimpse was caught of the pro-

PLATE IV

HAXEY HOOD GAME, 1932

A, The Lord ; B, The Lord's Wand ; C, The Leather Hood

cession, the church bells rang out merrily. This year, 1932, however, there was a shooting match in the morning and many clay-pigeons were brought down. At 2 p.m., the procession started at the old cross at the top of Haxey Lane and came up the village street. In Plate IV three Boggans are shown in ceremonial dress, red flannel coats and tall hats decorated with red flowers; the other Boggans are wearing red bands round their arms. The Fool stands on the base of the old cross; his face is smeared with soot and red ochre; his trousers are of sackcloth with pieces of red flannel stitched into it, in various shapes; he wears a red shirt, a tall hat decorated by the wing of a goose and red flowers; in his right hand he carries a short-stocked whip having a sock, filled with bran, attached to its thong. The wand of the Lord or senior Boggan consists of thirteen " celery " willows bound round thirteen times. The Lord carries the Hood, shown in Plate IV to be held temporarily by the Fool; the other Boggans carry a number of the sham hoods for use in the earlier stages of the game; six or more are shown in Plate IV. The first hood thrown is always thrown up on the half-acre on which, it is believed, Lady Mowbray's hood was blown away. The sham hoods are made of rolls of sacking, tied round with ribbons, but the Hood, called also the Sway Hood, is a length of stout rope firmly encased in leather and is used from year to year. At 4 p.m. this Hood was thrown up and then began the most strenuous part of the proceedings, the Sway [or tug-of-war] by two contending parties for possession of the Hood. In fair weather, there would be about 300 in the Sway but, in 1932, the weather was unfavourable and the crowd was smaller than usual. (*Lincolnshire Folklore*, Ethel H. Rudkin, Gainsborough, 1936, pp. 90-1.)

After making his speech, the Fool leads the way to the millfield, where Lady Mowbray's hood is believed to have been blown away and, on arrival at the field, the sham hoods are thrown to the crowd. Anyone who secures a hood and escapes without being touched by the Boggans, who carry long sticks, runs to the village and is entitled to free drinks at any inn he chooses to enter. At 4 p.m., the real Hood, 25 inches long and 9 inches in circumference, is thrown up ; then one end of the Hood is seized by partisans of one part of the Parish and the other end by those of the other part and the struggle at once becomes strenuous. The sport lasts till dusk and the victors carry the Hood to their part of the Parish, where it remains during the ensuing year. (*The English Illustrated Magazine*, December, 1903, vol. 30, 1904, pp. 270-2.)

Three men (mummers) have just left our door. They came from Haxey and this is what I gathered from them—that they stand on a stone and invite men to a big dinner, on the 6th of January. One man in scarlet jacket and wearing a hat adorned with artificial flowers was a lord ; he carried a large leather roll, called a hood, and thirteen willows bound into a rod. The lord was accompanied by a fool whose clothes were very grotesque ; he carried a mop. The third man, an attendant, carried a long staff. On the 6th of January, the church bells ring and the ceremony of " Swaying the Hood " takes place ; it lasts about three hours. The Hood is carried by the victors to a public house and is restored to the lord on payment of two shillings. The dinner takes place at the public house just mentioned. At one time, these mummers used to come in the evening and perform some play or make a speech ; this is not done to-day.—A correspondent to *The Standard*, writing from near Gainsborough. (*The Antiquary*, vol. 40, 1904, p. 36.)

The custom was celebrated on the 6th January, 1936 ; its essential phases were shown at a Watford cinema, on the 9th January, 1936 : the assembling of the spectators, the procession to the stone cross base, the Fool making a speech, the Boggans, the march to the field, and the struggle for the Hood.

HARTLEPOOL CUSTOM

[*Durham*] An anchor is dragged through the streets of Hartlepool, on Twelfth day, after the manner of the Fool Plough of husbandmen. (*An Historical, etc., View of the County Palatine of Durham*, E. Mackenzie and M. Ross, 2 vols., vol. 1, Newcastle-upon-Tyne, 1834, p. cxviii.)

GIFTS AND BEQUESTS

[*Dorset*] There is an old custom at Puddlehinton, Dorset, for the rector to give away, on Old Christmas day, annually, a pound of bread, a mince pie, and a pint of ale, to every poor person in the Parish. This distribution is made regularly to upwards of three hundred persons.—*Charity Commissioners' Report*, vol. 29, p. 108. (*Denham Tracts*, vol. 2, 1895, p. 91.)

POPULAR SAYINGS AND BELIEFS

[*Cheshire*] " Burn all the Christmas decorations in the shape of holly and ivy by Old Christmas day, or your house will be haunted by evil spirits all the year."—Luck, Good and Bad. Singular Village Customs in Cheshire, by Delta. (*Chester Courant, n.d.*)

[*Devonshire*] " When calves are weaned on the same day of the week as Old Christmas day happened to fall, they never get quarter-evil." In a particular instance, Old Christmas day fell on a Saturday and a farmer, who bought a calf on a Wednesday, arranged for the calf not to be taken away from its mother until the following Saturday. (*Trans. Devon. Assoc.*, vol. 38, Plymouth, 1906, pp. 94-5.)

" Child born upon Old Christmas day
Is good, and wise, and fair, and gay."

(*The Peasant Speech of Devon*, Sarah Hewett, 1892, p. 26.)

St. Distaff's Day
7th January

The day on which women resumed or made preparations for resuming their spinning, after the conclusion of the Christmas festive season, was called St. Distaff's or Rock [1] Day. The men amused themselves by burning the flax and tow used by the women who, in return, drenched the men with water. The fol-

---
[1] Rock = Distaff.

lowing is a poetic description written when the custom was popular :

> " Partly work and partly play
> Ye must on S. Distaff's day.
> From the plough soone free the teame,
> Then come home and fother them.
> If the Maides a-spinning goe,
> Burn the flax and fire the tow.
> Bring in pailes of water then,
> Let the Maides bewash the men.
> Give S. Distaff all the right,
> Then bid Christmas sport good night ;
> And next morrow, every one
> To his owne vocation."

(*Hesperides, Saint Distaff's Day*, Robert Herrick, 1648, ll. 1-14.)

TAKING DOWN CHRISTMAS DECORATIONS

These decorations have been taken down, by custom, on New Year's day, Candlemas, and Plough Monday, or, in parts of Lancashire, they have been taken down and used as fuel in making pancakes. The following is a record for taking down the decorations on St. Distaff's day.

[*Cornwall*] On the day after Twelfth day, in East Cornwall, all Christmas greenery comes down. Beware, however, of burning it, for this would be unlucky. I was once pulled back as if I were doing some ruthless deed when, in ignorance, I was about to put some Christmas holly on the fire. (T. Q. Couch in *Western Antiquary*, vol. 3, Plymouth, 1884, p. 193.)

WELL CUSTOMS

[*Scilly Isles*] About the middle of St. Agnes Island is a small well, called St. Warna's Well, which the inhabitants clean out on the day after Twelfth day and at which they pay their annual devotions and perform some mystic ceremonies, which are followed by feasting and amusements. They invoke St. Warna as a benefactress, who sends them wrecks and controls their fortunes.

St. Distaff's Day

(*A Natural and Historical Account of the Isles of Scilly*, Lieut. Robert Heath, 1750, pp. 89-90.)

Many aged people of the Island remember an annual day of rejoicing, in honour of St. Warna, which was celebrated by the discharge of fire-arms over the well. Water is still to be obtained from the shallow well as often as it is cleaned out. (*A View of the Present State of the Scilly Isles*, Rev. George Woodley, 1822, p. 329.)

Near St. Warna Bay, Agnes Island, is St. Warna's Well, once the most important spot in the Island but now an insignificant hole almost choked with dead bracken and leaves. According to tradition, St. Warna, in her coracle, put into the bay, at the end of her voyage from Ireland. (*The Isles of Scilly : Their Story, their Folk, and their Flowers*, Jessie Mothersole, 1910, p. 209.)

Plough Monday
First Monday after Twelfth Day

Just as, on St. Distaff's day, the women made preparations for resuming their spinning so, on Plough Monday, the men made preparations for resuming work in the fields ; for many, however, Plough Monday was a day of festivity associated mainly with the Fool Plough Procession. Plough Monday is not forgotten, but the old traditional custom of that day, celebrated regularly from year to year, is extinct. Performances during recent years, although intended to reproduce the old-time originals, are revivals.

[*Lincolnshire*] In Lincolnshire, at Carlton-le-Moorland and neighbouring villages, a band of farm-workers, representing the Doctor, the Fool, the Recruiting-Sergeant, the Lady, Dame Jane, the Farmer's Man, and Beelzebub, performed on Plough Monday, 8th January, 1934. (*The Lincolnshire Chronicle and Leader*, 3rd February, 1934.)

[*Yorkshire*] In Yorkshire, plough stots or mummers performed at Haxby and New Earswick, in 1930, on Plough Monday.

PLOW MONDAY IN THE CITY

[*London*] In accordance with ancient custom, Plow Monday was observed yesterday in the City. The Lord Mayor presided over a Court of Aldermen, in Grand Court of Wardmote, in the Guildhall. The Town Clerk presented the returns of the St. Thomas's day elections and, there being no objections, the Lord Mayor ordered the returns to be recorded. In the evening, the Lord Mayor and the Lady Mayoress gave the customary Plow Monday dinner. (*The Times*, Tuesday, 12th January, 1937, p. 7, *d*.)

THE PLOUGH MONDAY PROCESSION

The procession included a number of plough boys, stots, jags, or witchers who, in the guise of mummers, went about on Plough Monday, in order to obtain money and other donations to provide for a rustic feast. In olden times, a plough, sometimes blessed and perfumed by the clergy, was included in the procession and was drawn by oxen, suitably adorned, or more often by the plough boys, who were then called " plough bullocks." A plough was rarely seen in the procession after the year 1875.

Plate V, showing the Burringham Plough Boys of 1934, is an example from the collection of Mrs. E. H. Rudkin, of Lincoln, who made every effort and finally succeeded in obtaining a complete and correct reading of the characters from Mr. A. Lingo, of Burringham, probably the only person able to supply such information. Always reading from the left; we have in succession in the back row, a Hobby Horse ; Soldier ; Elsie Belsie Bug or Beelzebub ; Tom Fool ; two Hat Men, wearing tall hats decorated with ribbons and trinkets ; Besom Bet ; Sergeant ; a Hobby Horse. In the middle row, reading from the left are The Lady ; a Groom ; a Collector ; Joe Straw. In the front row, we have the Doctor, a Collector, and a Groom, in succession. Joe Straw is sometimes described as " Joe, stuffed with straw and having a goose-wing in hat." The Hobby Horse has its tail studded with tin tacks to prevent its being pulled.

Referring to the " tatters," a traditional feature in the Tom Fool's dress at Burringham, Scotter, and other places, Mrs. Rudkin says : " I have noticed a tendency, in Lincolnshire, to

PLATE V

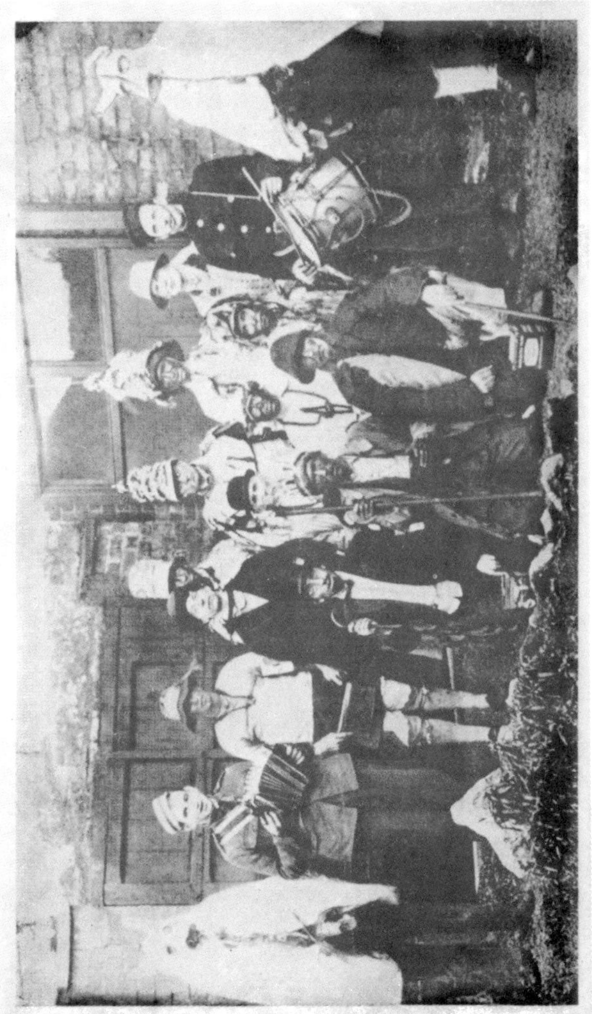

PLOUGH JAGS, BURRINGHAM, 1934

red and black in these tatters, red and black braid on horse harness and in the tails of cocks, mounted as finials on a thatched stack. Red is certainly the most popular colour; red always occurs in the brush of the centre ornament on a horse's head, and red is the dominant colour in the dress of the Boggans, in the Haxey Hood." [1]

[*Yorkshire*] In some parts of England, especially in the Whitby district, a party of sword dancers was included in the Procession. Sometimes, lads blowing cows' horns and, occassionally, the village blacksmith, carpenter, and others interested in the farming industry, joined the Procession.

RECORDS OF THE FOOL PLOUGH CUSTOM

[*Cambridgeshire*] Plough Monday is still observed at Cambridge by parties going about the town variously dressed in ribbons. Some parties include a female or a man in woman's clothes, and some of the parties have a plough. (*Time's Telescope* for 1816, pp. 3-4.)

After referring to the rapidly vanishing folk-lore of Cambridgeshire, it is stated that the Plough Monday proceedings are simple. Labourers go round, cracking whips and calling as if to plough teams, till the householder contributes to the fund for good cheer. In the Isle of Ely and district, I am informed, the plough procession used to be accompanied by seven characters : 1, the Humpty, who carried a hump, had a tail of plaited straw, horns, a black face, and a besom with which to persuade the unreasonable; 2 and 3, the King and the Queen, the latter a man in female dress; 4, a fiddler; 5, a purser to take charge of the contributions; and 6 and 7, men in tall hats, which were wound round with ribbons. The whole thing is apparently a survival of the elements from which sprang our drama. (*The East Anglian, etc.*, new series, vol. 12, Norwich, 1907-8, pp. 213-4.)

At Wisbech, as late as the 'fifties, young ploughmen carried a plough from house to house and asked for money. If none was

[1] This preference for red or red and black is noteworthy. Red especially has been a favourite colour of the Celtic races and Mrs. Rudkin's examples, as well as many others that might be given, deserve full consideration in relation to the origin of the customs mentioned above.

given, they ploughed up the scraper at the door. Plough Monday was so-called because the ploughmen's Christmas holiday ended then. (*The Times*, 25th August, 1933, p. 6, *e*.)

[*Derbyshire*] On Plough Monday, the Plough bullocks are occasionally seen. They are young men from the farm-houses, dressed up in ribbons, their shirts (for they wear no coats) literally covered with rosettes of various colours and their hats bound round with ribbons and decorated with every kind of ornament that comes in their way. The plough procession includes a plough, a band of music, the Fool and the Bessy. The Fool is dressed in the skin of a calf, with the tail hanging down behind; he carries a long stick, with an inflated bladder tied to one end, and uses it effectively on the shoulders of some of the spectators. The Bessy is usually a young man in female attire and covered with ribbons. When a donation is received, the gang dances round the plough, but if nothing is forthcoming, they plough up the ground.—Customs and Sports of the County of Derby, Llewellyn Jewitt. (*The Journal of the British Archæol. Assoc.*, vol. 7, 1852, pp. 201-2.)

[*Huntingdonshire*] The plough witchers came to my house, as usual, on the evening of Plough Monday, 9th January.—Cuthbert Bede. (*N. and Q.*, iv, 7, 1871, p. 53.)

[*Lincolnshire*] The following is an account of the highly developed Plough Monday gang of Alkborough, North Lincolnshire.

The old plough jag rhymes were completed with some from Whitton, by Mr. Edward Brown of Scunthorpe. He was born at Alkborough and was, for some years, one of the plough jags taking part in the Alkborough custom. The plough jags used to go to his house to dress. This was a long business, for the Gentlemen or Shirtmen in the gang always tried to dress as finely as they could, having ruffled shirts (hence Shirtmen) and top hats, covered with brooches, watch chains, and other jewellery, often to a value exceeding £5. So keen were the players that the young men who played the part of the Lady often let their hair grow long and, on Plough Jag day, the hair was curled, much in the style of a modern young lady.

An old plough jagger, who belonged to the West Halton gang, said that a tug-of-war was pulled over a bonfire, lighted in Normanby Hall yard, by the rival gangs of Alkborough, West Halton, Burton, and Flixborough. The winners called themselves Champions. While the tug-of-war was on, the mistletoe was brought out from the Hall and cast into the fire. The part of the Hobby Horse, at Alkborough, was taken for many years by one man; it was not wise to pull its tail, for this was generally well studded with pins and fish-hooks. The Horse always had a large bell suspended in front of it and was called Bang-up. In addition to the large bell, the gang carried small bells, a kettle-drum, and an old English accordion; the doctor carried a horn.

The Alkborough gang included two Gentlemen or Shirtmen, the Fool, Besom Betty, Doctor, Soldier, Lady, Indian King, Jane, Beelzebub, and the Hobby Horse. The Soldier assumes the part of a recruiting sergeant and Beelzebub carries a club under one arm and a frying-pan in his free hand.

Arriving in front of a house, the Fool knocks at the door, announces himself, and says that he will be followed by a few of his friends. Then the Soldier, Beelzebub, the Hobby Horse, and the Lady enter and say their parts. The speech of the Hobby Horse runs:

" In comes I who's never been before,
If you give me some of your best beer, I'll never come any more.
And I am hungry as well as dry
And should like a bit of your best pork pie."

The Lady says that she has so many sweethearts that she is at a loss whom to choose, upon which the Fool says : " It's me you want." The Lady gets hold of the Fool and says:

" This is the man, the very man
Who does my fancy take;
And as for all the others,
I freely will forsake.
He's handsome and he's shy
And I'll take him till I die."

The Fool then invites the company to the wedding, warning them that what they like they must bring with them.

The Indian King then enters and boasts of his prowess. The Soldier opposes him and refers to his own sword point. A duel follows and the Indian, wounded, falls to the ground. The Fool calls for the Doctor and, after an argument about the fee, which goes up from £5 to £15, the Doctor enters, but the Fool examines him as to how he became qualified. He declares that he can do almost anything in male and female achement, and, after more of this irrelevancy, he finally asserts that he can cure the Indian King, saying : " I'll drop a few drops of this magic mixture on the roots of his tongue and then he'll be as right as I am and that's about twopence to the shilling.

> This man's not dead, he's in a trance.
> Rise up Jack and we'll have a dance."

Then they dance with one another or with any one else in the house until Jane enters and orders the lads to clear out and she'll sweep the floor. Then Besom Betty enters and makes a speech like that used by Devil Doubt in some versions of the Play of St. George.

The Plough Jags finished by singing a song of which the following is a version :

> " Good master and good mistress
> As you sit round the fire,
> Remember us poor plough boys
> Who plod through mud and mire.
> The mud is so very deep
> The water is not clear.
> We'll thank you for a Christmas box
> And a drop of your best beer."

The Alkborough Plough Jag custom gradually died out after the year 1885. (From an account written by Mr. John Gott of Scunthorpe, Lincolnshire, and transmitted to Mrs. E. H. Rudkin of Willoughton, Lincoln.)

[*Northamptonshire*] The pageant varies in different places. At one time the plough was drawn by oxen decorated with ribbons. Sometimes, five persons precede the plough, which is drawn by boys having their faces blackened or reddled. The one who walks first in the procession is called the Master; he is grotesquely dressed and wears a large wig. Two are gaily attired in women's dress and two others have large hunches on their backs, a knave of hearts being sewn on each. These two are called Red Jacks or Fools. Each of the five carries a besom and one of them carries a box, which he shakes repeatedly among the spectators for donations for a feast. In some cases, they plough up the soil in front of houses whose inmates refuse to subscribe. (*Glossary of Northamptonshire Words and Phrases*, Anne Elizabeth Baker, 2 vols., vol. 2, 1854, pp. 123-4.)

Plough Monday was formerly observed in some of the villages in Northamptonshire by the ploughmen or, as they were called, plough witches, probably owing to their being attired in women's dress and having blackened and bearded faces. I have known ploughmen proceed to a neighbouring town and call upon tradesmen with whom their employers had dealings, and ask them for money. The custom of taking round a plough has been long discontinued in most villages. (*Northamptonshire Notes and Queries*, vol. 3, Northampton, 1890, pp. 152-3.)

[*Northumberland*] Men in gay attire draw about a plough, called the stot plough, to obtain contributions and when they receive a gift from a house visited by them they exclaim " Largess," but when they do not receive a gift from the house they plough up the ground in front of it. I have seen twenty men in the yolk of one plough. (*History of Northumberland*, William Hutchinson, vol. 2, 1798, p. 18 of the Appendix.)

[*Nottinghamshire*] In the Mansfield district, Plough Monday was celebrated regularly about the middle of the nineteenth century.

[*Staffordshire*] Plough Monday is still observed in some obscure villages in Staffordshire. The village in which I once resided still has a party of plough boys parading it on this day, dressed in gaudy rags and ribbons, accompanied by a clown carrying a horn, the Molly carrying a ladle, the Lady or Bessy, and the Can-bearer with the following rhyme displayed on his hat:

" This is the man that carries the can
And tots good beer to every man."

(*The Customs, Superstitions, and Legends of the County of Stafford*, Charles Henry Poole, *n.d.*, but later than 1875, pp. 15-6.)

[*Yorkshire*] Ploo or plough stots are farm servants having patched dresses and ribbon ends on hats and clothes; blowing cows' horns, they go round on Plough Monday, with a plough frame steered by the man last married. The youngest two lads act as drivers, the oldest two men as collectors, and the rest as horses. Almost extinct now, though one party, without plough, came into Wakefield, in 1865, but on the wrong Monday, *viz.* a week too soon. (*A List of Provincial Words in use in Wakefield*, William Stott Banks, 1865, p. 53.)

On Plough Monday, and some days following, there is a procession of country lads dragging a plough, who, since they do duty for oxen, are called " plough bullocks." They are dressed with their shirts over their jackets, with sashes of ribbons fixed across their breasts and backs, and knots or roses of ribbons fastened on their shirts and on their hats. Besides the plough draggers, there is a band of six in the same dress, furnished with swords, who perform the sword dance, while one or more musicians play on the violin or flute. The sword dance displays considerable ingenuity and is not without gracefulness. The dancers arrange themselves in a ring with their swords elevated; their movements and evolutions are slow and simple, at first, but gradually become more rapid and complicated. Towards the close, each one catches the point of his neighbour's sword and various movements follow, one of which consists in joining or plaiting the swords into the form of an elegant hexagon or rose, in the centre of the ring, which hexagon or rose is so firmly made that one of them holds it up above their heads without undoing it. The dance ends with taking it to pieces, each one laying hold of his own sword. During the dance, two or three of the company, called *Toms* or *Clowns*, dressed up as harlequins, in most fantastic modes, having their faces painted or masked, are making antic gestures to amuse the spectators, while another set, called *Madges* or *Madgy Pegs*, clumsily dressed in women's clothes and also painted or masked, go from door to door rattling old canisters, in which they receive money. Where they are well paid they raise a huzza; where they get nothing, they shout " hunger and starvation." When the party does not exceed forty, they seldom have a plough. Sometimes a kind of farce, into which songs are introduced, is acted along with the sword dance. The chief characters in this are the King, the Miller, the Clown, and the Doctor. Egton Bridge has long been the chief rendezvous for sword dancers in Whitby district. (*A History of Whitby*, Rev. George Young, 2 vols., vol. 2, Whitby, 1817, pp. 880-1.)

PLOUGH MONDAY IN OLDEN TIMES

Plough Monday was a rustic festival signalizing when, the ground being neither frozen hard nor too wet, ploughing may commence. More than three centuries ago, it was said that the ploughing of the soil should commence with the beginning of the year, which " with husbandmen is at Plow-day, being ever the first Munday after Twelfth-day, at which time you shall goe forth with your draught and begin to plow." (*The English Husbandman*, Gervase Markham, 1613, First Part, containing a Knowledge of the nature of every soil and how to plough it, chap. 5, lines 24-28 of the chapter.)

Plough Monday is a country phrase used by peasants who assembled to have a festive time, wishing success to the next harvest and a " God speed " to the plough, as soon as they began to break the ground.—*The British Apollo*, vol. 2, 1710, p. 92. (*Brand*, vol. 1, p. 508.)

[*Norfolk*] It is generally agreed that lights, called plow or plough lights, were maintained in many churches, before certain images, by husbandmen, in order to insure success in their labours. The following information is given in Blomefield's work: " Binham. Here were the lights of St. Mary, Tripudii de Westgate, and Tripudii de Market's hede.[1] These lights were maintained by a party of dancers at those places." It is also stated that the church was dedicated to the Holy Cross. (*An Essay towards a Topographical History of the County of Norfolk*, Francis Blomefield, 11 vols., vol. 9, 1805-10, p. 212, continued from vol. 3 by Charles Parkin.)

[*Cambridgeshire, etc.*] There are entries of money received from the Plough Monday ceremonies in the Accounts for many churches, *e.g.* Boxford Church, Cambridgeshire, Heybridge Church, Essex, Cratfield Church, Suffolk.

[*Suffolk; Lincolnshire*] In ancient times, the Church made Plough Monday an occasion for blessing the tilling of the soil. The plough used for the purpose was kept in church and was solemnly perfumed and blest before the Plough Monday procession started. The plough lights were kept up chiefly from the Plough Monday collections; in 1547, the wardens of Cratfield bought a plough at 8d. for this purpose. In 1548, Plough Monday festivities and wakes were abolished, but, in some villages, these church gatherings in connection with the Plough Monday custom continued after the Reformation; *e.g.* at Wigtoft, Lincolnshire, in 1575, the churchwardens received 20s. of " ye plougadrin." As a rule, the later collections were used for feasting the plough boys and their friends. (*Churchwardens' Accounts*, 1400-1700, J. Charles Cox, 1913, pp. 248-9.)

THE TOWN PLOUGH

There are available about five independent accounts of what is called the Town Plough. It seems to have been much larger and heavier than an ordinary plough and to have been used as an item in the means for obtaining money for parochial expenses. This use would be in accordance with parochial financial policy in olden times, when the whole or a large part of such expenses were paid out of the proceeds of church-ales, raffles, games, and sports; *e.g.* Aubrey informs us that in his grandfather's time, the church-ale of Whitsuntide paid the rates for the poor of

[1] Tripudium = the religious dance; the dance associated with the Church.

the Parish of Kingston St. Michael, Wiltshire. (*Brand*, i, p. 282.)

[*Northamptonshire*] Less than ten years ago, in the belfry of Castor Church, Northamptonshire, was an old town plough, roughly made, decayed, and worm-eaten. It was about three times as large as an ordinary plough. (*N. and Q.*, i, 7, 1853, p. 339.)

[*Eastern Counties*] At Duxford, Bassingbourne, and elsewhere in Cambridgeshire, the ceremonial plough, perhaps the old town or common plough, is still preserved. I believe there were lately ploughs also in Dry Drayton, Elsworth, and Long Stow churches. At North Elmham, Norfolk, the plough was known, 38 Henry VIII [1547], as the " Church-gate plough " and yielded a considerable sum for parochial purposes. At Braintree, Essex, there were Plow-wardens. The parish plough at Cratfield, Suffolk, was much in evidence on Plough Monday. (*The East Anglian, etc.*, new series, vol. 12, Norwich, 1907-8, p. 213.)

In some parishes in Cambridgeshire and other parishes, it appears that the town plough was kept in the church during the Commonwealth, but its removal was ordered after the Restoration, for, in a parochial visitation of part of Cambridgeshire shortly after the Restoration, orders were given for its ejectment from such resting-place. (*N. and Q.*, i, 6, 1852, p. 462.)

FAIR

[*Lincolnshire*] On Plough Monday, at Sleaford, is held annually the old, popular Plough Monday Fair, a business and pleasure fair which attracts many visitors from the agricultural district of which Sleaford is the centre. Business in agricultural produce, implements, tools, and articles of dress for all engaged in farming, gardening, and stock-rearing is brisk.

Straw Bear Tuesday
The Tuesday following Plough Monday

(*Cambridgeshire*) When I was at Whittlesey yesterday, 12th January, 1909, I had the pleasure of meeting a " straw bear," if not two, in the street. I had not been at Whittlesey on the day for nearly forty years and feared that the custom had died out. In my boyhood, the straw bear was a man completely swathed in straw, led by means of a string and made to dance before people's houses, in return for which money was expected. This always took place on the Tuesday following Plough Monday. Yesterday, the straw bear was a boy and I saw no dancing, otherwise there was no change. I was told that, two years ago, straw bears had been forbidden as a form of cadging; the police had also prevented people from taking round the plough, as they always did at Whittlesey when I was a boy. (*Folk-Lore*, vol. 20, 1909, p. 202.)

St. Hilary's Day
13th January

St. Hilary was bishop of Poitiers and is said to have died on the 13th January, 368. His name is best known in connection with the terms of the Law Courts and the Universities. The Law Courts' Hilary term commences on the 11th of January and the saint's day nearest to this date is St. Hilary's, which, in accordance with custom, gives its name to the term.

MAYORAL ELECTION

[*Yorkshire*] At Richmond, Yorkshire, on St. Hilary's day, the mayor for the following year of office is elected. (*British Popular Customs*, Thomas F. Thistleton Dyer, 1876, p. 44.)

POPULAR SAYING AND BELIEF

" St. Hilary's is the coldest day of the year."

All Souls' Mallard Day
14th January

[*Oxfordshire*] On this day, the Fellows and others of All Souls' College, Oxford, used to have a gaudy, with supper and copious draughts, in commemoration of a bird said to have been found

All Souls' Mallard Day

in an underground drain at the digging of the foundations of the College, about the year 1440.

Last Monday, 14th January, the 14th being always the day, was All Souls' Mallard. Formerly, the Mallardians used to ramble about the College, with sticks and poles, in quest of the Mallard and they had a Lord of the Mallard, but this has been left off many years. (*Thomas Hearne's Collections*, viii, p. 35, Manning MSS.) No date is given; T. Hearne died in 1735. The bird was said to have been a drake or wild duck or mallard, but grown to an enormous size, and this feature was punctuated by the frequent use of the word " swapping " applied to the bird, in the song of the evening entitled : *The Merry Old Song of the All Souls' Mallard*.

A controversy on the nature of this remarkable bird took place in the eighteenth century. As far as the incidents of this controversy are understood, the Mallardians maintained that the bird was a mallard (distinguished for its handsome plumage). However, an ornithologist, Francis Willughby, stated that a friend of undoubted fidelity told him that his father once had a goose known to be eighty years old and might have lived another eighty years, if it had not been killed. (*The Ornithology of Francis Willughby*, John Ray, Editor, 1678, p. 358.)

Using this statement, the Rev. John Pointer, of Slapton, Northamptonshire, said that if a goose were such a long-lived bird why not a drake or duck, although they differ in size, just as, for example, a rat and a mouse. This, he added, might help to give credit to our All Saints' Mallard. (*Oxoniensis Academia*, 1749.)

All this was considered, by the Mallardians, to be degrading to the memory of their Mallard and the Rev. John Pointer's suggestion was treated with contempt. The possible introduction of rats into the controversy may have had some effect.

St. Wulfstan's Day
19th January

[*Worcestershire*] Wulfstan, Bishop of Worcester, died on the 19th of January, 1095. For centuries, until recent times, the tomb of King John and the tombs of St. Wulfstan and St. Oswald were in the chancel of the Cathedral, that of King John being between the other two. These tombs were visited by pilgrims on 19th January, annually, until about the year 1700. They were visited in later times, until their removal, by many people from the Midlands who believed a local tradition that King John wished to be interred between St. Wulfstan and St. Oswald, because they would not fail to take him with them at the Last Day.

A note written in 1912, after information received from a verger of the Cathedral, gives the following record : " At an altar in the crypt, a service is held on 19th January, annually, and at no other time, in honour of St. Wulfstan."

St. Agnes' Eve and Day
20th-21st January

St. Agnes is the patroness of young girls, to whom the legend of her martyrdom appeals very strongly. By birth a Roman and by conviction a Christian, she refused to obey an order of a certain Prefect that she should marry his son. Soon afterwards, she was executed, at an early age, after insulting and cruel treatment, on 21st January, 303, during the reign of Diocletian. In conformity with her character, a snow-white lamb is a symbol for the saint.

The customs observed on her days relate to divinations, formerly carried out by girls, " who sighed for Agnes dreams, the sweetest of the year." [1] Many forms of these divinations have been practised, but a twenty-four hours' fast, commencing on St. Agnes' Eve, was a condition precedent to the completion of the divination and another important ceremony was that of the young girl's almost personal appeal to St. Agnes, which is recorded in some accounts of the divinations. These accounts show that the St. Agnes' divinations were very popular in the Northern Counties.

[1] *The Eve of St. Agnes,* Keats, stanza 7.

ST. AGNES LOVE DIVINATIONS

The Aubrey MSS. inform us that the girls had several magic secrets handed down to them by tradition, for the purposes of love divinations; *e.g.* take a row of pins, on St. Agnes' Night, 21st January, and pull out every one, one after another, saying a paternoster and sticking a pin in your sleeve, and you will dream of him or her you shall marry.

A lady informed Aubrey that, after practising a divination, she was favoured with a vision. About two years after, as she was in church, up popped a young Oxonian, in the pulpit, and as soon as convenient, she told her sister that this was the very face of the man she saw in her dream. Aubrey adds that he became her husband. (*Time's Telescope* for 1830, pp. 55-6.) Aubrey seems to have known a bevy of ladies who had remarkable experiences.

[*Derbyshire, etc.*] It is not so long ago that the following divination was practised by girls in Derbyshire and Yorkshire. The girl who wished to test her future, on St. Agnes' Day, prepared herself by a twenty-four hours' fast, beginning at midnight on the 20th and ending at midnight on the 21st. During this time, she took nothing except pure spring water and she would not, on any account, speak to anyone about the divination and not even mention it aloud to herself. At midnight, on the 21st, she retired to bed, without breaking her fast, and rested on her left side, saying three times the following lines :

> " Saint Agnes be a friend to me,
> In the gift I ask of thee ;
> Let me this night my husband see."

Her dreams ought to be about her future husband. If she should dream of more than one man, she would marry an indefinite number of times ; if she does not dream of a man, she will never marry. This divination was very popular. (*Long Ago : A Journal of Popular Antiquities*, Alex. Andrews, Editor, vol. 2, 1874, p. 80.)

[*Durham, etc.*] St. Agnes' Fast is thus observed throughout Durham and Yorkshire. Two young girls, each desirous of dreaming about their future husbands, must abstain through the whole of St. Agnes' Eve from eating, drinking, or speaking, and must avoid even touching their lips with their fingers. At night they are to make their dumb-cake, so-called from the rigid silence which attends its manufacture. Its ingredients, flour, salt, water, must be supplied in equal proportions by the girls, who must also take equal shares in the baking and turning of the cake and in drawing it out of the oven. After dividing the cake into two equal parts, each girl takes a part, carries it upstairs, walking backwards all the time and, after eating her half-cake, jumps into bed in hopes of seeing her future husband in her dreams. (*Notes on the Folk-Lore of the Northern Counties of England and the Borders*, William Henderson, 1879, pp. 90-1.)

[*Lincolnshire, etc.*] A method of finding out the identity of a future husband is to take a handful of barley on the Eve of St. Agnes, and scatter it under an apple tree, repeating the lines :

"Barley, barley, I sow thee
That my true-love I may see ;
Take thy rake and follow me."

or other words of similar meaning. The figure of the future husband is supposed to follow and rake up the seed the girl has scattered. (*County F.L.*, vol. 5, *Lincolnshire*, Mrs. Gutch and Mabel Peacock, 1908, p. 130.)

A divination known in the north of England and formerly very popular in Scotland, especially among the mountain peasantry, commenced on St. Agnes' Eve. Girls and youths met together at 12, midnight, went to a certain corn-field and threw in some grain, repeating a few lines. In the case of a girl the lines were :

"Agnes sweet and Agnes fair,
Hither, hither, now repair ;
Bonny Agnes, let me see
The lad who is to marry me."

It is asserted that St. Agnes grants the prayer and the likeness of the destined bridegroom (or bride) is seen in a mirror on this very night. (*Time's Telescope* for 1832, pp. 14-5.)

[*Norfolk, etc.*] The dumb-cake is or has been made as far south as Norfolk. A friend tells me that his mother, when a girl, with another young girl, duly made their dumb-cake in perfect silence, walked to their bed backwards, laid their stockings and garters crosswise, and their shoes " going and coming," and then sitting up in bed began to eat the cakes, which were very small ones, made in thimbles. Still, the girl in question, with her mouth full of cake, exclaimed, " I can't eat it," and this broke the spell. The cake was exceedingly salty. (*Notes on the Folk-Lore of the Northern Counties of England and the Borders*, William Henderson, 1879, p. 91.)

The following record gives two recipes, each of which would apparently be very effective in producing a nightmare.

[*Northumberland*] The procedure is different in Northumberland. There, a number of girls, after a day's silence and fasting, will boil eggs, one apiece, extract the yolk, fill the cavity with salt, and eat the egg, shell and all, and then walk backwards, uttering this appeal to the saint :

> " Sweet Agnes, work thy fast,
> If ever I be to marry man,
> Or man be to marry me,
> I hope him this night to see."

Or, the following lines may be used :

> " Fair St. Agnes, play thy part,
> And send to me my own sweetheart,
> Not in his best or worst array,
> But in the clothes of every day,
> That I to-morrow may him ken,
> From among all other men."

A raw red herring swallowed, bones and all, is said to be equally effective. Northumbrians sometimes adopt this plan to get a glimpse of their future wives. (*Notes on the Folk-Lore of the Northern Counties of England and the Borders*, William Henderson, 1879, p. 91.)

Girls on going to bed, on St. Agnes' Eve, place their shoes on the floor, at right angles to each other, and repeat the following lines :

> " I place my shoes in form of a T,
> Hoping my true love to see ;
> Not dressed in his best array,
> But in the clothes he wears every day."

—Stamfordham. (*County F.L.*, vol. 4, *Northumberland*, M. C. Balfour and Northcote W. Thomas, 1904, p. 54.)

On St. Agnes' Eve, take a sprig of rosemary and a sprig of thyme and sprinkle them three times with water. In the evening, put one in each shoe and place one shoe on one side of the bed and the other shoe on the other side. Repeat the following lines when you retire to rest and your future husband will appear :

> " St. Agnes that's to lovers kind
> Come ! ease the trouble of my mind."

(*English Folk Rhymes*, G. F. Northall, 1892, p. 112.)

A ST. AGNES' EVE VOW

[*Yorkshire*] The village maidens considered it a most binding vow to remain true to their sweethearts if they washed their garters in St. Cedd's Well, at Lastingham, on the Eve of St. Agnes. (*The Evolution of an English Town*, Pickering, Gordon Cochrane Home, 1915, p. 220.)

PENNY CROFT WELL, UTTOXETER

[*Staffordshire*] This well, associated with divination ceremonies, is situated in The Flatts, in the Parish of Uttoxeter. The water of this well was believed to possess medicinal and occult properties. Annually, the people of the district held a festival, adorned the well with boughs and flowers, and danced and sang in its honour. According to an old legend, the maid who looked into its depths, on St. Agnes' Eve, would see the likeness of her future husband reflected from the surface of the water. (*Midland Weekly News*, 23rd September, 1893.)

St. Vincent's Day

22nd January

St. Vincent, a Spaniard by birth, perished at Valencia on the 22nd January, in the year 304.

It was considered to be a good omen for the sun to shine on his day and a direction that such a phenomenon should be remembered is given in an old Latin sentence: *Vincenti festo si Sol radiet memor esto*, quoted in *Brand*, i, p. 38.

If the sun shine at all on St. Vincent's day, it is quite a good omen, for

" If on St. Vincent's day the sky is clear,
More wine than water will crown the year."

(*Weather Wisdom from January to December*, compiled by Wilfrid Allan [1889], pp. 11-12.)

St. Paul's Eve

24th January

[*Cornwall*] An old custom used to prevail on St. Paul's Pitcher day, as St. Paul's Eve was called, in Cornwall. The tin miners would leave their work, set up a pitcher full of water, pelt it with stones until it was broken and then go to an inn, there to fill and refill a fresh pitcher with ale and pass the rest of the day in revelry. This custom is considered by some writers to be a relic of a custom commemorating the first smelting of tin ore, but others say that it was a protest by the miners against regulations enforcing them to drink water when they were at work. As late as the year 1859, the boys of Bodmin used to parade the town with pitchers, which they threw into every open doorway, shouting the words, " Paul's Eve and here's a heave." (*Daily Chronicle*, 24th January, 1906.)

A very old custom is observed by the youths of Mawgan in Pydar, Cornwall, on St. Paul's Eve. They parade the neighbourhood in gangs and throw all the broken earthenware they can collect into people's doorways, saying: " Paul's Eve and I will heave." I learn that a similar custom used to be observed in almost every parish in Cornwall, but that it gradually died out during the last century. (*Western Antiquary*, vol. 3, 1884, p. 19.)

The first red-letter day in the tinners' calendar is Paul's Pitcher day, 24th January, which is marked by a very curious and inexplicable custom [throwing at pitchers containing water]. This custom is observed not only among tinners but also among the mixed mining and agricultural people of Bodmin and the seafaring people of Padstow. At Bodmin, the boys are accustomed, on St. Paul's Eve, to slink along the streets and throw a pitcher, usually stolen and filled with rubbish, into any house whose door is left open. On entering a house, I have, more than once, stumbled over the broken pieces of a " Paul's pitcher." (T. Q. Couch in *Western Antiquary*, vol. 3, 1884, p. 67.)

On St. Paul's Eve, the lads of Blisland collected old sherds and threw them at the door of any who had been teasy. (T. Q. Couch in *Western Antiquary*, vol. 3, 1884, p. 91.)

This record, which mentions sherds and refers to an action directed against someone whose conduct was annoying or irritating, relates to a custom similar to that celebrated, especially on Shrove Monday evening, in Devonshire and Cornwall; *see* Shrove Monday in Vol. I, 1936, pp. 5-6.

St. Paul's Day

25th January

LAND TENURE CUSTOM

[*London*] Sir William de Baud, on Candlemas Day, 1274, granted to the Dean and Chapter of St. Paul's that, in consideration of 22 acres of land by them granted within their manor of Westley, in Essex, to be inclosed into his park at Curingham, he would provide for ever, upon the Feast Day of the Conversion of St. Paul, in winter, a good doe (and upon the Feast of the Commemoration of St. Paul, in summer, a good buck) and offer the same at the High Altar. The doe to be brought at the hour of Procession and through the Procession, and the bringer, a man, to have nothing. (*A Survey of London*, John Stow, 1720, vol. 1, book 3, pp. 164-5.)

The reception of the doe and buck was solemnly performed till the time of Elizabeth, at the steps of the choir, by the canons of St. Paul's in their sacred vestments and with garlands of flowers on their heads. (*Ancient Manorial Customs, Tenures, etc., of the County of Essex*, Richard Stephen Charnock, 1870, p. 5.)

POPULAR SAYINGS AND BELIEFS

In olden times, popular sayings and beliefs, deduced from observations on the weather phenomena of St. Paul's day, were considered to be exceptionally reliable. The first of the sayings and beliefs cited below is from an ancient authority on farming; the second is similar to a saying and belief recorded by Thomas Passenger in his *Shepherd's Kalendar*, or the Citizen's and Countryman's Daily Companion, published and sold at the Three Bibles and Star, London Bridge, about the year 1680.

" If St. Paul's is fair and bright, the harvest will be good; snow or rain on that day foretells famine; and, if misty, shortage of cattle." (*The Second Booke of the English Husbandman*, Gervase Markham, 1615, p. 8.)

[*Cornwall*] " If Paul's Fair be fair and clear,
We shall have a happy year;
But if it be both wind and rain,
Dear will be all kinds of grain.
If the winds do blow aloft,
Then wars will trouble this realm full oft;
If clouds or mist do dark the sky,
Great store of birds and beasts shall die."

These lines were obtained from a Bodmin man who could not be supposed to have learnt them from books, although they are known, in various forms, in England, and also in continental countries. At Bodmin, there is a charter fair on St. Paul's day; this explains the first line of the saying. (T. Q. Couch in *Western Antiquary*, vol. 3, 1884, p. 193.)

[*Worcestershire*]

" If St. Paul's be fine and clear,
It betides a happy year,
But if it chance to snow or rain,
Dear will be all sorts of grain."

(*Glossary of West Worcestershire Words*, E. L. Chamberlain, 1882, p. 37.)

The above sayings, primarily intended for farmers, agree in foreshadowing a good harvest or a happy year (phrases practically synonymous) if the weather on that day happens to be fair and bright. The weather of the 25th of January, 1936, in West Hertfordshire and East Buckinghamshire, may be described as follows: cloud 100 per cent., all day; calm; fog or mist; degree of humidity, near to dew-point. The absence of fair and bright weather on St. Paul's Day, 1936, gives no positive forecast, but events after that day were consistent with the nature of the popular sayings to this extent that 1936 was a cheerless and anxious year for farmers, whose crops were saved from ruin, only by a remarkable late improvement in the weather before harvest time. The prophecy that cloud or mist on St. Paul's day is followed by great mortality among birds, cattle, and other animals appears to have been falsified by events, in 1936. In some past years, there have been destructive outbreaks of disease among animals or, as in the winter of 1916-7, a large scale annihilation of fieldfares, song thrushes, goldcrests, tits, blackbirds, and other wild birds, but such a disaster did not occur in 1936. The other forecasts given by the popular sayings are scarcely applicable to the events of that year.

On St. Paul's Day, 1937, there was sunshine in the morning; then it became dull and rainy for the rest of the day. For the year 1937, to July, it may be said that the hay crop has been good and, although the wheat crop seems to be thin, prospects are improving.

FAIR

[*Cornwall*] St. Paul's day fair, at Bodmin, was granted by charter, dated Westminster, 30th April, 36 Eliz. 1594, together with a court of piepowder. (*The Bodmin Register*, Bodmin, 1827, pp. 165-6.) The fair is still held.

King Charles' Day
30th January

[*Northumberland, etc.*] Until recently a muffled peal was rung annually, on 30th January, at Newcastle-upon-Tyne, in commemoration of the death of King Charles I; also, an extract from the church books of Colne, for 1710, reads: " Paid for ringing on ye martyrdome of King Charles . . . 1s." (*A Book about Bells*, Rev. George S. Tyack [1898], pp. 205 and 241.)

[*Nottinghamshire*] At Newark, distinguished for its loyalty, there is a regular custom, observed also on Good Friday, of raffling for oranges on the 30th January, annually. (*Time's Telescope* for 1826, p. 17). The custom was discontinued about the year 1870.

January

POPULAR SAYINGS AND BELIEFS

" As the days lengthen,
So does the cold strengthen."

This old saying, often true, applies to January and also February.

" A January spring
Is worth nothing."

" January freezes the pot by the fire."

Another form of this saying, not so good, is: " January freezes the pot on the fire."

" The blackest month in all the year
Is the month of Janiveer."

" May in Janiveer,
Janiveer in May, I fear."

Another form, not so good, gives March instead of May.

"A green Yule makes a full churchyard." The week beginning the 5th of January is the one to which this saying specially refers. It is usually much colder after the winter solstice, but if the early part of January is mild, fierce cold later becomes fatal to the weakly. (Author's MS. Notes.)

[*Derbyshire*] "If you see the first moon of the year through a glass [mirror], there will be a death in your family during the year. (*Memorials of Old Derbyshire*, J. Charles Cox, Editor, 1907, p. 361.)

[*Suffolk*] "The grass that grows in Janiveer
Grows no more all the year."

—New Suffolk Garland, 1866, p. 168. (*County F.L.*, vol. 1 (2), *Suffolk*, The Lady Eveline Camilla Gurdon, 1893, p. 163.)

[*Worcestershire*]

"He who, in January, sows oats
Gets gold and groats."

St. Bride's Day
1st February

In England, we call this saint St. Bride; in Ireland, she is called St. Bridget and this name is commonly used in the Isle of Man. In ancient times, her memory was held in great honour by the British races and the races of northern Europe. She is said to have been born in Louth, or in Armagh, about the year 450, and to have died about the year 520. She was interred in Kildare Church, where a continually burning light is said to have been maintained in her honour, until the thirteenth century. St. Bride is usually represented holding a cross, with a flame near her.

[*Isle of Man*] On the Eve of the Saint's day, a custom was kept up in her honour, in many parishes in the Isle of Man, called Laa'l Breeshey, in Manx. This custom was very popular and consisted in standing in the doorway of the house, with a bundle of green rushes, and inviting St. Bridget to enter and stay the night. The rushes were then laid down for the comfort of the Saint. (*An Historical and Statistical Account of the Isle of Man*, Joseph Train, 2 vols., vol. 2, Douglas, 1845, p. 116.)

[*Midland Counties*] It is a common belief, especially in the Midlands, that dew collected from plants and applied to the face rejuvenates and improves the features and a cutting, not dated nor identified, records that dew gathered and used on St. Bride's day will make old people young and improve the features.

WEATHER OMEN

[*Worcestershire, etc.*]

" If February Calends be summerly gay,
'Twill be winterly weather on the Calends of May."

(*Glossary of West Worcestershire Words*, E. L. Chamberlain, 1882, p. 37.) In various forms, this omen was common knowledge in many counties.

Candlemas Eve and Day
1st and 2nd February

This festival was held in commemoration of the Purification of the Virgin; it was an important festival of the Church and, on its day, the church bells were rung. Many devotional and ritualistic ceremonies were performed and a characteristic feature of the festival was the large number of candles used in its celebration. Several popular customs were celebrated, many Candlemas sayings, beliefs, and omens were current among the people, and Candlemas fairs were numerous.

[*Suffolk*] Candlemas day was so called because, on that day, all the candles and tapers to be used in the church during the year were consecrated. (*County F.L.*, vol. 1 (2), *Suffolk*, The Lady Eveline Camilla Gurdon, 1893, p. 51.)

Candlemas day is so called because lights were distributed and carried about in procession or because the use of lighted tapers, practised all the winter at Vespers and Litanies, ceased till the next All-Hallowmass. It is called the Day of Presentation in the Temple; it is called the Holy Day of St. Simeon and also the Day of Purification, and is more than an ordinary day among women and, therefore, is called the Wives' Feast Day. (*The Antiquities of the Common People*, Henry Bourne, Newcastle, 1725, pp. 170-1.)

From the earliest times, our English forefathers gathered together in their parish churches, on Candlemas day, for the blessing of the candles and for the procession with lighted tapers. Ælfric, the homilist and translator, who died about the year 1050, speaks of the feast, in his days, and the celebration remained the same till the Reformation. He says: "It is appointed in the ecclesiastical observances that we, on this day, bear our lights to church and let them there be blessed." (*Parish Life in Mediæval England*, Abbot Gasquet, 1906, p. 168.)

CANDLEMAS CUSTOMS

In olden times, parishioners attended church on Candlemas day, when wax candles and tapers were consecrated, lighted, distributed to the officers of the church and members of the congregation, and then carried in procession. The consecrated candles, when lighted, were believed to be protective against evil spirits and storms, and the larger the candle and the more brightly it burned the more powerful the protection. The custom was discontinued in the churches of London and in many churches throughout the country, on Candlemas Day, 1547-8.

[*Nottinghamshire*] It was customary, at one time, in the villages bordering on the Trent, to decorate churches and houses, on Candlemas day, with branches of box and to light up a number of candles in the evening, as being the last day of Christmas festivity. (*Journ. British Archæol. Assoc.*, vol. 8, 1853, p. 231.)

TAKING DOWN CHRISTMAS DECORATIONS

It was customary to take down Christmas decorations on Candlemas Eve and replace them with box. On Candlemas Eve, it was said :

> " Down with the Rosemary and Baies,
> Down with the Mistletoe ;
> Instead of Holly, now upraise
> The greener Box for show."

(*Hesperides, Ceremonies for Candlemas Eve*, Robert Herrick, 1648, ll. 2-5.)

[*Eastern Counties*] Every berry and every particle of the leaves of evergreens used for decorating the house, at Christmas, must be removed on Candlemas Eve ; if they are allowed to remain, some misfortune will certainly happen to the family. (*Vocabulary of East Anglia, etc.*, Robert Forby, 1830, p. 415.)

[*Staffordshire*] Christmas decorations are taken down on Candlemas day and are usually burnt, but at Stone Mill, forty to fifty years ago, they were always given to the cows to eat, in order that they might not cast their calves. (*Notes on the Folk-Lore of North Staffordshire*, [W.] Wells Bladen, . . . p. 34.)

If every remnant of Christmas decoration is not cleared out of church before Candlemas day, there will be a death that year in the family occupying the pew where a leaf or berry is left. An old lady, whom I knew, was so persuaded of the truth of this superstition that she would not be content to leave the clearing of her pew to the church cleaners but used to send her own servant, on Candlemas Eve, to see that no leaf or berry was left in her own seat. (*The Book of Days*, R. Chambers, Editor, vol. 2, Edinburgh, 1883, p. 53.)

THE CHRISTMAS BRAND AND CANDLEMAS EVE

A brand from the Yule-log of the preceding Christmas was kept till Candlemas Eve, when it was lighted and allowed to burn till sunset. It was then put out and kept for lighting the Yule-log for the next Christmas festivity.

CANDLEMAS AND SNOWDROPS

[*London, etc.*] Many people, both in London and various parts of the country, think it unlucky to bring snowdrops into the house. The snowdrop is dedicated to the Virgin and at the Feast of the Purification, or Candlemas, there used to be a procession of girls in white, singing :

" The Snowdrop, in purest white array,
First rears her head on Candlemas Day."

(*N. and Q.*, vol. 160, Jan. to June, 1931, p. 160.)

[*Shropshire*] A Shropshire custom was the " purification " of the house, on or about Candlemas day, by placing within it a bunch of snowdrops or Christ's flowers ; this was called " the white purification." Snowdrops are called " Candlemas bells " and an old rhyme says that the snowdrop first raises her head on Candlemas day. The snowdrop is also called the " Fair Maid of February " and the " Purification Flower." (Author's Notes.)

MANORIAL AND OTHER TENURE CUSTOMS

[*Cornwall*] In accordance with an old custom, the Reeve of the Manor of Samburne attended on Saturday, Candlemas Day, at Godolphin Hall, near Helston, to demand his lord's dues, which are payable on Candlemas day. At a few minutes to seven, on Saturday, the Reeve arrived and, proceeding to the old oaken door under the portico, said aloud : " Oh, yes ; Oh, yes ; Oh, yes. Here come I, the Reeve of the Manor of Samburne, to demand my lord's dues, eight groats, and a penny in money, a loaf, a cheese, a collar of brawn, and a jack of the best ale in the house. God save the Queen and the lord of the Manor." After each phrase " Oh, yes," he knocked the door with a stick. These ceremonies were repeated at the inner door of the quadrangle and, for the third and last time, in the grand old kitchen. The dues are paid by the Duke of Leeds to the St. Aubyn family to whom, in default of an heir, the estate reverts. After the ceremony was over, Mr. Rosewarne, the present genial tenant, entertained the spectators to breakfast.—*Western Daily Mercury*, 9th February, 1884. (*Western Antiquary*, vol. 3, 1884, pp. 208-10.)

[*Yorkshire*] At Horbury, Yorkshire, a custom affecting rights of common and called " Candlemas Gills " is celebrated annually. On this subject the historian of Wakefield, Mr. John Hewitt, wrote me : " On Candlemas day, at Horbury, every ratepayer is entitled to receive a gill of ale, that is half a pint, or what is more commonly called a " glass of ale," at an inn in the township. I got a Candlemas Gill myself last February (1873) at the Fleece Inn, where many before me had done the same." The custom originated about a century ago, estimating from the year 1874, when Horbury commonlands were inclosed and it was necessary to make some compensation to the commoners in consideration of loss of rights of free pasturage on the lands. (*Long Ago : A Journal of Popular Antiquities*, Alex. Andrews, Editor, vol. 2, 1874, p. 81.)

It may be mentioned that Candlemas day is one of the four terms of the year in Scotland, and that in England, especially in the counties of the Lake District, Candlemas is sometimes the time, not only for commencing and terminating tenancies of farms, but also for settling the year's accounts.

[*Cheshire, etc.*] The Cheshire custom of tenure of a farm is to enter on and leave the land on a Candlemas day and the houses, farm buildings, garden, and boozing field or pasture adjacent to the cows' stalls, on old May day. (*A Glossary of Words used in the County of Chester*, Robert Holland, 1886, pp. 38-9.)

The great army of farmers mostly take their lands or begin their year from Candlemas, 2nd February. They give or take possession of the land on that day, an old custom that has lately been legalized in the Agricultural Holdings Act. (*Folk-Lore: Old Customs and Tales of my Neighbours*, Fletcher Moss, Didsbury and Manchester, March, 1898, p. 31.)

[*Cumberland*] At Candlemas, the season in some districts for making annual settlements of accounts, ale-posset was eaten with great solemnity.—Ancient Customs and Superstitions in Cumberland. (*Trans. Historic Soc., Lancashire and Cheshire*, vol. 10, 1858, p. 104.)

[*Dorset*] The usual plan for letting a dairy farm, in Dorset, stipulated that the tenancy began at Candlemas and, after notice given before All Saints' day, terminated at the following Candlemas. (*The History and Antiquities of the County of Dorset*, John Hutchins, new edition, 4 vols., Westminster, 1861-73.) This record is worth keeping but, unfortunately, the reference is incomplete. After several searches, I cannot say on which of the 2,000 or more pages, the record is to be found. There are indexes, but they are, *e.g.* of Persons, Pedigrees, Arms.

[*Lake District*] Candlemas was the end of the farmers' financial year, when all accounts were settled. All interest on loans became due and most of the farms and tenements were let to be entered upon at that time. No accounts were settled at any other time than Candlemas.—Old Customs and Usages in the Lake District. (*Trans. Cumberland Assoc.*, Keswick, 1876, p. 116.)

[*Westmorland*] Agricultural rents, in Westmorland, are usually made payable half-yearly: at Candlemas, Lammas; Lady Day, Michaelmas; or 25th April, 25th October. (T. H. Little, in a letter, dated 22nd July, 1916.)

I find that the cross-quarter day, Candlemas, is quite as generally used, in this locality, as the more widely-recognized quarter-day of Christmas.—Westmorland. (J. F. Curwen, in a letter, dated 5th September, 1916.)

[*Yorkshire*] In the Huddersfield district, the custom in connection with farm tenancies is to give up the land on Candlemas day, 2nd February, and to leave the buildings on the following first day of May. (J. Bates, in a letter, dated 1917.)

THE INNS OF COURT CANDLEMAS CUSTOM

[*London*] Candlemas was the day of Hilary Term on which no business was transacted. The Day was a Grand Day at the Inns of Court, a Collar Day at St. James's, and a Gaudy or Joy Day at Oxford and Cambridge. (*Time's Telescope* for 1814, p. 35.)

On Candlemas Day, an ancient and quaint custom, called " Dancing round our Coal Fire," used to be celebrated by the judges, benchers, and others. Apparently, the dance itself took place towards the end of the celebration.

" Saturday, 2nd February, being Candlemas Day, there was a grand entertainment at the Temple Hall. The company included the Judges, Sergeants-at-Law, the Prince of Wales (incog.), the Earl of Macclesfield, and the Bishop of Bangor. Mr. Baker was Master of the Ceremonies. At night, there was a comedy, entitled " Love for Love," acted by the company of His Majesty's Revels from the theatre in the Haymarket. The ancient ceremony of the Judges dancing round our coal fire and singing an old French song was performed with great decency. The societies of the Temple presented the comedians with £50. (*Gentleman's Magazine*, vol. 4, February, 1734, p. 103.) According to custom, the dance would be three times round the fireplace.

BLIDWORTH ROCKING CUSTOM

[*Nottinghamshire*] The rocking of the last-baptized infant by the vicar in an ancient cradle bedecked with flowers and surrounded by candles, before the altar at Blidworth, near Mansfield, took place in February, 1923, and following years. This was a revival, after an interval of at least a century, of an ancient custom which is alleged to date back to the thirteenth century. Revivals of old customs have been of late remarkably numerous and the collector of folklore ought to record carefully the dates of such revivals, to prevent inquirers being misled into supposing that every detail is a copy of ancient practice and so being drawn to false conclusions. (*English Folklore*, Arthur Robinson Wright, 1928, p. 46.)

Observing an ancient custom, on Candlemas day, the Rev. J. Lowndes, vicar of Blidworth, rocked a baby in an old cradle, in the chancel of Blidworth Church. (*Daily News*, 3rd February, 1930.)

DISTRIBUTING GIFTS AND BEQUESTS

[*Suffolk*] Inscribed on his gravestone at Woodbridge, Suffolk, is the direction by George Carlow, who died in 1758, apparently, that on the 2nd day of February, for ever, twenty shillings' worth of bread be given, on the stone, to the poor of the town. This ceremony was duly performed on Candlemas day, the 2nd of February, 1937, as shown in Plate VI, under the supervision of the rector and churchwardens.

[*Yorkshire*] On the feast of St. Stephen, large goose pies are made, all of which they distribute among their needy neighbours, except one pie, which is carefully kept and not tasted till Candlemas.—N. Yorkshire. (*Gentleman's Magazine*, vol. 81, 1811, pp. 423-4.)

POPULAR SAYINGS AND BELIEFS

[*Cheshire, etc.*]

" A farmer should, on Candlemas day,
Have half his corn and half his hay."

—Cheshire and Staffordshire. (*Folk-Lore: Old Customs and Tales of my Neighbours*, Fletcher Moss, Didsbury and Manchester, March, 1898, p. 32.) This precautionary procedure is based on an assumption that winter is half over at Candlemas.

[*Cornwall*] A Cornish saying expresses a belief that Candlemas day is unlucky for sailing.—Seafaring usages. (*All the Year Round*, 1st February, 1879.)

[*Hertfordshire*] The sowing of beans is usually done at Candlemas, according to the old saying:

" At Candlemas day,
It's time to sow beans in the clay."

PLATE VI

Photo: W. H. Needs.

DISTRIBUTION OF LOAVES AT WOODBRIDGE, CANDLEMAS DAY, 1937

(*The Modern Husbandman*, William Ellis, Farmer at Little Gaddesden, Hertfordshire, 8 vols, vol. 8, 1750, p. 309.)

[*Lincolnshire, etc.*] An old farming friend of mine who had farmed in Lincolnshire, Nottinghamshire, and Derbyshire for more than fifty years, said that the following rhyme always stood good and certain :

" If Candlemas day comes blithe and gay,
You may saddle your horse and buy some hay,
But if Candlemas day comes rugged and rough,
You may use fodder away, for you'll have fodder enough."

—Thomas Radcliffe. (*Country Life, n.d.*)

[*Norfolk*]

" The farmer should have, on Candlemas day,
Half his stover, and half his hay."

—E. S. Taylor, St. Margaret, Norfolk. (*N. and Q.*, i, 11, 1855, p. 239.)

Stover = litter, or hay spoilt in the making.

" The farmer should have, on Candlemas day,
Half his turnips and half his hay."

(*The Norfolk Garland*, John Glyde, Junr., 1872, p. 153.)

[*Norfolk, etc.*]

" When Candlemas day is fine and clear,
A shepherd would rather see his wife on the bier."

—Proverbs, Adages, and Popular Superstitions still preserved in the Parish of Irstead, Rev. John Gunn. (*Trans. Norfolk and Norwich Archæol. Society*, vol. 2, Norwich, 1849, p. 294.) This saying is, or was, well known in many other counties besides Norfolk.

" On Candlemas day, if the thorns hang a-drop,
Then you are sure of a good pea crop."

I had this from an old shepherd named Balderstone who, on a foggy Candlemas day, told it to me, and certainly the pea crop that year was remarkably good. (*N. and Q.*, i, 11, 1855, p. 421.)

[*Nottinghamshire*] On Candlemas day, Christmas decorations should be burned. Old women in Nottinghamshire call it

"Blaze day." (*Household Tales*, Sidney Oldhall Addy, 1895, p. 111.)

[*Worcestershire*]

"Candlemas day,
Every good goose should lay."

(*Notes and Queries for Worcestershire*, John Noake, 1856, p. 239.) This saying, in various forms, is known in Buckinghamshire, Herefordshire, Lincolnshire, Norfolk, Nottinghamshire, Shropshire, Warwickshire, and Worcestershire. Geese begin to lay during the first fortnight in February.

"It is unlucky to keep Christmas holly about the house after Candlemas day; after that day, Satan himself will come and pull it down." (Miss E. J. Ladbury's MS. notebook, Worcestershire.)

[*Yorkshire*] "Candlemas-crack lays many a brave sailor on his back." Stormy weather is generally expected about Candlemas and such weather was called Candlemas-crack.—Hornsea, East Yorkshire. (*County F.L.*, vol. 6, *East Riding of Yorkshire*, Mrs. Gutch, 1912, pp. 213-4.)

"A Can'lemas crack
Lays mony a sailor on his back."

(*Yorkshire Dialect Poems*, F. W. Moorman, 1916, p. 118.)

I have no note of locality for the following saying: "Better to see a wolf enter the fold than the sun shine on Candlemas day." —M. C. Jones, Scraps of English Folk-Lore in Collectanea, Cambridgeshire. (*Folk-Lore*, vol. 24, 1913, p. 237.) This seems to be a unique saying and belief. The disclaimer referring to locality may mean that no note of a Cambridgeshire locality was available or no note of any locality.

The following sayings, in various forms are common knowledge:

"The snow won't stay after Candlemas day."

"On Candlemas day,
Throw candle (and candlestick) away."

WEATHER OMENS

Among the Candlemas weather omens is one which has been known for centuries throughout England and in many other countries. This omen is recorded in the old couplet :

> " Si Sol splendescat Maria purificante,
> Major erit glacies post festum quam fuit ante."

This may be translated : " If the sun shine on Candlemas day, the cold will be more intense after the festival than before it."

An old seventeenth century almanack gives the following :

> " After Candlemas day, the frost will be more keen,
> If the sun shines bright, than before it has been."

Another form of the omen reads :

> " When on the Purification the sun hath shin'd,
> The greater part of winter comes behind."

Anon. (*N. and Q.*, i, 7, 1853, p. 599.)

The following old Scottish couplet is very expressive :

> " If Candlemas is fair and clear,
> There'll be two winters in the year."

> " Foul weather is no news, hail, rain, and snow
> Are now expected and esteemed no woe ;
> Nay, 'tis an omen bad the yeomen say,
> If Phoebus shows his face the second day."

(*County Almanack*, 1676, February.)

This weather omen, intended primarily for shepherds, predicts an intensification of wintry conditions after Candlemas day, if the sun happens to shine on that day. On Candlemas day, 1936, there was no sunshine and it rained in the afternoon. After Candlemas, the weather was similar to that experienced before it, *i.e.* cold, almost sunless, and decidedly unfavourable for shepherds, farmers, and everyone else. It would have been consistent with the nature of the omen, if the weather had improved after Candlemas, but there was no such improvement. Examining the application of the omen in terms of the Old Style, it may be said that on Old Candlemas day, 14th February, 1936, there were a few hours sunshine, but the weather after that day presented no intensification of wintry conditions.

The weather for Candlemas day, 1937, may be described as follows: Sunshine in the morning, becoming dull and, at 3.30 p.m., rainy.—West Herts. From Candlemas day till the last week of February, the weather was dull and rainy. Wintry weather set in during the last week of the month and snow fell from about 7 a.m. till 10 a.m. on Sunday, 28th February, 1937. Afterwards, during the greater part of March, wintry weather continued and snowstorms were frequent throughout most of England; the frost was intense and many deaths were caused by the cold. The weather was so unseasonable that all were pleased to welcome the advent of April and bid farewell to a very cold March, reputed to have been the coldest March for a long series of years. If that was the result of sunshine on Candlemas day, we may all agree that the Candlemas day omen has shown its reliability, at least for the year 1937. A similar conclusion follows from a consideration of the weather on Old Candlemas day, 1937, on which day also there was sunshine.

[*Devonshire*] " When drops hang on the fence on 2nd February, icicles will hang there on 14th March." " If a storm comes on 2nd February, spring is near, but if that day be bright and clear, the spring will be late." (*Nummits and Crummits*, Sarah Hewett, 1900, pp. 106-7.)

[*Gloucestershire*] " If it rains on Candlemas day, it will rain for about forty days after."—Minchinhampton, My charwoman, aged 45, January, 1916. (Miss J. B. Partridge.)

[*Norfolk*]
"As far as the sun shines in on Candlemas day,
So far will the snow blow in before old May."
(*N. and Q.*, i, 11, 1855, p. 239.)

[*Surrey*] The old folks used to say: " As far as the sun shone into the house on Candlemas day, so far would the snow drive in before the winter was over."—A labourer, 2nd February, 1882. (*A Glossary of Surrey Words*, Granville Leveson Gower, English Dialect Society, 1893, p. 8.)

Candlemas

FAIRS

In olden times, fairs were held at East Looe, Evesham, Lyme Regis, Pontefract, and Reading, on Candlemas day; the Reading fair is still held on that day. At Stamford, there was a Candlemas fair and, at York, an Old Candlemas fair for all kinds of cattle and also an Old Candlemas line fair; to-day, at York, a fair is held on the Thursday before Old Candlemas day.

[*Berkshire*] At Reading, there are four fairs, one on the 2nd of February, chiefly for the sale of horses and cows. (*The History and Antiquities of Reading*, Charles Coates, 1802, p. 456.)

(*Cornwall*) East Looe has four fairs, annually, by Charter apparently dated Edward I. One of these is held on Candlemas day and on the day before and after this day. These fairs were formerly important but are now insignificant. (*Topographical and Historical Sketches of the Boroughs of East and West Looe*, Thomas Bond, 1823, p. 142.)

[*Lincolnshire*] The Charter granted to the Borough of Stamford by James II, in 1685, grants a fair and a court of piepowder on the Tuesday next before the 2nd of February. The fair was for the sale of horses and all kinds of cattle, chattels, and merchandise of all kinds. (*The History of Stamford*, John Drakard, Stamford, 1822, p. 92.)

A fair, the representative of the above, is still held at Stamford, on the Tuesday before the 13th February.

[*Worcestershire*] The Evesham fair, held on the 2nd of February, was chiefly for the sale of strong, black horses for which the Vale of Evesham was famous. This fair was held in the year 1840, but there are no data available to show when it was discontinued. Evesham has two fairs, both in October.

[*Yorkshire*] At Candlemas fair, Pontefract, the Corporation was entitled to receive 4d. per stand. (*The History of the Ancient Borough of Pontefract*, Benjamin Boothroyd, 1807, p. 452.)

St. Blase's Day
3rd February

St. Blase has been long regarded as the patron saint of woolcombers and many others engaged in the woollen industry. The customs celebrated on his day were associated with pageants, usually of an expensive and splendid kind, organized at Bradford, York, Bury St. Edmunds, Norwich, and other large cities and towns engaged in the woollen trade.

It is said that St. Blase was Bishop of Sebaste, in Cappadocia; that he was patron saint of Cappadocia, Armenia, and Ragusa; that he suffered martyrdom in the year 316, and that, before his death, was lacerated by means of iron implements, this operation being suggestive of that of wool combing.

His name is spelt in many different ways, *e.g.* Blase, Blasius, Blaze, and Blaise; the name Blase will be used here, except when one of the other names is required by the nature of a record.

COLCHESTER AND COGGESHALL CELEBRATIONS

[*Essex*] The following records give details of the woolcombers' procession, at Colchester, and of the weavers' procession, at Coggeshall, towards the end of the eighteenth century. The Coggeshall record does not mention St. Blase and the dates for the processions were later than the 3rd of February.

Colchester Woolcombers' Procession, 13th March, 1792. Order of procession: Two leaders with flags; Drums and fifes; Jason with the Golden Fleece; Argonauts, two and two; Two flags; Band of music; Shepherd and Shepherdess; Sheep shearer; Woolsorter; Bishop Blase and chaplain; Combmaker; Two comb pots, etc., followed by the Cavalcade. Time of starting, 9 a.m.; bells ringing, etc.

Coggleshall Weavers' Procession, 15th June, 1791. Order of procession: Two leaders; Two ensign bearers; Flemings, two and two; Union flag; Drums and fifes; King Henry II; Band of music; Shepherd and Shepherdess; Sley maker; Shackle maker; Loom maker; Jack of Newbury; Fleecy Care, etc., followed by the Cavalcade. Start at 8 a.m. (Programme

St. Blase's Day

copies in *The East Anglian, etc.*, vol. 1, Lowestoft, 1864, pp. 41-2.)

NORWICH CELEBRATIONS

[*Norfolk*] In Norwich, a pageant of great splendour was displayed in honour of St. Blase and the woollen industry; a pageant of this kind was organized in 1783, when a procession was formed which went along the chief streets of the city. Led by trumpeters and forty Argonauts on horseback there followed representations of the Golden Fleece, Hercules, Peace, Plenty, and the banner of Britannia. Next followed Jason, Castor and Pollux, Bishop Blase, his chaplain, and several orators who delivered appropriate speeches in every street on the route. Seven companies of woolcombers on foot and five on horseback brought up the rear. There was a Bishop Blase pageant in 1836, when the foundation stone of the Norwich Yarn Factory was laid, but this was a revival of the custom. (*Memorials of Old Norfolk*, Hugh J. Dukinfield Astley, 1908, pp. 268-9.)

NORTHAMPTON CELEBRATIONS

[*Northamptonshire*] The last observance in the town of Northampton was in the year 1804, when the procession paraded the principal streets. The procession included the following characters: Jason, carrying the Golden Fleece; Bishop Blase, in mitre and black gown; Shepherd and Shepherdess; Masters on horseback; Sorters, with helmets, wands, tassels, and scarves. The procession halted at various places where the orators, alternately, recited a poem of quite modern composition, praising St. Blase and explaining the different processes of the woollen industry. Money was collected and afterwards spent on a dinner or social entertainment. (*Glossary of Northamptonshire Words and Phrases*, Anne Elizabeth Baker, vol. 2, 1854, pp. 417-21.)

BURY ST. EDMUNDS CELEBRATIONS

[*Suffolk*] This day, Monday, 3rd February, 1777, being the anniversary of Bishop Blase, the same was observed in Bury St. Edmunds, in a manner far surpassing anything of the kind ever seen. The procession consisted of between 200 and 300 woolcombers on horseback, in uniforms properly decorated, Bishop Blase, Jason, Castor and Pollux, a band of music, drums, and colours, all in keeping with the greatness of the woollen industry. —From a contemporary Common Place Book in MS. (*The East Anglian, etc.*, vol. 1, Lowestoft, 1864, p. 31.)

HADLEIGH CELEBRATIONS

Many cities and towns used to organize pageants in honour of St. Blase and the woollen industry. Pageants of this kind used to be held at Hadleigh on the 3rd February, within the memory of living persons. People in or connected with the woollen trade paraded the town and a female, dressed as a shepherdess, rode in state in a post-chaise, carrying a lamb in her lap. (*The East Anglian, etc.*, vol. 1, Lowestoft, 1864, p. 48.)

GUILDFORD CELEBRATIONS

[*Surrey*] The Feast of St. Blase was, to the people of both Guildford and Godalming, the great festival of the year. On the 3rd of February, there were great processions both here and at Godalming. Solemn High Mass at St. Mary's Church, conducted by the Dominican Friars, opened the day's proceedings; alms were given to the poor; bonfires blazed on the hills; and there was an entire cessation of labour throughout the day. In 1222, the Council or Parliament of Oxford prohibited all servile work on the 3rd of February and, wherever the woollen industry flourished, this prohibition was specially observed. The proceedings in honour of the woollen industry and St. Blase maintained their hold on the people down to Stuart times, even when the woollen industry showed signs of steady and rapid decadence. (*Guildford in the Olden Time*, George C. Williamson, Guildford, 1904, p. 117.)

BRADFORD CELEBRATIONS

[*Yorkshire*] The splendour of the Bradford festival on St. Blase's Day was unsurpassed. In 1811, 1818, and at previous septennial periods, there was much pomp and festivity but the splendour of the last celebration, in 1825, was greater than before. The different trades began to assemble at 8 a.m. and were

St. Blase's Day

drawn up in marching order in Westgate. At about 10 a.m. the procession started in the following order: A herald bearing a flag; wool-staplers on horseback, each horse carrying a fleece; worsted spinners and manufacturers on horseback and wearing white stuff waistcoats each with a white stuff sash and a sliver over the shoulder; merchants on horseback with coloured sashes; guards, apprentices and masters' sons mounted and dressed in showy costumes. Then came bands of musicians, impersonations of the King and the Queen, Jason, Medea, and St. Blase, followed by a shepherd and shepherdess, woolsorters mounted and having ornamented caps and coloured slivers. Following these were comb-makers, charcoal-burners, woolcombers with wool wigs, dyers with red cockades, blue aprons, and crossed slivers of red and blue, and also several bands of musicians at intervals. The number of persons in the procession was about 800. In accordance with ancient custom a poem in honour of the woollen industry was read at certain parts of the line of march, which was traversed by about 5 p.m. The popularity of St. Blase at Bradford is indicated by the fact that a full-sized representation of the saint is carved in stone at the principal entrance of the Bradford Exchange.—*The Leeds Mercury*, 5th February, 1825. (*Old Yorkshire*, William Smith, Editor, vol. 2, 1881, pp. 150-4.)

YORK CELEBRATIONS

York, 9th Feb. Wednesday being the anniversary of St. Blase, Bishop of Sebaste, in Armenia, the woolcombers and others concerned in the woollen industry in this city made a grand procession through most parts of the city in the following order. Bishop Blase, represented by Francis Whitefield, clothed in a black gown, a mitre on his head, a prayer-book in his left hand, a comb full of wool in his right hand, and his horse led by two black boys. He was preceded by his secretary, also on horseback, with a drawn sword, who made a speech at several parts of the route to the honour of the saint and the woollen trade. Next in order were a shepherd and shepherdess, a band of music, three men with flags and garlands made of wool of various colours, many men walking in double file, wearing shirts and wigs made

134   *Calendar Customs*

of the finest wool, cross-belts and sashes of coloured wool, and carrying white rods decorated with tufts of wool. (*Whitehall Evening Post*, 12th February, 1768, a cutting from which is opposite p. 46 of Joseph Haslewood's copy of *Brand*, 1813 edition.) The year is not clearly written but seems to be 1768.

MASHAM CELEBRATIONS

The feast in honour of St. Blase was formerly held here annually, on 3rd February, when it was duly commemorated by the woolcombers by a supper and drinking, for the "jolly combing-boys were always thirsty souls." This was the course pursued in ordinary years but, on special occasions, something more imposing, as a spectacle, was attempted. On these special occasions a band of music led a grand procession not only through the streets of the town of Masham but also those of other neighbouring towns. The procession was composed of master woolcombers on horseback, each wearing a white sliver of wool; woolsorters, also on horseback, each carrying a fleece before him and bright and glittering shears; the shepherd and shepherdess dressed in green and carrying shepherds' crooks; St. Blase, on horseback, dressed in his mitre and full canonicals, bearing an open Bible in one hand and a wool-comb in the other, attended by guards, and attendants, and accompanied by a chaplain, who acted the part of an orator. These were followed by the working woolcombers and others connected with the trade, on foot, in shirts as white and as neat as women's hands could make them, each gaily decked with cross-belts, sashes, and bracelets composed of parti-coloured slivers of wool. As if by way of contrast, the rear of the procession was brought up by an old charcoal-burner, with grimy face and a short tobacco-pipe in his mouth, smoking like a steam engine, and riding an ill-favoured mule with trappings to match the rider. The cavalcade presented— with the glittering paraphernalia, and other emblematic figures representing Jason and the Golden Fleece, etc., which were used on the occasion—a novel and imposing appearance, and created no little interest in the district. At certain places on the route the procession stopped and the orator made a grandiloquent speech

St. Blase's Day

extolling the value of the woollen industry, the honour due to St. Blase (to whom he gracefully extended his hand and who as gracefully acknowledged the compliment), and the benefits, resulting from the success of the industry, to the town of Masham. Then, the oration having been delivered, the company sang a song in honour of St. Blase, as follows :

" My friends, the day of Bishop Blase is here—
The joyful'st day we have in all the year,
Wherein all tradesmen may rejoice and sing—
From a woolcomber to the greatest King.

When first the art of combing—it was found
By Bishop Blase—through England it did sound,
And therefore he shall canonized be,
Amongst the Saints, to all eternity.

Ten thousand spinners, and twice ten thousand too,
By our brave art have daily work to do ;
Who from their wheels send forth such pleasant noise
In honour of we jolly combing boys.

Go ! ask the weaver who was the first trade,
Whose approbation here it may be had—
For what fine stuffs or serges could there be,
Without the art of combing mystery ?

Here's a health unto our masters, we'll begin,
And then we'll drink a health unto the King.
What one invents the others do support—
Whilst Indians mourn, we true Britannians sport."

(*History and Antiquities of Masham and Mashamshire*, John Fisher, 1865, pp. 465-8.)

ST. BLAZEY

[*Cornwall*] This place is said to be where St. Blaze landed in this country; his effigy is preserved in the church, which is dedicated to his memory. An annual festival is held in the parish, on the 3rd of February, in honour of the Saint, as patron of the woollen industry. (*Time's Telescope* for 1830, p. 106.)

FIRES ON ST. BLASE'S DAY

On the anniversary of St. Blazius, 3rd February, it is still the custom, in many parts of England, to light up fires on the hills on St. Blayse night, a custom anciently taken up, perhaps, for no better reason than the jingling resemblance of his name to the word Blaze.—Dr. Percy, in his notes on the Northumberland Household Book, p. 333. (*Brand*, i, p. 52.).

In olden times, women went about in holiday mood, on St. Blase's day, and set fire to the wool and distaff of any woman they found at work, spinning on that day.

FAIRS

[*Sussex*] An old record for Boxgrove, Sussex, reads : " The proffet of one ffaire there holden on St. Blase's day woorth yerely 10s." The church of Boxgrove is dedicated to St. Mary and St. Blase. The fair still continues to be held on February 14th which is February the 3rd, Old Style. (*Sussex Archæol. Society's Collections*, vol. 9, Lewes, 1857, p. 225.)

[*Somerset*] A fair, date 3rd February, is held at Axbridge, Somerset.

St. Valentine's Eve and Day
13th and 14th February

The most popular saint of lovers, known as St. Valentine, has a day of commemoration in spring, a special period for courtship. Valentinus was a common Roman name and there were several saints of that name. One of these was a priest at Rome who is said to have been executed during the reign of Claudius Gothicus, on the 14th of February, in the year 269 ; another was a bishop, in Umbria, who is said to have been executed on the 14th of February, in the year 273. In such circumstances, identification of St. Valentine would be very difficult.

ST. VALENTINE'S DAY SENTIMENT

The customs celebrated on St. Valentine's day have been influenced, in an especial degree, by sentiment and in some of its popular sayings and beliefs no regard is paid to facts. The popular saying that, on St. Valentine's day, every bird chooses its mate, used to be treated as if it were an axiom. Still, it should be remembered that the saying is more than five centuries old and the popular ideas about birds, at that early time, must have been very vague and, what is more important, a concise and plausible saying about their breeding-habits would be accepted readily. Some birds, *e.g.* the missel thrush, the partridge, and the blackbird, pair during February and the average time for the partridge is about 20th February.

As late as the days of Herrick and Pepys, much importance was attached to another popular saying, that a maiden would marry the first bachelor whom she met on the morning of St. Valentine's day. The result of this belief, if it were put into operation, would soon show that marriages were not necessarily made in Heaven. However, a maiden of those times would be astute enough to avoid meeting anyone she did not wish to marry, and there were many who, like Mrs. Stuart, later Duchess of Richmond, would not marry by chance but only by choice.

ST. VALENTINE'S EVE AT NORWICH

[*Norfolk*] The approach of the happy day is heralded by advertisements headed " Valentines," all printed in very large type, announcing the offers for sale, at the shops and stores, of a great variety of presents. This is but the prelude to the real fun, which begins on the advent of St. Valentine's Eve. The streets swarm with carriers and baskets laden with treasures; bang, bang goes the knocker and away rushes the banger, after depositing upon the door-step a package from the basket of stores. Anonymously, St. Valentine presents his gifts, labelled only with " St. Valentine's Love " or " Good Morrow, Valentine." Many packages contain valuable presents, but some contain presents of little or no value wrapped up in a large package, the size of which is due to the use of numerous wrappers. This mockery is punctuated by the mottoes on the wrappers—" Persevere "; " Never despair "; " The brightest jewels are in the deepest mine "; " Happy is he that expecteth nothing." A local newspaper cutting of 1872 states that the new arrangement by which parcels not exceeding 12 oz. in weight can be sent through the post has had an effect in the Norwich district, and we hear that about 150,000 letters passed through the Norwich Post Office from Tuesday evening to Wednesday evening. Our tradesmen did a good business, ranging in value from a halfpenny wooden doll to a seventy-guinea piano, which the " Valentine " declined to accept. (Abridged from an account of *How they keep St. Valentine's Eve in Norwich, n.d.*, by Mrs. Madders.)

In additon to sending valentines by post, a peculiar custom is observed at Norwich and other places in Norfolk, on St. Valentine's Eve. The custom followed by all classes is to place a present on the door-step of the house of the favoured one, ring the bell or bang the knocker and run away. So general is the custom that some thousands of pounds are expended annually in purchasing suitable presents for office, domestic, or personal use. The local papers advertise the " valentines," the walls display printed placards for the same purpose, and the city crier, with a loud voice and a loud bell, proclaims the advantages offered in the valentine departments of rival shops. The presents, sent in the secret manner described, include cakes, oranges, confections, squeaking dolls, work-boxes, fancy bags, cutlery, silver pencil-holders, magnificent books, colours, drawings, drawing instruments, puzzles, dissected maps ; indeed, I have known a great library chair come in this way. The inmates of the house on whose door-step a package is laid try, by all means, to ascertain who sent it, but the most they can do is to read the letters or the words, " G. M. V." or " Good Morrow, Valentine," on the package, which has been sent carefully and anonymously.—John Wodderspoon, Norwich. (*N. and Q.*, i, 1, 1850, p. 293 ; i, 10, 1854, p. 5.)

ST. VALENTINE'S DAY IN OLDEN TIMES

The very old saying and belief about birds choosing their mates on St. Valentine's day was mentioned in the fourteenth century by Chaucer in his *Parliament of Birds* ; in the fifteenth century, in the *Paston Letters* ; and, in the seventeenth century,

St. Valentine's Eve and Day 139

by Herrick in his *Hesperides*. The saying is also mentioned, here and there, in many other publications.

The poem by John Lydgate, written in honour of Queen Katharine, consort of Henry V, refers to an English custom of men making their choice, apparently by chance.

The Paston Letters, 1422-1509, represent the correspondence of an East Anglian family and are more informative. They show that a custom of choosing others of the opposite sex as Valentines was practised, in the fifteenth century, in England. In a letter from Dame Elizabeth Brews to John Paston, February, 1477, it is stated: " And, cosyn, uppon Fryday is Sent Valentyne's Day, and every brydde chesyth hym a make."[1] Another letter, February, 1477, reads: " Unto my ryght welebelovyd Valuntyn, John Paston, Squyer, be this bill delyvered." This letter was from Margery Brews, daughter of Dame Elizabeth Brews, and later Mrs. John Paston. A third letter February, 1477, is signed:

" Be your Voluntyne,[2]

Margery Brews."

(*The Paston Letters*, 1422-1509, James Gairdner, Editor, 1900, pp. 169-172.)

In the seventeenth century a development of the custom of choosing Valentines was not only popular but expensive. Pepys has several notes on the seventeenth century custom. They are best told in his own language; the following notes are from Lord Braybrooke's edition of the *Diary*, 1828:

14th February, 1666-7. This morning came up to my wife's bedside (I being up and dressing myself) little Will Mercer to be her Valentine, and brought her name written upon blue paper in gold letters, done by himself very prettily, and we were both well pleased with it. But I am also this year my wife's Valentine and it will cost me £5, but that I must have laid out if we had not been Valentines. (Vol. 3, p. 147.)

16th February, 1666-7. I find that Mrs. Pierce's little girl is my Valentine, she having drawn me; which I am not sorry for,

---

[1] Every bird chooseth him a mate.
[2] Be your Voluntyne = I am, your Valentine.

it easing me of something more that I must give to others. But here I do first observe the fashion of drawing mottoes as well as names; so that Pierce who drew my wife did draw also a motto and this girl drew another for me. What mine was I forget, but my wife's was " Most courteous and most fair," which might be very pretty. (Vol. 3, p. 148.)

23rd February, 1667-8. This evening came up my wife, who willingly showed me her jewels, including a Turquie ring set with diamonds, my Valentine's gift to her for the year. (Vol. 4, p. 50.)

22nd February, 1660-1. My wife to Sir W. Batten's and there sat awhile, he having yesterday sent my wife half-a-dozen pairs of gloves and a pair of silk stockings and garters for her valentines. (Vol. 1, p. 179.)

26th April, 1667. The Duke of York having once been Mrs. Stewart's Valentine, did give her a jewel of about £800 and my Lord Mandeville, her Valentine this year, a ring of about £300. (Vol. 3, p. 204.) (*Memoirs of Samuel Pepys*, Richard Griffith Neville, Baron Braybrooke, Editor, 2nd edition, 5 vols, 1828.)

The custom of selecting personal valentines and giving costly presents began to lose its popularity before the end of the seventeenth century, one reason for this being the expense attaching to the custom. In accordance with the title of his book, Bourne does not mention this costly form of the custom but says that there was a custom, in his time, never omitted by the common people, to draw lots, which they called Valentines, on the Eve of St. Valentine's day. The names of a selected number of one sex were, by an equal number of the other sex, put into a vessel and then everyone drew a name which was called her or his Valentine and was looked upon as a good matrimonial omen. He adds that there was a rural tradition that every bird chooses its mate on St. Valentine's day and he seems to believe that this was the origin of the custom. (*The Antiquities of the Common People*, Henry Bourne, Newcastle, 1725, pp. 174-5.)

" Valentine's day is drawing near
 And both the men and maids incline
 To choose them each a Valentine."

(*Poor Robin's Almanack*, for 1757.)

St. Valentine's Eve and Day

Before the end of the eighteenth century, the artistically made card, or its equivalent, bearing a short love poem, began to be popular and the old and expensive custom of choosing personal valentines continued to decline until it became evanescent about the middle of the nineteenth century. Still, as long as the ordinary valentine displays an old phrase, such as, for example, " Dearest mine, will you be my Valentine ?", a reference, intended or implied, to the old custom, will remain.

The following records relate to some old-time valentines displayed at an exhibition of valentines, opened on 13th February, 1929, at the Victoria and Albert Museum.

The earliest valentine in the exhibition is dated 1760; it is an amorous effusion beginning :

" Charming Chloe, look with pity
On your love-sick swain."

Many of the 300 exhibits, which have been lent by Mrs. Willoughby Hodgson, Miss Jane Samuels, Mr. Gerald S. Hervey, Mr. Guy Little, and the St. Bride Foundation Institution, are hand-painted in elaborate designs. (*Daily News*, 14th February, 1929.)

There will be seen in the South Kensington exhibition a valentine, from Mr. G. S. Hervey's collection, which is dated 1800 and seems to be one of the best examples of the valentine at its purest and shyest. It is a pretty cut, hand-coloured, of a swain peeping through a hedge at his mistress, who, seated on a rustic bench, is reading his valentine, " I want my dear maid a sweet partner for life ; so tell me in earnest if you'll be my wife." (*The Observer*, 10th February, 1929.)

St. Valentine's day, the festival of romance, falls due in a week's time. It has faded in popularity since this home-made valentine (Plate VII) was sent by the fourth Duke of Portland, in 1847, to a Miss Betsy Keates. Its appeal, expressed verbally in part and pictorially in part, reads : " If you love I as I love you, no knife shall cut our love in two." (*Daily Express*, 7th February, 1929.)

ST. VALENTINE'S DAY IN MODERN TIMES

During the past hundred years, the St. Valentine's custom has changed much in popularity and type of valentine sold. Throughout England, during a period including the years 1850-1880, numerous valentines of different types were displayed, the courteous, the sentimental, the comic, the satirical, and the vulgar or offensive, which was rarely enclosed in an envelope and admirably suited for rousing the resentment of the recipient. This was true for the period 1870-85, when valentines enclosed in neat cardboard boxes and displaying silk of delicate shades, artistically cut lace-paper, and roses, violets, and words in bright colours, silver, and gilt, were at their best. However, the increasing unpopularity of the offensive type of valentine and the increasing popularity of Christmas and picture cards reduced the sales of the superior types of valentine so that, during the period 1898 to 1904, in Watford and the adjacent district, the valentine custom was at a low level as regards popularity, and there does not appear to have been any important revival; valentines were sold in small numbers in 1930 and 1933. To give even an approximately accurate account of such changes, it would be necessary to limit the scope of the inquiry to a single city, town, or district, for what would be true for any one of these would not necessarily be true for another.

[*London*] In London, especially the West End, increased interest was shown in 1929, 1930, and 1936, when large numbers of valentines were sold and the celebrations in the hotels were highly popular.

On 13th February, 1929, an inquirer was informed, by a sales girl at a West End store, that a lot of valentines were being sold, most of the customers being young women. She also mentioned what would be a novel and useful type of valentine, called a " Love's Thermometer." (*Daily News*, 14th February, 1929.)

On 2nd February, 1930, it was announced that Messrs. Raphael Tuck and Sons, Ltd., had published a series of valentine cards. (*The Observer*, 2nd February, 1930). This was a correct forecast of the popularity of St. Valentine's Day, 1930, when many valentines were sold.

PLATE VII

VALENTINE
SENT BY THE FOURTH DUKE OF PORTLAND TO A MISS BETSY KEATES, 1847

St. Valentine's Eve and Day

Revival of interest in St. Valentine's Day was reflected in London hotels last night. At the Savoy there were nearly 1,000 guests, and valentines, specially written to order, were distributed. At the Royal Palace Hotel, a valentine almost a century old, with Cupid in a petticoat, was an attraction. Men enjoyed wearing French top hats of scarlet, green, and gold and women wore poke bonnets from Paris. (*Daily News*, 15th February, 1930.)

In Leap Year, 1936, the number of valentines sold was very great and the Postmaster-General issued special valentine telegram forms.

Thousands of "Valentine Telegrams," for delivery on the special form with a golden envelope, introduced by the Postmaster-General, were handed in at London post offices to-day. (*The Evening News*, 14th February, 1936.)

ST. VALENTINE'S DAY COUNTY RECORDS

[*Herefordshire*] The custom of sending valentines is dying out but is not yet extinct. (*The Folk-Lore of Herefordshire*, Ella Mary Leather, Hereford, 1912, p. 96.)

[*Lancashire*] St. Valentine's day received a merry welcome from the country swains and maidens who at that time became associated with their partners for the year. The selection was made by writing the names of an equal number of each sex on separate slips of paper, and then arranging them in two lots, one representing the males and the other the females. The females drew from the male lot and the males from the female lot, so that each person had two sweethearts and the final pairing was effected by arrangement. After the selection had been completed, the youths gave treats and dances to their sweethearts and wore their billets for several days. (*History of the Fylde of Lancashire*, John Porter, Fleetwood and Blackpool, 1876, p. 97.)

[*Lincolnshire*] On the 14th of February, we duly sent and received vollantines—valentines we set down as an alien affectation. One verse which we were fond of scrawling to each other is too universally known for me to quote ; it refers to the redness of the rose and the blueness of the violet, but there is another favourite which I will not withhold, as it refers to the significance of colours, a subject of no small interest :

> " If you love me, love me true ;
> Send me a ribbon and let it be blue.
> If you hate me, let it be seen ;
> Send me a ribbon and let it be green."

—G. J., June 29, 1878. (*County F.L.*, vol. 5, *Lincolnshire*, Mrs. Gutch and Mabel Peacock, 1908, pp. 187-8.)

Valentine's day is dead and gone. The modern Christmas cards have all but supplied the place of the valentines, many coarse and vulgar, which were common enough twenty years ago, *i.e.* 1879, and I do not think that, at any time, Valentine's day had in Marshland the importance it had farther north. (Rev. R. M. Heanley in *Saga Book of the Viking Club*, vol. 3, 1902, p. 41.)

[*Northumberland*] The pleasing custom of sending love missives on St. Valentine's day, some years ago, rendered this one of our most popular festivals. Twenty or thirty years ago, every country swain and his sweetheart exchanged valentines. These usually took the form of a fanciful design on paper, displaying a picture of a cupid in the centre, a suitable verse below, surrounded by a border of paper lace-work. Thousands of these were sent by post on St. Valentine's day. In many country places in Northumberland, lads sometimes made their own valentines by drawing a true-lover's knot or a Catharine wheel, painted in colours, red, white, and blue, on a nice sheet of paper, not forgetting a suitable amatory effusion. Of late years, however, the old valentine has been quite superseded by Christmas and picture post cards.—Rothbury and Whittingham. (D. D. Dixon, MS. *n.d.* [about 1905].)

[*Yorkshire*] St. Valentine's day was duly observed in Morley, fifty years ago, but the message of affection was not conveyed by means of elaborately designed and highly artistic cards. The message was generally a written one and was slipped under the door where the recipient lived.[1] (*Morley : Ancient and Modern*, William Smith, 1886, p. 142.)

[1] The same procedure used to be followed by boys at Polperro, Cornwall. (*Western Antiquary*, vol. 3, 1884, p. 207.)

At one time, St. Valentine's morning was of such momentous meaning that all work was neglected in houses and mills in Honley, until the postman arrived. Now we no longer see those embroidered works of art containing charming combinations of sentiment and bathos, so well known years ago. Modern lovers now despise the go-between of St. Valentine, and Cupid's emblems have given place to Christmas cards and good wishes. (*The History of Honley, etc.*, Mary A. Jagger, Huddersfield, 1914, pp. 127-8.)

THE FORLORN MAIDEN

[*Derbyshire*] If a lass is not kissed or is not visited by her sweetheart, on St. Valentine's day, she is said to be dusty and the villagers sweep her with a broom or a wisp of straw. She is bound to cast lots with other girls and, if chance favours her, draws the name of her future husband out of an old top hat. Mr. Pendleton, the writer of an article on *Superstitions in the Peak*, tells me, in a letter, that the custom was observed on the morning of St. Valentine's day, in the middle of the last century. (*Sheffield Daily Telegraph*, article on *Superstitions in the Peak*, quoted in *Memorials of Old Derbyshire*, J. Charles Cox, Editor, 1907, p. 370.)

HUNTING THE WREN

[*Suffolk*] The custom of hunting the wren on St. Valentine's day is not entirely out of use. (*The History and Antiquities of Suffolk, Thingoe Hundred*, John Gage, 1838, footnote, p. xxvii.)

ST. VALENTINE'S GIFT CUSTOMS

These customs of giving Valentine buns, money, apples, and oranges, to children and old people, are numerous and varied. They will be arranged in three groups and described under the subordinate headings, *St. Valentine's Buns*, *Valentining*, and *The Leicestershire, etc., Gift Customs*; overlapping of subject-matter will be avoided, as far as possible.

ST. VALENTINE'S BUNS

[*Leicestershire ; Rutland*] In Leicestershire, lozenge-shaped buns, with currants and caraways, and called Shittles, are given to children and old people, notably at Glaston, on St. Valentine's day. The bakers call them "Valentine buns." (*Old English Customs extant at the Present Time*, P. H. Ditchfield, 1896, p. 54.)

[*Northamptonshire*] In Peterborough and some of the villages in the northern part of the county, sweet plum buns were, and I believe are still, made and called "Valentine buns." I am told that, in some villages, these buns are given by sponsors to their godchildren, on the Sunday before and after St. Valentine's day. (*Glossary of Northamptonshire Words and Phrases*, Anne Elizabeth Baker, vol. 2, 1854, p. 374.)

[*Rutland*] At Market Overton, Rutland, every 14th of February, it has been the custom from time immemorial to give buns to all the children in the village. Some years ago, there were seven donors, but with lapse of time the number has decreased and now I am the only one left; when I am gone, the custom will probably die out altogether. The buns are now known as "Valentine Buns" but, within my remembrance, they were called "Plum Shittles," being of an oval shape, like a weaver's shuttle.—Edward Cosall, Market Overton. (*Leicestershire and Rutland Notes and Queries*, John and Thomas Spencer, Editors, vol. 3, April 1893-July 1895, 1895, p. 159.) The Editors add that Plum Shuttles, pronounced Shittles, are still eaten, on St. Valentine's day, at Uppingham, Rutland.

VALENTINING CUSTOMS

For centuries past, it was customary for persons, especially children, to go from door to door, on St. Valentine's day, and sing or repeat a few lines in order to obtain money, cakes, or fruit. These customs present numerous differences in details but, with very few exceptions, they are closely associated by having in the lines, sung or recited, the phrase "Good morrow, Valentine," or an equivalent phrase announcing that the children are celebrating St. Valentine's day.

[*Essex, etc.*] These customs have been popular in many counties, Essex, Norfolk, Suffolk, Cambridgeshire, Northamptonshire, Oxfordshire, Devonshire, Buckinghamshire, Worcestershire, and others.

[*Essex*] I first heard, at Sheering, Essex, the queer old rhyme :

"Good Morrow to you, Valentine,
Curl your hair as I curl mine,
One before and two behind ;
Good Morrow to you, Valentine."

It is commonly sung all about here on St. Valentine's day, but I never remembered having heard it near Epping nor Ongar.—Folk-Lore in Essex and Herts. (*Essex Review*, vol. 5, Chelmsford, 1896, p. 148.)

[*Suffolk*]

"Good Morrow, Valentine,
Change your luck an' I'll change mine,
We are ragetty, you are fine,
So prar gon us a Valentine.
Good Morrow, Valentine,
Curl your hair as I curl mine,
One before and two behind,
An' prar gon us a Valentine."

This song is still sung in remote villages in Suffolk. Young people go round on Valentine's Eve with a lantern on a pole. A turnip is scooped out and a face made on it ; a candle is put inside ; and the children have pennies given to them.—Suffolk. (*Spinning Days and Olden Ways*, Lois A. Fison, . . . pp. 32-3.)

[*Cambridgeshire, etc.*] The children go round the village in couples, or three or four together, and sing :

"Good morning, Valentine ;
Curl your locks as I do mine,
Two before and three behind.
Good morning, Valentine."

Of course, pennies, cakes, or oranges are expected.—Duxford and Ickleton, M. C. Jones. (*Folk-Lore*, vol. 24, 1913, p. 234.) These customs are of a type in which a reference to the curling of hair is introduced. Similar customs have been recorded for High Roding, Essex (*Old English Customs extant at the*

Present Time, P. H. Ditchfield, 1896, p. 56), and for Meldreth, Cambridgeshire (*N. and Q.*, vi, 4, 1881, p. 258.)

The following are Northamptonshire and Buckinghamshire customs associated by the sentence, " First 'tis yours and then 'tis mine."

[*Northamptonshire*] The children of the villages go in parties and repeat at each house a valentining rhyme, two forms of which are the following :

" Good morrow, Valentine !
First its yours and then its mine.
So please give me a valentine."

or

" Morrow, morrow, Valentine !
First 'tis yours and then 'tis mine.
So please to give me a valentine.
Holly and ivy tickle my toe,
Give me red apple and let me go."

(*Glossary of Northamptonshire Words and Phrases*, Anne Elizabeth Baker, vol. 2, 1854, p. 373.)

[*Buckinghamshire*] In a Buckinghamshire village, to the present day, the boys go round for pence to every house, singing :

" Good morrow to you, Valentine,
First 'tis yours and then 'tis mine,
I'll thank you for a Valentine."

(*Notes on the Folk-Lore of the Northern Counties of England and the Borders*, William Henderson, 1879, p. 94.)

[*Oxfordshire*] At Islip, I have heard the children sing the following lines when collecting pence on St. Valentine's day :

" Good morrow, Valentine,
I be thine and thou be'st mine,
So please give me a valentine."

(*Popular Rhymes and Nursery Tales*, James Orchard Halliwell 1849, p. 239.)

[*Worcestershire*] In Armscote, a Worcestershire hamlet, the children sang these words :

> " Morrow, morrow, Valentine,
> I'll be yourn if you'll be mine,
> Please to give me a valentine."

They always begged for apples, which were saved to make apple fritters on Shrove Tuesday. (*Folk-Lore*, vol. 26, 1915, p. 94.)

These Islip and Armscote rhymes have as a distinct feature the second line of each rhyme.

[*Norfolk*] Another group of rhymes, having as a distinguishing feature the words " God bless the baker," belongs especially to the county of Norfolk. For Billingford, Norfolk, the following rhyme is recorded :

> " Good morrow, Valentine,
> A happy new year ;
> A pocket full of money,
> And a cellar full of beer.
> Good morrow, Valentine,
> God bless the baker,
> You be the giver
> And I'll be the taker."

(Rev. J. G. Lambert, Rector of Billingford, October, 1914.)

At Ryburgh, Norfolk, children go round for contributions, saying :

> " God bless the baker ;
> If you will be the giver
> I will be the taker."

(*N. and Q.*, iv, 5, 1870, p. 595.)

[*Northamptonshire*] The boys and girls of Ecton used to come round, on St. Valentine's day, with a very short rhyme :

> " Morrow, morrow, Valentine,
> Empty your purse and fill mine."

(*Northamptonshire Notes and Queries*, vol. i, Northampton, 1886, p. 149.)

[*Oxfordshire*] The following rhyme seems to refer to an old popular belief that St. Valentine influences the weather :

> " To-morrow, to-morrow, Valentine,
> Mr. March has laid his line.
> Please give us a valentine."

—Bucknell, Oxfordshire. (*Oxfordshire Archæological Reports* for 1903, Banbury, 1904, p. 34.)

[*Devonshire*] On St. Valentine's day, a girl sometimes addresses the first young man she meets :

> " Good morrow, Valentine, I go to-day,
> To wear for you what you must pay,
> A pair of gloves next Easter day."

New gloves are generally sent on Easter Eve by the young man chosen to make such a present. The girl and the young man are, as a rule, not strangers to each other.—8th January, 1833. (*The Borders of the Tamar and the Tavy*, Anna Eliza Stothard, afterwards Bray, vol. 2, Plymouth, 1879, pp. 118-9.)

[*Northamptonshire*] Children go in parties, on St. Valentine's day, from house to house, repeating the following rhyme :

> " Good morrow, Valentine,
> Parsley grows by savoury,
> Savoury grows by thyme,
> A new pair of gloves on Easter day,
> Good morrow, Valentine."

(*Glossary of Northamptonshire Words and Phrases*, Anne Elizabeth Baker, vol. 2, 1854, p. 374.)

[*Berkshire*] In Berkshire, the boys repeat the following rhyme, on St. Valentine's day :

> " Knock the kittle agin the pan,
> Gie us a penny if 'e can.
> We be ragged and you be fine,
> Plaze to gie us a valentine.
> Up wi' the kittle and down wi' the spout,
> Gie us a penny and we'll gie out."

(*Old English Customs extant at the Present Time*, P. H. Ditchfield, 1896, p. 55.)

St. Valentine's Eve and Day

THE LEICESTERSHIRE, ETC., GIFT CUSTOMS

[*Leicestershire*] It is an ancient custom at Beaumanor, Leicestershire, the residence of William Herrick, Esq., that all children living within the township of Woodham and Beaumanor who made their appearance there on St. Valentine's day, shall receive one penny as a valentine and, on their return to Woodham, a half-penny at the Rev. W. Riley's. On Wednesday morning week, the customary assemblage took place and, after a variety of youthful sports, 228 children received the usual penny from the proprietor of Beaumanor. (*The Leicester Chronicle*, 24th February, 1849.)

On St. Valentine's morn, the children would be astir early, eager to go to the great house for a "valentine." Assembled in groups before the front door of the mansion, they piped forth their greeting:

" Good morrow, Valentine,
A piece of bacon and cheese
And a bottle of wine.
If you've got a penny in your pocket
Slip it into mine.
We used to come at eight o'clock
And now we come at nine."

The children received coppers or Valentine buns. T. R. Potter, in his *History of Charnwood Forest*, says that he saw as many as three hundred children, on one such occasion, going to Beaumanor. The art of making Valentine buns is not yet forgotten in the neighbourhood of Melton. (*Bygone Leicestershire*, William Andrews, Editor, Hull, 1892, pp. 117-8.)

[*Essex*] At High Roding, Essex, a bright, new sixpence is given to every child in the Parish who presents himself or herself at the Ware Farm, at 8 a.m., on St. Valentine's day. (*Old English Customs extant at the Present Time*, P. H. Ditchfield, 1896, p. 56.)

DIVINATIONS

On St. Valentine's eve and day, the carrying out of divinations, usually love divinations, was general, especially in country villages. The divinations varied greatly in detail but many necessitated secrecy and a visit to the village churchyard about the time of midnight. It would seem that just as Valentine customs were suggestive of the church and its altar, so there was a sentimental attachment to divinations whose ceremonies were centred about the village church. At any rate, such divinations were popular.

[*Derbyshire*] At Ashbourne, Derbyshire, a young woman who wishes to know who is to be her future husband goes to the churchyard at midnight and, when the clock strikes twelve, commences to run round the church, repeating the lines:

> " I sow hemp seed, hemp seed I sow,
> He that loves me best
> Come after me and mow."

Having, in this way, run round the church twelve times, without stopping, the figure of her lover is believed to follow her. (*Journ. British Archæol. Assoc.*, vol. 7, 1852, p. 209.)

A custom prevailed, years ago, in country farm and other houses, in Derbyshire, for a girl to peep through the keyholes of house doors, before opening them on St. Valentine's day, when, if she saw a cock and a hen in company, the event was believed to be so favourable that it could be safely concluded that she would be married before the end of the year. (*Long Ago: A Journal of Popular Antiquities*, Alex. Andrews, Editor, vol. 1, 1873, p. 81.)

[*Devonshire*] In Devonshire, the peasants and others believe that if a man or woman goes to the porch of a church, on St. Valentine's Eve, waits there till half-past twelve with some hemp seed in his or her hand and, at that time, goes homewards scattering the seed on either side and repeating these lines:

> " Hemp seed I sow, hemp seed I sow,
> She (or he) that will my true love be,
> Come, rake this hemp seed after me,"

his or her true love will be seen behind, raking up the seed just sown, in a winding-sheet. (*N. and Q.*, i, 5, 1852, p. 55.) It

St. Valentine's Eve and Day

seems to be inexplicable why a winding-sheet is introduced into such a ceremony.

In many of the villages in Devonshire, girls pluck yarrow from a man's grave, in the belief that if they repeat a few lines commencing :

" Yarrow, sweet yarrow, the first I have found,
And in the name of Jesus I pluck it from the ground,"

and place the yarrow under the pillow, their lovers will appear in their dreams. (*Bygone Days in Devon and Cornwall*, Mrs. H. P. Whitcombe, 1874, p. 23.)

Those who are averse to visiting a churchyard at night may carry out the following divination, provided the time be St. Valentine's Eve or Midsummer Eve. A bowl of water must be provided and also a number of small pieces of paper, on each of which is written a different letter, the whole alphabet being represented. Then the shoes must be placed in the form of the letter T and the following words must be said :

" I place my shoes like the letter T,
In hopes my true love I shall see,
In his apparel and his array,
As he is now and every day."

A reversal of the shoes and a second recitation of these lines followed by another reversal and a third recitation of the lines completes the first stage of the divination. The pieces of paper are laid, face downwards, on the surface of the water in the bowl and the girl practising the divination retires to rest. Next morning, she looks into the bowl and should any of the pieces of paper be seen to be turned over so as to expose a letter or letters, such are believed to indicate the initials of her lover's name. (*Folk Rhymes of Devon*, William Crossing, 1911, p. 148.)

The following divination used to be practised but no locality is given for it. The use of the pillow, bay leaves, and rose water is evidence that the divination was a very old one.

On Valentine's day, take two bay leaves, sprinkle them with rose water and place them on your pillow, in the evening. When you go to bed, put on a clean night-gown turned inside out and, lying down, say softly :

" Good Valentine, be kind to me ;
In dreams, let me my true love see."

Then, go to sleep as soon as you can, in expectation of seeing your future husband in a dream. (*Popular Rhymes and Nursery Tales*, James Orchard Halliwell, 1849, pp. 219-20.)

In a passage, often quoted but still interesting, a young lady describes three experiments, made on the same St. Valentine's Eve, in order to identify her future partner. She pinned five bay leaves to the corners and the centre of her pillow ; rolled up clay in small pieces of paper, on which she had written the names of her lovers, and put the papers in water ; she retired to rest after eating a hard-boiled egg, including shell, the yolk having been removed and replaced by salt. She emphasized the fact that she had a preference for a Mr. Blossom—and the piece of paper bearing his name was the first to rise to the surface of the water. (*Connoisseur*, no. 56, dated about 1755 ; *Brand*, i, p. 58 ; *Time's Telescope* for 1814, pp. 32-3.)

POPULAR SAYINGS AND BELIEFS

" You will marry the man or woman, as the case may be, whom you meet first on St. Valentine's day."

This old and widely-known saying and belief is well expressed by the lines :

" Last Valentine, the day when birds of kind
Their paramours with mutual chirpings find,
I early rose, just at the break of day,
Before the sun had chas'd the stars away.
A-field I went, amid the morning dew,
To milk my kine (for so should housewives do).
Thee first I spy'd, and the first swain we see,
In spite of fortune shall our true love be."

(*The Shepherd's Week*, Thursday, John Gay, 1714, lines 37-44.)

Before the poet wrote the above lines, many ladies had decided that their selection in matrimony would not depend on the drawing of Valentines, but only on free choice.

" St. Valentine's is the birds' wedding day." This quaint, rustic saying is widespread and very old; it is referred to by Chaucer in his *Parliament of Birds*, 1381 :

> " Ye know wel how, seynt Valentyes day,
> By my statut and by my governaunce,
> Ye come for to chese [1]—and flee your way—
> Your makes,[2] as I prik [3] yow with pleasaunce."

(*The Parlement of Foules*, ll. 386-9, *The Student's Chaucer*, Prof. W. W. Skeat, Editor, Oxford, 1897, p. 106.)

" St. Valentine's is a lucky day."

[*Worcestershire*] " If you meet a single man first on Valentine's day, it is a sign you will never want for clothes, throughout the year; if a married man you will want for them." (Mrs. Edward Salt, Standon Rectory, Staffordshire; from a Suckley maid-servant.)

" Snowdrops should not be brought into the house before St. Valentine's day, if you wish to be married during the year."

" St. Valentine's day, sow your beans in the clay."

This saying, or mere variations of it, is known in Rutland, Staffordshire, Shropshire, Oxfordshire, and other counties.

> " By Valentine's day,
> Every good hen, duck, and goose should lay ;
> By David and Chad,
> Every hen, duck, and goose should lay, good or bad."

—Warwickshire. (*Folk-Lore*, vol. 24, 1913, p. 239.)

This saying, in various forms is known in many counties, Warwickshire, Lincolnshire, Buckinghamshire, Norfolk, Nottinghamshire, Staffordshire, and several others.

WEATHER OMENS

" So far as the sun shines into your house on Valentine's day, so far will the snow drive in on May day."

[1] chese = choose.   [2] makes = mates.   [3] prik = urge.

"If the wind is in the west on Valentine's day and the trees hang a-drop, it is a sign of good weather for the shepherd." (From Miss Matthews' Oral Collection.)

St. Valentine is supposed to influence the weather, as appears from the old saw:

"In Valentine, March lays her line."

(*Glossary of Northamptonshire Words and Phrases*, Anne Elizabeth Baker, vol. 2, 1854, p. 374.)

FAIRS

At Bath, Biggleswade, Devizes, Dorchester, Kings Lynn, and Wymondham, fairs are held on the 14th of February.

[*Dorset*] Old Candlemas Hiring Fair, Dorchester, 14th February. Hiring is still done, 1911, according to an inn-keeper, a native of Dorchester. (Miss J. B. Partridge.)

[*Kent*] A century ago, an important fair for the sale of cattle was held at Bromley, Kent, on 14th February. (*The History, Antiquities, etc., of the Parish of Bromley, Kent*, Charles Freeman, Bromley, 1832, p. 23.)

[*Norfolk*] Kings Lynn St. Valentine's fair is an ancient charter fair for six days' pleasure and business; it is said that its charter directs that the fair should begin on the day of St. Valentine. The fair is held in Tuesday Market Place, the market, meanwhile, being accommodated near the Guildhall. As at most East Anglian fairs, there are set up the usual paraphernalia of a pleasure fair and a great display of agricultural machinery and tools, and also general merchandise. The opening is ceremonial and, in 1930, was performed by Lord Fermoy, Mayor of Kings Lynn. The fair is usually called "Lynn Mart," "Mart" being an ancient name used in connection with the fairs of a few other towns, *e.g.* Gainsborough and Boston.

[*Wiltshire*] A fair is held at Devizes, on the 14th of February, in Monday Market Street. It is popularly called "Candlemas Fair" or, more correctly, "Old Candlemas Fair."

February

POPULAR SAYINGS AND BELIEFS

" February fill dyke."

In many parts of England, February is not a dyke-filling month. Rainfall measurements in Hertfordshire, during the period 1840-1909, showed that February was, next to March, the driest month of the year and was not remarkable for heavy rainstorms. (*Trans. Herts. Nat. Hist. Soc.*, vol. 15, 1915, p. 204.) For the dry year 1921, the rainfall for the county was 0.2 inch and for the year 1930 was 0.68 inch.

" If in February, there be no rain,
'Tis neither good for hay nor grain."

" February's rain swells the grain."

" February's flood does good."

" All the months 'n the year
Curse a fair Februeer."

" If February be white
It's the better to like."

This saying expresses a belief that snow in February is advantageous.

" Thou cauld, gloomy February."

" A warm day of February is a dream of April."

" A February Saturday is good for merchants, lovers, and seamen."

WEATHER OMEN

" Much February snow
A fine summer doth show." (Worcestershire).

St. David's Day

1st March

[*London*] St. David, the patron saint of Wales and founder of the See of St. David, died about the year 550. He is often represented preaching on a hill, with a dove on one of his shoulders. A well-known popular custom celebrated on his day is that of wearing the leek and one of the popular spectacular ceremonies, in London, is the presentation of leek emblems to officers, non-commissioned officers and men of the Welsh Guards, on St. David's day.

DISTRIBUTING BEQUESTS

[*Huntingdonshire*] At Godmanchester, one quarter of good malt and one quarter of good barley were distributed to the poor on the first of March, annually, under the terms of Upchurch's Charity, 1570, and one quarter of barley under the terms of Thomas East's Charity on the first of March, annually. Both distributions have ceased; East's distribution was last made in the year 1810. (*The History of Godmanchester*, Robert Fox, 1831, p. 344.)

DIVINATION

[*London*] Early on the 1st of March, girls of the village of Steban Hethe, now called Stepney, used to go to Goodman's Fields in search of a blade of grass of a reddish tint. The fortunate finder of such a blade of grass would, it was believed, obtain the husband of her wishes within the month. (*Time's Telescope* for 1823, p. 56.)

POPULAR SAYINGS AND BELIEFS

[*Lancashire*] I have often heard my grandmother say: "On the 1st of March, a peck of fleas is left at every door." She was a Lancashire woman. (*N. and Q.*, x, 2, 1909, p. 277.)

St. David's Day

[*Shropshire*] " The devil shakes a bag of fleas at everybody's door, on the 1st of March." This has been often heard in Shrewsbury. (*Bye-Gones relating to Wales and the Border Counties*, Oswestry and Wrexham, 1899-1900, p. 344.)

[*Devonshire*] A house-maid advised Mrs. Hewett not to open her bedroom window on the 1st of March, and said that she had heard that the black army always came down Exeter Hill, in swarms, on that day. (*The Peasant Speech of Devon*, Sarah Hewett, 1892, p. 52.)

[*Gloucestershire*] " I don't want the black soldiers in." This was said by an old villager who was most careful to keep every window shut, on the 1st of March, lest fleas should enter; he said that he didn't want the black soldiers in. (From one of his women-neighbours, at Minchinhampton, to Miss J. B. Partridge, 1915.)

[*Sussex*]

" If from fleas you would be free,
On 1st of March, let your windows closed be."

This was said by a nurse to Mrs. Latham. (*Sussex Archæol. Society's Collections*, vol. 33, Lewes, 1883, p. 240.)

[*Norfolk*]

" Sow beans and peas on David and Chad,
Be the weather good or bad."

(*The Norfolk Garland*, John Glyde, Junr., [1872], p. 157.) A similar saying, referring to peas only, was commonly known in Worcestershire.

" First comes David, then comes Chad,
Then comes Winneral as though he were mad.
White or black
Or old house thack."   Thack = thatch.

This saying refers to the stormy weather commonly experienced at the beginning of March. The first two lines of the saying are known in Suffolk, but St. Winwaloe, whose anniversary falls on the 3rd of March, is there called Winnold and not, as in genuine Norfolk, Winneral. The Norfolk saying means that, at this season of the year, there will be snow, rain, or wind, suggested by " old house thack." (*The Norfolk Garland*, John Glyde, Junr., [1872], p. 155.)

[*Northumberland*]

" Upon St. David's day,
Put oats and barley in the clay."

(*County F. L.*, vol. 4, *Northumberland*, M. C. Balfour and Northcote W. Thomas, 1904, p. 175.)

[*Suffolk*]

" First comes David, then comes Chad,
Then comes Winnold as if he were mad."

(*County F. L.*, vol. 1 (2), *Suffolk*, The Lady Eveline Camilla Gurdon, 1893, p. 163.)

[*Worcestershire*]

" By Valentine's day, every good goose should lay,
But by David and Chad, both good and bad."

(*Glossary of West Worcestershire Words*, E. L. Chamberlain, 1882, p. 37.)

FAIR

[*London*] In Church Street, in the Lambeth Church district, a fair was held annually, until within a few years back, on St. David's day; it was called " Taffy's Fair," from the numbers of Welsh people who visited it. (*The History and Antiquities of the Parish of Lambeth*, Thomas Allen, 1827, p. 342.)

St. Chad's Day
2nd March

St. Chad (Ceadda) became Bishop of Mercia about the year 669 and had his See at Lichfield. He died in the year 673. Many churches have been dedicated to his memory and, as the patron saint of medicinal springs, several wells and springs of importance have been named after him, such as, for example, an old London well near King's Cross, called St. Chad's Well, and Chadwell Springs, sources of the New River.[1] Some of St.

[1] *Wolverhampton Chronicle*, [no date given] (*The Antiquary*, vol. 1, 1880, p. 129).

St. Chad's Day

Chad's sacred relics are in Birmingham R. C. Cathedral, which is dedicated to St. Chad.

Chad pennies and farthings used to be paid on the high altar of Lichfield Cathedral; *see* vol. 1, 1936, p. 150.

Popular sayings and beliefs for St. Chad's day, *see* St. David's day.

St. Winwaloe's Day
3rd March

[*East Anglia, etc.*] By various names, Winwaloe, Winneral, Winnold and Winnal, this saint is known in East Anglia; it is said that he lived in the sixth century. On the question whether or no there were more than one saint of the name, authorities are not agreed. It is said, however, that more than one Cornish church bears the name of the saint, that traditions concerning him are contradictory, and that there may well have been more than one saint of the name. (*The Book of Saints*, compiled by the Benedictine Monks of St. Augustine's Abbey, Ramsgate, 1931, p. 272.)

[*Cornwall*] Gunwalloe Church is said to have been dedicated to St. Winwallo, Abbot of Tauracum, whose festival is on the third of March. (*Magna Britannia*, David and Samuel Lysons, vol. 3, 1814, p. 126.)

Popular Sayings and Beliefs. *See* St. David's day.

FAIR

[*Norfolk*] Winnold Fair is of very great antiquity. Kept originally at Whinwall or Winnold, a hamlet in the Parish of Wereham, it is mentioned as early as 1337 and is probably as old as the early part of the thirteenth century. After the dissolution of West Dereham Abbey, to which, at that time, the Fair belonged, the holding of the Fair was continued because it was useful. Soon afterwards it was transferred to the adjoining Parish of Wimbotsham and was held there until about the end of the eighteenth century, when it was again removed, this time to

Downham Market, where it has been held ever since. (*Norfolk and Norwich Chronicle*, 3rd March, 1897; Blomefield's *History of Norfolk*, [Parkin], vol. 7, 1807, pp. 507-9.)

The ancient fair of St. Winwaloe was removed to Downham Market, in 1797, where it still flourishes as the great horse-fair of West Norfolk. (*Memorials of Old Norfolk*, Hugh J. Dukinfield Astley, 1908, p. 265.)

St. Piran's Day
5th March

[*Cornwall*] The patron saint of miners, St. Piran or St. Perran, is said to have lived near Padstow, Cornwall. He was one of the most popular of Cornish saints.

The tinners of Cornwall held some holidays peculiar to themselves: the White-Thursday before Christmas and St. Piran's day are deemed sacred in the mining districts. (*The History of Cornwall, etc.*, Rev. R. Polwhele, 7 vols., vol. 2, 1816, p. 132.)

The 5th March, known as St. Piran's day, sanctions a suspension of all work by the tinners, and this has been followed from time immemorial until within the last few years. It is supposed that St. Piran communicated to the tinners' ancestors valuable information about the metallurgy of tin. (*Bygone Days in Devonshire and Cornwall*, Mrs. Henry Pennell Whitcombe, 1874, p. 188.)

There is a saying in the Meneage district that metal won't run within the sound of St. Keverne bells. Keverne is supposed to be the same as Piran. (*The Age of the Saints*, William Copeland Borlase, Truro, 1893, p. 24.)

THE FIRST FRIDAY IN LIDE

[*Cornwall*] This, the first Friday in March, is another tinners' holiday. It is marked by a serio-comic custom of sending a boy to the highest hillock of the works and allowing him to sleep there as long as he can, the length of his sleep to be the measure of the afternoon nap of the tinners throughout the ensuing twelve months. Lide is an obsolete term for the month of March and is preserved in old proverbs, such as, for example, " Ducks won't lay till they've drunk Lide water."—Cornish Feasts and Feasten Customs, Miss M. A. Courtney. (*Folk-Lore Journal*, vol. 4, 1886, p. 221.)

THE FIRST MONDAY IN MARCH

[*Hampshire, etc.*] On this day, in Hampshire, Berkshire, and adjoining counties, shoemakers ceased working by candlelight and performed a ceremony called " wetting the block." (*The Every-Day Book*, William Hone, vol. 2, 1866, pp. 235-6.)

10th March

POPULAR SAYINGS AND BELIEFS

" Mists or hoar frosts on the 10th of March betoken a plentiful year, but not without some diseases."—*The Shepherd's Kalendar or the Citizen's and Countryman's Daily Companion*, Thomas Passenger, Three Bibles and Star, London Bridge, about 1680. (*N. and Q.*, i, 8, 1853, p. 50.)

[*Devonshire*] " If it does not freeze on the 10th of March, a fertile year may be expected." (*Nummits and Crummits*, Sarah Hewett, 1900, p. 109.)

St. Constantine's Day

11th March

[*Cornwall*] This saint, tradition says, was the son of Padarn, a king of Cornwall but, resigning the crown, he became a priest and devoted himself to work in the west of Scotland. He died about the year 576.

Adjoining St. Merran or Harlyn-warren, in ancient times, was a village with a chapel or, as it is said, a parish church, dedicated to St. Constantine. His festival was kept,[1] until very lately, at St. Merran, by an annual hurling match when, by immemorial custom, the owner of Harlyn supplied the silvered ball. We are

[1] Here, Mag. Brit., III, p. 226, says " March 9th," but March 11th was St. Constantine's day.

informed, on good authority, that a cottage in Constantine was held for many generations under the owners of Harlyn, by the annual render of a Cornish pie, made of limpets, raisins and sweet herbs, on the feast of St. Constantine. (*Magna Britannia*, David and Samuel Lysons, vol. 3, 1814, p. 226.)

PENNY-LOAF DAY

[*Nottinghamshire*] During the siege of Newark, March 1643, Hercules Clay, who lived in Market Place, dreamed on three separate occasions that his house was on fire. After the third dream, he aroused his household and left the house. Soon after, a bomb from the parliamentary artillery fell on the house. After this escape, he bequeathed £200 to the Corporation of Newark, in trust, to pay the interest on £100 to the vicar of Newark for his preaching of a sermon on the 11th of March, annually, to commemorate the testator's escape, the remaining interest to be used in paying for penny loaves to be given to those who applied for them, a penny loaf to every applicant. Formerly, the loaves were given away at the church and later at the Town Hall. The applicants entered the Hall in single file and remained locked up until all the loaves had been distributed. (*Nottinghamshire Facts and Fictions*, collected and edited by John Potter Briscoe, Principal Librarian, Nottingham Free Library, Nottingham, 1876, pp. 10-11.)

St. Gregory's Day
12th March

St. Gregory, Pope Gregory the Great, patron of scholars, died on the 12th of March, 604. He sent Augustine and his monks, as Christian missionaries, to England. His day used to be noted by husbandmen, who called it the " Farmer's day."

SOWING ON ST. GREGORY'S DAY

[*Lancashire*] The farmer and the cottager deem it necessary, in order to obtain a good crop of onions, to sow the seed on St. Gregory's day, which is called " Gregory-gret onion." (*Lanca-*

shire Folk-Lore, John Harland and T. T. Wilkinson, 1867, p. 140.)

Onion seed was always sown on St. Gregory's day. (*The History of the Parish of Kirkham*, Henry Fishwick, 1874, p. 208.)

St. Patrick's Day

17th March

[London] St. Patrick, Bishop of Armagh and patron saint of Ireland, died about the year 464. A well-known popular custom celebrated on his day is that of wearing the shamrock and one of the popular spectacular ceremonies, in London, is the presentation of shamrock to officers, non-commissioned officers and men of the Irish Guards, on St. Patrick's day.

The flower-sellers of London used to sell large quantities of shamrock, Wood-sorrel Oxalis (*Oxalis acetosella*, Linn.) or, much more commonly, White Clover (*Trifolium repens*, Linn.), on St. Patrick's day.

St. Benedict's Day

21st March

St. Benedict, the founder of western monachism, was born about the year 480, and died on the 21st of March, 543. The date, 21st March, is important in the fixing, for any given year, of the date of Easter Sunday.

AN OLD CARNIVAL

[Yorkshire] Fifty years ago, many thousands of people from neighbouring towns and villages used to assemble, annually, on the 21st of March, at Hessleskew, for horse-racing, cudgel play, football and other games. When playing football, each side contested for the honour of carrying the ball home. This carnival is now held for horse-racing.—M. Foster. (*Old Yorkshire*, William Smith, editor, 4 vols., vol. 3, 1882, pp. 11-12.)

POPULAR SAYING

" If peas are not sown by Benedick,
They had better stay in the rick."

WEATHER OMEN

[*Surrey*] " Where the wind is at twelve o'clock, on the 21st of March, there she'll bide for three months afterwards."—Near Farnham. (*Memoirs of a Surrey Labourer*, George Bourne, 1907, p. 289.) Three months is a long time for direction of the wind to remain constant.

Lady Day
25th March

On this day, the Salutation of the Virgin Mary by the Angel was commemorated. In ancient times, the day was kept with much solemnity; at the present time, it is, for many, a term for the payment of rents and for commencing and terminating tenancies. In ancient times, such terms varied in different parts of the country and, among their number, were term days not commonly used now, such as, for example, Martinmas, Easter, Candlemas, St. Andrew's, Lammas and Hock Day. The change from this complicated system, as it existed in the thirteenth century, to the more modern one, was effected to a large extent before the year 1500. During such period of evolution, Lady Day was sometimes a quarterly or half-yearly rent day but often Christmas, Easter, Martinmas, Michaelmas, St. Andrew's and Midsummer served as regular rent days.

[*Worcestershire*] The nature of the change may be illustrated by a consideration of the records, chiefly the *Inquisitiones post Mortem* for the County of Worcester, which tend to show that, in the thirteenth century, Michaelmas, Martinmas, St. Andrew's, Lady Day and Hock Day were important money-rent days and that for rents payable in produce, Easter, Midsummer, Michaelmas and Christmas were important rent days and, after these, Martinmas, Lady Day (payments in fish, barley, malt), St. Andrew's, Lammas Day, St. Margaret's and St. Kenelm's.

Lady Day

Taking account of the times of payment of rents in money and in produce, it appears that Michaelmas, Martinmas, Midsummer, Easter and Christmas were the most important and, next to these, Lady Day and St. Andrew's. Then Lady Day and St. Andrew's became more important and Martinmas, Christmas and Easter less important.

A noteworthy entry, dated 1294, for Dudley and Kidderminster, relates to the rents of free tenants payable at the two terms, Michaelmas and the Annunciation in March. Then, for the year 1316, it is recorded that at Comberton, Stoulton, Elmley Castle, Salwarp, Droitwich, Acton Beauchamp, Inkberrow and other places, free tenants and, in some cases, customary tenants, paid at " the four terms," viz. St. Andrew, Lady Day, Midsummer and Michaelmas.

The places mentioned in the above records are situated in all parts of the county, north, east, south, west and central, and the records indicate the decreasing importance of Martinmas. Later records, for the fourteenth and fifteenth centuries, show that St. Andrew's lost its importance and that Christmas became one of the four terms together with Midsummer, Michaelmas and Lady Day.

POPULAR SAYINGS AND BELIEFS

" When our Lord falls on our Lady's lap,
Then England beware of a sad mishap."

This refers to a hypothetical event to take place when Easter Sunday falls on the 25th day of March; *see* vol. 1, 1936, pp. 103-4.

" If on St. Mary, it's bright and clear,
Fertile is said to be the year."

FAIRS

[*Devonshire*] From time immemorial to within the last fifty years, young girls stood in the market places, on Lady day, awaiting a chance of being hired as servants. The custom prevailed very recently at Holsworthy, Okehampton, and South Molton, but has been discontinued. (*The Peasant Speech of Devon*, Sarah Hewett, 1892, p. 82.)

[*Gloucestershire*] Tetbury and Chipping Sodbury, Gloucestershire, are the only places, so far as I can learn, where Lady-day hiring was done in the county. Both places had hirings at Michaelmas as well and this was the general rule. (Miss J. B. Partridge.)

[*Oxfordshire*] More than a century ago, at Bampton, an ox-roasting fair was held on or about Lady day.

[*Worcestershire*] An ox-roasting statute fair used to be held at Alvechurch, on Lady day. (*The Rambler in Worcestershire*, John Noake, 2 vols., 1851-4, vol. 1, p. 217.) According to former residents of Alvechurch, such fair has been held since John Noake's time, but not annually.

March

POPULAR SAYINGS AND BELIEFS

" April borroweth three daies of March and they are ill." (*Remaines of Gentilisme*, John Aubrey, 1686-7, Folk-Lore Soc. edition, 1881, p. 95.)

Lady Cumming set out from Edinburgh for London on the first of the borrowing days, towards the end of March, 1709. These days are so called because they are generally attended with very blustering weather, which inclines people to say that they would wish to borrow three days from April in exchange for those last three days of March. (*N. and Q.*, i, 5, 1852, pp. 278-9.)

I remember hearing, when a child, in the north of Ireland, an explanation of what is a common interchange of character between March and April, towards the close of March and the beginning of April. " Give me," says March, " three days of warmth and sunshine for my poor lambs, whilst they are too tender to bear the roughness of my wind and rain, and I will repay them when the wool is grown." (*N. and Q.*, i, 5, 1852, p. 342.)

" March borrowed of April
Three days and they were ill.
The first was rain, the second snow,
The third such a wind as never did blow."

(*N. and Q.*, iii, 3, 1863, p. 288.)

> " March does from April gain
> Three days and they're in rain;
> Returned by [to] April in 's bad kind,
> Three days and they're in wind."

(*Brand*, ii, p. 43.)
[*Northumberland*]

> " March borrowed of Aperhill
> Three days and they were ill."

The popular notion is that they were borrowed from April by March with a view to the destruction of a number of innocent lambs. (*Northumberland Words*, Richard Oliver Heslop, 2 vols., vol. 1, 1892, p. 85.)

[*Yorkshire*] The old dalesfolk hereabouts believed that the first three days of April were the borrowing days. These days were repayments by March of three fine days which could have been borrowed from April only: for March to produce three fine days of itself was not in the natural order of things. Even the repayment was made in typical March weather, for

> " The first will see rain, the second snow,
> The third as rough a day as ever did blow."

—Mr. H. Foster, Sedbergh. (Printed cutting; only means of identification, " Times about 1929," in ink.)

[*Hertfordshire*] While it would be difficult to decide upon the fundamental idea on which these sayings were based, it may well be that they emanated from shepherds anxious about the safety of their lambs. The sayings set out above are consistent with the main facts about the weather of the late part of March and the early part of April. In some years, *e.g.* 1917 and 1936, the weather of the early part of April was strikingly similar to that of the late part of March but, usually, the average temperature in the early part of April is nearly 2° F. higher than that of the late part of March and the outlook is brighter. The weather of the last few days of March is sometimes very destructive; the most violent storm in Hertfordshire and adjacent counties, during the past 75 years, occurred on 28th March, 1916, when about 25,000 trees, chiefly elm and beech, were blown down in Hertfordshire alone.

[*Devonshire*] " A damp, warm March will bring much harm to the farm." (*Nummits and Crummits*, Sarah Hewett, 1900, p. 109.)

[*Scilly Isles*] There are weatherwise proverbs among the fishermen, *e.g.* " You may look for six weeks' weather in March " is a hit at the variable character of that month. (*The Isles of Scilly: Their Story, their Folk and their Flowers*, Jessie Mothersole, 1910, p. 98.)

" March many weathers."

" March, the storm month."

> " March winds and April showers
> Bring forth May flowers."

" Many flies in March cause sheep to die."

" A peck of March dust is worth a king's ransom." In various forms this saying is well-known from Cornwall to Northumberland. In the south-east of England, March is one of the dry months of the year.

> " Much March dust and a shower in May
> Make the corn green and the fields gay."

" As mad as a March hare."

In Mr. Mayhew's *London Labour and the London Poor*, Part 33, p. 112, a collector of hare-skins says: " Hare-skins is in, leastways I c'lects them, from September to the end of March, when hares, they says, goes mad." (*N. and Q.*, i, 4, 1851, p. 208.)

Hares are very timid and easily become excited and wild; March, too, is their rutting season. At any time, however, hares are easily startled. An old sportsman informed the Editor of *Notes and Queries* that, in the month of March, when the winds are usually high, hares quit their cover to avoid the continual disturbance arising from the falling of decayed twigs and the rustling of dried leaves. (*N. and Q.*, ii, 8, 1859, p. 514.)

All Fools' Day
1st April

The custom celebrated on this day, observance of which has not been wholly abandoned, is of an amusing and good-tempered kind, but it is necessary for the one practising it to have regard for the 12 o'clock rule which, by custom, limits the period of celebration to the morning of the 1st of April; this rule was regularly observed in many counties. Among the numerous means employed in celebrating the custom, the following may be mentioned: the loose shoe lace; the something out of your pocket; the empty egg-shell inverted in an egg-cup; the envelope enclosing a blank sheet; the pencil with a rubber point; the note for delivery to a false address; the non-existent bus terminus; the strap-oil; the " Life of Eve's Mother "; the 2nd edition of " Cock Robin "; the pigeon's milk; the memory powder. The seven means last mentioned exemplify the most ancient phase of the custom, that of sending persons on a useless or foolish errand.

When or how this April-fooling custom originated may never be known and the following lines:

> " The first of April, some do say,
> Is set apart for All Fools' Day,
> But why the people call it so,
> Nor I nor they themselves do know,"

are as true to-day as they were in 1760, when they appeared in *Poor Robin's Almanack*. It may be asserted, however, that the earliest available record of celebration of the custom is dated 1698 and there is nothing in that record, *see* p. 173, to suggest that the custom was not ancient at that time.

COUNTY RECORDS

[*Berkshire*] The custom of making one an Aayprul Vool, on the 1st of April, before noon, obtains throughout Berkshire. (*A*

Glossary of Berkshire Words and Phrases, Major B. Lowsley, English Dialect Society, 1888, p. 37.)

[*Cheshire*] An April fool is called an April gawby in west Cheshire, an April gobby in central Cheshire, and an April gob in Macclesfield. (*A Glossary of Words used in the County of Chester*, Robert Holland, English Dialect Society, 1886, p. 9.)

[*Cornwall*] The custom is celebrated in Cornwall as elsewhere. Children are sent by their school-fellows for pigeon's milk, memory powder, strap-oil, or with a note directing the recipient to send the fool further. When a boy succeeds in taking-in another, he shouts after him, " Fool, fool, the guckaw." —Miss M. A. Courtney's Paper on Cornish Customs. (*Folk-Lore Journal*, vol. 4, 1886, p. 224.) Guckaw = cuckoo.

[*Cumberland and Westmorland*] Sending people on foolish errands is practised in the Lake District, on the 1st of April, and victims of the custom are called April noddies. (*Trans. Cumberland Assoc.*, Keswick, 1876, p. 118.)

To be an April noddy, a person must be induced to go somewhere on an imaginary or foolish errand. (Communicated by Mr. Edward M. Wilson, Cambridge, 7th November, 1936.)

For May geslins or goslings, *see* p. 242.

[*Durham*] During my boyhood, in Durham, I was sent, with many another urchin, to the chemist for a pennyworth of oil of hazel and received it from the stout hazel stick hidden behind the shopman's counter. Sometimes the victim is directed to ask for strap oil, but "hunting the gowk" is more fully carried out by sending the victim from place to place with a letter in which was written

" The first and second of Aprile,
Hound the gowk another mile." Gowk = cuckoo.
(*Notes on the Folk-Lore of the Northern Counties of England and the Borders*, William Henderson, 1879, p. 92.)

[*Hampshire*] After 12 o'clock, noon, the one trying to observe the custom was, by the rule to be followed, an April fool. This is expressed in the Hampshire rhyme :

" April Fool's gone past,
You're the biggest fool at last ;

When April Fool comes again,
You'll be the biggest fool then."

(*N. and Q.*, i, 12, 1855, p. 100.)

[*Herefordshire*] A boy would often be told to go to a chemist and ask for strap-oil or to a farm-house for some pigeon's milk. Anyone may be made an April fool before noon. (*The Folk-Lore of Herefordshire*, Ella Mary Leather, Hereford, 1912, p. 99.)

[*Lancashire*] A guttering-peg is an unknown article for which April fools are sent on the first of April. (*A Glossary of Rochdale-with-Rossendale Words and Phrases*, Henry Cunliffe, Manchester, 1886, p. 44.)

[*Lincolnshire*] During the morning of the 1st of April, the fun was fast and furious, at Grantham, but tricksters calmed down in the afternoon when their victims had a right of reply in :

" Twelve o'clock is past and gone
And you're a fool for making me one."

—*Grantham Journal*, 29th June, 1878. (*County F.L.*, vol. 5, *Lincolnshire*, Mrs. Gutch and Mabel Peacock, 1908, p. 194.)

[*London*] A very early record is to be found in Dawks's *News-Letter* for the 2nd April, 1698, informing us that " yesterday being the 1st of April, several persons were sent to the Tower Ditch to see the lions washed."—Alfred T. Robbins. (*N. and Q.*, xi, 7, 1913, p. 357.)

I read in a newspaper, five or six years ago, that several persons went to the Tower, on the 1st of April, with cards of admission, purporting to be signed by the Warden, to see the annual ceremony of washing the lions. They bought the cards for a penny each, at a ballad shop in Seven Dials.—C. E. (*N. and Q.*, ii, 10, 1860, p. 395.)

[*Norfolk*] It is still a custom to send people on foolish errands, before noon on 1st April ; *e.g.* for a penn'orth of Lob-lolly or some elbow grease. (Miss Matthews' Oral Collection.)

[*Northumberland*] The custom of making April gowks is still extant in the parishes of Rothbury and Whittingham. If a person attempts to make another an April gowk, after the hour of twelve, saying " Oh, ye April gowk! " the intended victim replies " April gowk day's past and gone and you're a fool and I'm none"; again, the other replies quickly " Up the tree an' down the tree, you're a fool as well as me." (MS. notes by D. D. Dixon.)

At Wooler, Northumberland, those who thus resisted being made feul gowks on " Feul Gowk day," the 1st of April, replied :

" The gowk and the titlene sit on a tree,
You're a gowk as weel as me."

(*Folk-Lore of British Birds*, Rev. Charles Swainson, 1886, p. 122.) Titlene is a generic name and refers to the hedge-sparrow or other bird whose life-history is closely associated with that of the cuckoo.

[*Yorkshire*] If anyone should attempt to make an April noddy after mid-day, on the 1st of April, the reply is :

" April noddy's past and gone,
You're a fool an' I'm none."

—Swaledale. (*County F.L.*, vol. 2, *North Riding of Yorkshire, York, and the Ainsty*, Mrs. Gutch, 1899, p. 247.)

Once a boy was sent on the 1st of April to a bookseller's shop, Bridlington, for " The Life of Adam's Grandfather." (*Folk-Lore of East Yorkshire*, John Nicholson, 1890, p. 13.)

On the 1st of April, the youths of our town delight in making as many April fools as they can. (*The History and Antiquities of Morley*, William Smith, 1876, p. 92.)

April Fool's Day is not much observed now. (*Morley : Ancient and Modern*, William Smith, 1886, p. 142.)

In Honley, the custom of sending people on useless errands, on April the first, has fallen into neglect, except among children. (*The History of Honley, etc.*, Mary A. Jagger, Huddersfield, 1914, p. 128.)

These records support evidence from other sources indicating that the custom lost most of its popularity during the period 1870-85.

NOTES ON THE CUSTOM

An annual custom of inducing a person to perform a useless or foolish act, on the 1st of April, or at a time near that date, has been celebrated in various countries, *e.g.* France, Sweden, Portugal and India. A romantic story of the second century, adumbrates an alleged annual custom of fooling people. Briefly, Byrrhæna informs Lucius that, on the day next following, an ancient, annual custom of propitiating Risus, god of Laughter, would be celebrated by her fellow-citizens alone among mankind.[1] She invites him to attend and adds that the god would be more propitious and the laughter would be increased. Quite true ; Lucius attends and is derided. (Lucii Apulei *Metamorphoseon Libri XI*, J. Van der Vliet, Lipsiæ, 1897, Liber II, Cap. 31.)

Referring to the English custom, a writer, apparently Dr. Samuel Pegge, says that it was probably an indigenous custom of our own, that a new year used to begin on the 25th of March and, since important English customs usually lasted eight days, the 1st of April would be the last day of the new-year festivities and a day of great hilarity. (*Gentleman's Magazine*, vol. 36, 1766, p. 186.) *The Ency. Brit.*, 14th edition, 1929, states that, in some way, the custom may be a relic of those once universal festivities which began on New Year's day, O.S., and ended on 1st April. *Chambers' Ency.*, new edition, 1935, suggests that it is a relic of some ancient Celtic custom.

The French custom in one of its aspects, is of special interest ; this aspect is illustrated by George Augustus Sala with the aid of a cartoon and its explanation :

> " Baptiste, why do you not answer the bell ?
> Because to-day is the first of April and I
> thought you wanted to make a fool of me."

(*Paris Herself Again in* 1878-9, George Augustus Sala, 2 vols., vol. 2, 1879, p. 275.) The other aspect of the French has no counterpart in the English custom and consists mainly in sending, anonymously, dainty presents made up to represent fishes. This custom is described by the phrase, " Donner quelqu'un un poisson d'Avril " = to make an April fool of somebody, and is illustrated, on p. 276 of Mr. Sala's volume, just cited,

---

[1] *soli mortalium ... propitiamus* seems to refer to the Hypatæi, Thessaly.

by a sketch of a Grisette carrying a fancy basket filled with objects representing small fishes.

POPULAR SAYING AND BELIEF

[*Norfolk*]
" If it thunders on All Fools' day,
It brings good crops of corn and hay."
—Norfolk. (Miss Matthews' Oral Collection.)

FAIR

[*Derbyshire*] At Buxton, a fair is held on the 1st of April, annually.

St. Richard's Day
3rd April

[*Worcestershire*] This day was celebrated at Droitwich in honour of Richard de la Wich, a native of Droitwich and Bishop of Chichester. The celebration was discontinued a few years before John Leland visited Droitwich, about the year 1540. Referring to the most important salt spring then at Droitwich, he says : " Some say that this springe did fayle in the tyme of Rich. de la Wich, B. of Chichester, and that, after his intercession, it was restored to the profit of the old course. In token whereof or from the Honour that the Wichmen and Salters had unto this Richard, their Countriman, they used of late times on his day to hang about this Salt Springe or Well, once a year, with tapestry and to have drinking games and revels at it." (*The Itinerary of John Leland the Antiquary*, 9 vols., Oxford, 2nd edition, vol. 4, 1744, pp. 105-6, folio 184*b*.)

[*Sussex*] This day, 3rd of April, St. Richard of Chichester's day, commemorates Richard de la Wich, Bishop of Chichester and is one of the English saints' days (not numerous) in the Calendar of the English Church. It was formerly specially observed at Chichester, with religious ceremonies. (*Sussex Archæol. Society's Collections*, vol. 33, Lewes, 1883, p. 243.)

CUCKOOS AND THE CALENDAR

There are popular sayings relating to the times of arrival of the cuckoo and many of such sayings include references to the times of holding fairs where the sayings are current. The following examples are given in chronological order.

14TH APRIL

[*Sussex*] " An old woman takes a cuckoo in her basket to Hefful [Heathfield] Fair and there lets it out." (*Sussex Archæol. Soc. Collections*, vol. 33, Lewes, 1883, p. 243.)

The tradition in East Sussex is that an old woman goes to Heathfield Fair and there lets a cuckoo out of a bag. (*A Dictionary of the Sussex Dialect*, W. D. Parish, Lewes, 1875, p. 32.)

In Sussex, it is believed that a certain old woman has charge of all the cuckoos and fills her apron with them in the spring. If she is in good humour, she allows several to take flight at Heathfield fair, 14th April. (*Folk-Lore of British Birds*, Rev. Charles Swainson, 1886, p. 112.)

The average date of arrival of the cuckoo in Sussex is the 14th of April, called " Cuckoo day " in Sussex. Heathfield fair is called " Cuckoo fair."

15TH APRIL

[*Hampshire*] At Beaulieu, Hampshire, the day on which Beaulieu fair is held, is called " Cuckoo day." There is a local proverb : The cuckoo goes to Beaulieu fair to buy a greatcoat, because he arrives about that time. (*A Glossary of Hampshire Words and Phrases*, Sir William Henry Cope, Bart., English Dialect Society, 1883, p. 22.)

[*Northamptonshire*] In Northamptonshire, the 15th of April is called Cuckoo day. (*Folk-Lore of British Birds*, Rev. Charles Swainson, 1886, p. 112.)

20TH APRIL

[*Worcestershire*] " You never hear the cuckoo before Tenbury fair nor after Pershore fair." (*Glossary of West Worcestershire Words*, E. L. Chamberlain, 1882, p. 38.)

Early in the third week in April, I said to a Worcestershire labourer, " I have not yet heard the cuckoo." His reply was : " It won't be Tenbury Fair for four days to come. You never hear the cuckoo before Tenbury Fair nor after Pershore Fair." (*N. and Q.*, ii, 1, 1856, p. 429.) Tenbury Fair is on the 20th of April and Pershore Fair on the 26th of June.

21ST APRIL

[*Bedfordshire*] They still have a saying in Bedfordshire that the cuckoo is never heard till Bedford Fair day, the 21st April. (*The Bedford Record*, 12th May, 1931.) This is a late date for Bedfordshire. I have no records for Bedfordshire but, for Hertfordshire, an early recorded date of arrival of the cuckoo is 12th April, 1904, St. Albans.

St. George's Day
23rd April

Patron saint of England, Portugal and Aragon, St. George has been long enrolled in the list of saints by the Western and the Eastern Churches ; many churches have been dedicated to his memory ; and, during the Crusades and later campaigns, his name was very popular in the camp and on the battlefield. In later times, St. George's Chapel, Windsor, was founded, the Order of the Garter, the badge of which is the " St. George," was instituted by Edward III, and for many years the banner of the saint waved from many a ship on every sea. St. George was an officer serving under the Emperor Diocletian and, about the year 300, refusing to abandon Christianity, suffered martyrdom, apparently at Nicomedia. Little more seems to be known of the saint but, as the researches of eminent scholars progress, it is probable that the honour due to his name will be increased. The story of St. George and the Dragon is comparable with the mythical stories of Perseus and Beowulf, the killing of the dragon being symbolical of the triumph of noble ideals over those which are base and treacherous.

ST. GEORGE'S DAY IN OLDEN TIMES

Leicester, Norwich, London, York, Chester, Reading, Chichester, Worcester and other cities and towns used to perform solemn ceremonies or hold festivities in honour of St. George; in many parish churches, equestrian statues of St. George were erected and, on his day, people of fashion often wore blue coats.

[*Berkshire*] In the Churchwardens' Accounts for St. Laurence's Church, Reading, under the heading " Charges for St. George, 1536," are entries relating to an effigy of St. George and his horse. These entries refer to three calf-skins and two horse-skins; the making of the loft on which the effigy stood; the iron for supporting the horse; and St. George's coat, roses, bells, girdle and daggers. (*The History and Antiquities of Reading*, Rev. Charles Coates, 1802, p. 221.)

[*Cheshire*] The famous Chester races, now held on the Roodee in May week, used to be held on St. George's day until about the year 1811; they are the modern representatives of ancient races and sports in which men, boys and horses competed for prizes, on St. George's day. In 1609, Robert Amery of Chester had three silver cups[1] made, mainly at his own expense, to be competed for in a race, called the " St. George's Race," to be held on the Roodee, on St. George's day, annually. At its inauguration, in 1610, there was a long procession on horseback, of characters representing Fame, Mercury, Chester, St. George, Peace and other ideals; the Mayor and other civic dignitaries also attended. The St. George's Race was transferred, in the seventeenth or the early part of the eighteenth century, to Farndon. (*The History of the County of Chester*, George Ormerod, 3 vols., vol. 1, 1882, p. 384; *Magna Britannia*, David and Samuel Lysons, vol. 2, 1810, p. 588.)

[*Leicestershire*] At Leicester, there used to be a St. George's Guild and, on St. George's day or another later day, chosen by the Mayor and Corporation, one of the chief solemnities of the town was celebrated; this was called " Riding the George."

---

[1] Three bells, in Ormerod's *Cheshire*.

The inhabitants were bound, subject to being liable to pay a fine, to attend the Mayor and Corporation to ride against [meet] the King, or for " Riding the George," or for any other thing at the pleasure of the Mayor. (*Leicestershire and Rutland Notes and Queries*, vol. 1, Leicester, 1891, p. 112.)

In a fragment of a roll of expenses incurred by the Chamberlains of the town is an item " 1536-41. Itm paid for dryssyng the dragon . . . 4s," and another entry " 1553-4. Itm for dressyng and . . . sent Georgs harnes . . . 6s. 8d." (*A Chronicle of St. Martin in Leicester*, Thomas North, 1866, pp. 136 and 240.)

[*Norfolk*] At Norwich, there was a Guild of St. George and in many of the city pageants representations of St. George and the Dragon were assigned prominent positions.

Who that has seen a Norwich Guild procession, twenty years ago, does not remember " Snap, Snap," as necessary to the Mayor as his gold chain ? The terror and the delight of children, the representation of the Dragon, which used to be borne, like a barbarian monarch in a Roman triumph, at the head of the civic procession, opening its wide jaws to receive contributions. The man who walked under the scaly hide flourished the long, forked tail and pulled the string which moved the dreadful head and jaws. These are gone and so are the whifflers who, dressed in blue and red silk, led the procession and by means of the wonderful evolutions of their swords kept off the crowd from his worship. (*Edinburgh Review*, vol. 77, 1843, pp. 143-4.)

[*Sussex*] The Merchant Guild of Chichester had St. George as its patron and Bishop Sherburne settled land on the fraternity, the rent to be used to buy a quarter cask of choice wine to be stored near the cross at Chichester. On St. George's day, part was consumed by the fraternity and, after a service in the Chapel of St. George and the anthem in the Cathedral, the remainder was consumed by the populace. Then the Master of the Revels held up a horn-glass and shouted *Consummatum est*. (*Sussex Archæol. Society's Collections*, vol. 33, Lewes, 1883, pp. 244-5.)

[*Worcestershire*] An old record, apparently of the sixteenth century, refers to the payment of 16d. to four minstrels from Worcester, who performed at Crowle, on the morn of St. George's day. (*The Monastery and Cathedral of Worcester*, John Noake 1866, p. 160.)

[*Yorkshire*] Formerly, on St. George's Field, York, now cut through by the approach to the new bridge, was celebrated the festival of its patron saint. Here, pageants were exhibited and, at their conclusion, a sermon was preached from a pulpit to an audience sitting on forms and benches provided for the occasion. (*Yorkshire in Olden Times*, William Andrews, editor, Hull, 1890, p. 42.)

ST. GEORGE'S DAY IN RECENT YEARS

[*Buckinghamshire*] Towards the end of last century, an increasing interest in St. George's day was shown and, in many localities, especially Stratford-on-Avon, the interest was enhanced by the remembrance of the date of Shakespeare's birthday, on or near 23rd April. It was an indication of the change that was taking place that, on St. George's day, 1902, at a village near the Chilterns, between Tring and Dunstable, school children, six years of age and upwards, explained joyfully that they had a holiday and were keeping St. George's day.

[*Worcestershire*] In 1914, St. George's Day was celebrated ceremoniously in many towns and villages. At Kidderminster, for example, on the 23rd April, 1914, the well-known flag of St. George waved over the municipal buildings, the churches of St. Mary and of St. George, and some of the town mills. Arrangements were made for the enjoyment of the children and a civic procession to, and service at, the Parish or Minster Church of St. Mary was arranged for the following Sunday morning, in honour of St. George's Day. (*The Kidderminster Shuttle*, 25th April, 1914.)

On St. George's Day, 1936, the annual service of the Order of St. Michael and St. George was held at St. Paul's. There were other ceremonies, not only in honour of the saint but commemorative of important national events, whose anniversaries fall on St. George's Day. Many towns celebrated the day in a manner similar to that above described for Kidderminster, roses and St.

George's flags were worn, and in numerous villages the flag of St. George waved over the village church.

FAIRS

In past times, many St. George's fairs were held, *e.g.* at Bewdley, Campden, Chichester, Hatfield, Penrith, Modbury and Ipswich.

[*Gloucestershire*] An old list of Gloucestershire fairs records the holding of fairs, annually, at Campden, on St. George's day. (*The History and Description of the City of Gloucester, etc.*, G. W. Counsel, Gloucester, 1829, p. 246.)

[*Sussex*] A charter of James II, dated 1685, granted a fair to be held yearly at Chichester, on St. George's day and two days after, together with a court of pie powder. (*The History of Chichester*, Alexander Hay, Chichester, 1804, p. 593.)

[*Worcestershire*] Of the four Bewdley fairs, the one held on St. George's day is still a good fair. (*The Rambler in Worcestershire*, John Noake, 2 vols., 1851-4, vol. 1, p. 130.)

St. George's fair at Bewdley and the St. George's fairs of Hatfield and Penrith are still held.

[*Devonshire*] The fair at Modbury, known as St. George's fair, is held on the 4th of May or Old St. George's day and continues for nine days. Within the last fifty years, it was the custom in the town to hang out a holly bush from private houses; the bush served the purpose of an excise license, during the fair, which was one of the most important in the district. Within living memory, the fair afforded the only opportunity of purchasing cloth in the town. Travelling braziers attended the fair and did a lot of trade. (*History of Devonshire*, R. N. Worth, 1886, p. 242.)

At Modbury, on the 3rd of May, being the Eve of Old St. George's day, even though it falls on a Sunday, the portreeve and borough officers assemble in the centre of the town, once the market cross. The crier calls out " O yes " three times, requests silence to be kept, and then the proclamation of the fair follows. The glove is then hoisted on the market bell stand and the company adjourns to an inn, where a bread and cheese supper is prepared. (*Western Antiquary*, vol. 1, Plymouth, 1882, p. 140.)

[*Suffolk*] At Ipswich, a fair is held, annually, on Old St. George's day, the 4th of May, for toys and miscellaneous articles. (MS. note dated 1830.) There is still a fair at Ipswich early in May.

St. Mark's Eve
24th April

Most of the popular customs that have been celebrated in England, on St. Mark's Eve, are divinations concerning marriage, sickness and death. The divinations relating to marriage are numerous and the means employed in their operation are very varied, ranging from hemp seed to church windows. Most of the divinations relating to sickness and death are associated with the watching of the church porch at midnight.

For the sake of convenience in description, the following classification will be used, it being understood that church-porch watching was sometimes resorted to in order to obtain a forecast of marriage and that, occasionally, the ashes on the hearth were used for the same purpose. Marriage and death divinations have been commonly practised, especially in Lincolnshire and Yorkshire.

DIVINATIONS RELATING TO MARRIAGE

1. Barn-watch.
2. Basins and water.
3. Chemise near fire.
4. Church windows.
5. Churchyard grass.
6. Dumb cake.
7. Farthing candle.
8. Garters and shoes.
9. Haystack and ring.
10. Hemp-seed.
11. Looking-glass and candle.
12. Pewter pots.
13. Sage leaves.
14. Supper-watching.
15. Wells.

DIVINATIONS RELATING TO SICKNESS AND DEATH

a. Ashes on the hearth.
b. Chaff-riddling.
c. Church-porch watch.

1. BARN-WATCH

[*Derbyshire*] To see the vision of your future wife, sit on a strike in the barn, on St. Mark's Eve at midnight, when she will walk in at one door and out at the other. A man said that he once saw his future wife in this way, and another man saw a pick-axe and a spade, which forecast that he would remain unmarried.—Derbyshire. (*Household Tales*, Sidney Oldhall Addy, 1895, p. 73.)

2. BASINS AND WATER

[*Norfolk*] On the Eve of St. Mark, place three basins in a row, leave one empty, pour clear water into another and dirty water into the remaining third basin. After blindfolding a girl, change her position and guide her to the basins so that she can dip her fingers into one of the basins. If she should select the empty basin, she will remain unmarried; if that containing clear water, she will be a bride; and if she dips into the dirty water, she will be a widow.—Norfolk. (Miss Matthew's Oral Collection.)

3. CHEMISE NEAR FIRE

[*Eastern Counties*] A girl, wishing to make use of this divination, washes her chemise and places it, turned inside out, before the fire in a room the outer door of which is left open. Sitting in a corner of the room, the girl should not speak after 11 o'clock but wait, watching the chemise, until 12 o'clock, in expectation of seeing the form of her future husband enter and turn the chemise.

[*Norfolk*] Some years ago, the servant at a house on Yarmouth Quay duly carried out this divination but a sailor, learning what was going on, entered the room and then vanished with the chemise. Next morning, she saw the chemise hanging from one of the vessels near the Quay. (*Notes on the Folk-Lore of the Northern Counties of England and the Borders*, William Henderson, 1879, pp. 101-2.)

4. CHURCH WINDOWS

[*Lincolnshire*] When making use of this divination, a youth or girl walks round the church, at dead of night, on St. Mark's

Eve, looking into each window, in succession, in expectation of seeing, in the last window, the face of his or her future partner in life. (*Bygone Lincolnshire*, William Andrews, editor, 2 vols., vol. 2, 1891, p. 90.)

5. CHURCHYARD GRASS

[*Lincolnshire*] The late Venerable William Brocklehurst Stonehouse, Archbishop of Stowe and Vicar of Owston, in the Isle of Axholme, furnished the author with the following record obtained in his own parish. Repair to the nearest churchyard as the clock strikes twelve and take from a grave, on the south side of the church, three tufts of grass, the longer and ranker the better, and on going to bed place them under your pillow, repeating three several times :

" The Eve of St. Mark by prediction is blest,
Set therefore my hopes and my fears all to rest.
Let me know my fate, whether weal or woe,
Whether my rank is to be high or low ;
Whether to live single or to be a bride,
And the destiny my star doth provide."

Should you have no dream that night, you will be single and miserable all your life. If you dream of thunder and lightning, your life will be one of great difficulty and sorrow. (*A Glossary of Words used in the Wapentakes of Manley and Corringham*, Edward Peacock, English Dialect Society, 1877, p. 211.)

6. DUMB CAKE

Divination by means of the Dumb cake has been especially associated with All Hallows' Eve, 31st October, the Eve of All Saints' Day. For St. Mark's Eve, however, there are records of divination by means of the cake in Cambridgeshire, Lincolnshire, Norfolk, Northamptonshire, Suffolk and Yorkshire.

[*Lincolnshire*] Mrs. H. and another girl made a dumb cake on St. Mark's Eve. Both had to assist in doing each part of the performance ; both went to the dairy to get the materials ; both took hold of the bowl ; both helped to get the flour ; both got some water and rinsed the bowl ; both helped to make the cake and roll it. A line was then drawn across the cake and the initials of each girl placed on the cake, on opposite sides of the line. During the whole time, strict silence was maintained and, while the cake was being baked, the two girls stood upon something never stood on before. Then, a sudden gust of wind swirled round the house and put them to flight. This nullified the proceedings. (*Lincolnshire Notes and Queries*, vol. 2, 1890, p. 44.)

[*Suffolk*] On the night of the 24th April, girls bake a dumb cake made of an egg-shell full of salt, an egg-shell full of wheat meal and an egg-shell full of barley meal. It must be baked before the fire, a little before 12 o'clock at night; the girl must be quite alone, must be fasting and not a word must be spoken. The door must be left open. At 12 o'clock exactly, the sweetheart will come in and turn the cake. (*Vocabulary of East Anglia, etc.*, Robert Forby, 1830, p. 408.)

7. FARTHING CANDLE

On St. Mark's Eve, a party of males or a party of females place a lighted pigtail or farthing candle on the floor; the candle must be a stolen one. They then sit in silence, eyes directed to the flame. When it begins to burn blue, the intended lovers will appear to cross the room. The doors and cupboards must remain unlocked. (*The Dialect of Craven*, William Carr, 2nd edition, 1828.)

8. GARTERS AND SHOES

Miss M. writes: Mrs. Laughton used to tell me that it was an old custom, on St. Mark's Eve, to pin your garters to the wall and put your shoes going and coming. This having been done, you would see your sweetheart in a dream. (Miss Matthews' Oral Collection.)

9. HAYSTACK AND RING

[*Yorkshire*] In Barker *v.* Ray, Court of Chancery, 2nd August, 1827, a deponent swore that a woman, named Ann Johnson, went to the deponent and said, " I will tell you what I did to know if I could have Mr. Barker. On St. Mark's night, I ran round a haystack nine times, with a ring in my hand, calling out 'Here's the sheath but where's the knife?' When I was running round the ninth time, I thought I saw Mr. Barker coming home, but he did not come home that night, but was brought home from the Blue Bell, at Beverley, the next day." (*The Table Book*, William Hone, 1866, p. 494.)

10. HEMP-SEED

[*Norfolk; Suffolk*] This divination was used in Norfolk and Suffolk. Precisely at midnight, the girl practising the divination went alone into the garden and scattered hemp-seed, saying:

" Hemp-seed I sow,
Hemp-seed grow;
He that is my true love,
Come after me and mow."

The figure of the future husband is believed to appear, with a scythe and in the act of mowing. (*Vocabulary of East Anglia, etc.*, Robert Forby, 1830, p. 408.)

11. LOOKING-GLASS AND CANDLE

[*Norfolk*] If a maiden sits before her looking-glass in her bedroom, at midnight on St. Mark's Eve, with a candle in a far corner of the room, giving only a dim light, and repeats these lines :

" Come lover, come lad,
And make my heart glad,
For husband, I'll have you,
For good or for bad,"

she will presently see the shadow of her future husband appear in the glass. (Miss Matthews' Oral Collection.)

12. PEWTER POTS

[*Suffolk*] Two girls wash the hearth-stone perfectly clean, before going to bed; two clean pewter pots are whelmed down at the outermost corners; then the girls retire backwards, undressing and getting into bed backwards and, of course, in perfect silence. In the morning, they will find something under the pewter pots to tell them the trades of their future husbands. —Suffolk. (*County F.L.*, vol. 1 (2), *Suffolk*, The Lady Eveline Camilla Gurdon, 1895, p. 97.)

13. SAGE LEAVES

[*Lincolnshire*] A girl who gathers 12 sage leaves, one by one, as the clock strikes at midnight, on St. Mark's Eve, will see a semblance of her future husband; another form of the divination specifies red sage. (*County F.L.*, vol. 5, *Lincolnshire*. Mrs. Gutch and Mabel Peacock, 1908, p. 136.)

14. SUPPER-WATCHING

According to a popular belief, any girl who "watches her supper," on St. Mark's Eve, will see the spirit of the man she will wed enter the room at midnight. Each girl who undertakes to keep watch must have a separate supper laid and a separate candle and all talking must cease before midnight. The room must be one with a door in one wall and a window in another; both must be open. The spirit enters by the door and leaves by the window. (*Folk-Lore*, vol. 2, 1891, p. 511.)

[*Yorkshire*] On St. Mark's Eve, Thursday, 24th April, 1796, a girl living at a public house in Mill Street, Hull, and two other girls, celebrated the divination custom known as "supper-watching." On the Friday she became very ill, and died on the Saturday. It is believed that, during the celebration of the custom, she received a shock which was fatal.—*The Hull Advertiser*, 25th May, 1796. (*N. and Q.*, xi, 3, 1911, p. 246.)

15. WELLS

[*Lincolnshire*] The Maiden Well at North Kelsey is visited by unmarried females on St. Mark's Eve. A young servant, native of Kelsey, informed W. F. not many years ago, that the procedure was to walk towards the Well backwards and go round it three times in the same way, then kneel down and gaze into the water, in which the devotee will see her lover looking up out of the depths. (*The Antiquary*, vol. 31, 1895, pp. 372-3.)

St. Mark's Eve

DIVINATIONS RELATING TO SICKNESS AND DEATH

a. ASHES ON THE HEARTH

[*Yorkshire*] On St. Mark's Eve, the ashes are riddled or sifted on the hearth for the purpose of obtaining any impression they may receive before morning. Should any member of the family be destined to die within a year, it is believed that his or her shoe will be traced on the ashes. (*A Glossary of Words used in, etc., Whitby*, Francis Kildare Robinson, 1876, p. 6.)

b. CHAFF-RIDDLING

[*Yorkshire*] A method of divination has been used in Yorkshire, commonly called " cauff-riddling," and was thus practised. The barn-doors were set wide-open, a riddle and some chaff were procured and the inquirers about the future went into the barn at midnight and in turn commenced the riddling. If the riddler be doomed to die during the year, two persons will be seen passing the open doors and carrying a coffin ; in the other case, nothing will be seen. Not many years ago, two men and a woman went to a barn near Malton, on St. Mark's Eve, to riddle cauff. The rules were duly observed ; the men riddled in turn but nothing was seen. Then the woman began to riddle and very soon all saw the ominous pair of coffin-bearers ; the men rushed out but could not see anything unusual. The woman died within a year. This story was told to my informant by one who knew the persons concerned and spoke of them by name. (*Notes on the Folk-Lore of the Northern Counties of England and the Borders*, William Henderson, 1879, pp. 52-3.)

c. THE CHURCH-PORCH WATCH

The primary object of this divination, so characteristic of St. Mark's Eve, was to ascertain who, among the parishioners, were destined to pass away during the next twelve months. Those who wished to obtain such information went to the church porch late on St. Mark's Eve and waited there until after the striking of the midnight hour. The climax was reached about that time, when, it was believed, a funereal procession of those destined to die during the next twelve months would be seen to pass into the church and remain there. Wherever practised, in England, the divination was much the same; sometimes it was believed, the procession included apparitions of those who would be seriously ill or would marry during the twelve months.

[*Derbyshire*] At Dronfield, an old man used to watch in the church porch, on St. Mark's Eve, at midnight. (*Chantrey Land*, [Village of Norton], Harold Armitage, 1910, p. 330.)

[*Lincolnshire*] In the year 1634, two men watched, on St. Mark's Eve, in the church porch at Burton, Lincolnshire. The moon was shining brightly but, about midnight, a strange darkness came over them; they became spellbound and were nearly frightened to death on seeing what appeared to be a series of ghosts entering the church. As soon as they could, they hurried away. Later, they concluded that the forecast indicated the early deaths of four adults and an infant, and this was in accordance with events in Burton during the ensuing twelve months. —Gervas Holles in the Landsdowne MSS., British Museum. (*Time's Telescope* for 1828, pp. 89-90.)

There is still a widespread belief that by sitting in the church porch on St. Mark's Eve, 24th April, at midnight, one may see pass by and enter the church the spirits or *simulacra* of all who will die in the parish during the coming twelvemonth. Just before I left Wainfleet, at the close of 1889, my Men's Guild were discussing the question of " Second Sight " and a very intelligent mechanic got up and said that there was one night in the year when anyone, who had brass enough, could do it, and proceeded to state that the parish clerk and sexton of his own parish, Theddlethorpe, had always " set out St. Mark's Eve, aiming to know how much he'd addle in happin foak up t' year, an' he were nivver far out in his reckonin', an' I knaw as it's gospel trewth, for bimebye he'd hardlins set hisself down afore he sets eyes on his own sen goin' in with a whap an' he taakes hisself off whoam in a rare moil an' tells his missus he were as good as dead, an' he were dead come a fortnight an' I were at the berryin'. I allus had a bit o' hanklin' after tryin' it mysen, but feyther tellt me not to hev nought to do with sich loike carryings on, for if I nobbut got agate o' the job, I'd be tied to go a thruff wi' it ivery year till I seed mysen an' all, an' that's a sought as 'ud mak any chap dither an' shaake."—Paper on the Vikings: Traces of their Folk-Lore in Marshland, The Rev. R. M. Heanley. (*Saga Book of the Viking Club*, vol. 3, 1902, p. 43.)

[*Norfolk*] Robert Staff, who used to keep the Maid's Head at Stalham, opposite to the church, told Mrs. Lubbock that he and two other men had been able to tell who were going to die or be married in the course of the year. They watched the church porch on St. Mark's Eve. Those who were to die went into the church singly and stayed there and those who were to be married went in, in couples, and came out again.—Proverbs and popular superstitions still preserved in the Parish of Irstead. (*Norfolk Archæology*, vol. 2, Norwich, 1849, p. 295.)

[*Northumberland*] Young rustics will sometimes watch, or pretend to watch, in the church porch, through the night of St. Mark's Eve, with a view to seeing the ghosts of those who are to die the next year pass by them, which they are said to do in their usual dress. The watchers are a terror to the neighbourhood. (*A Glossary of North Country Words*, John Trotter Brockett, Newcastle upon Tyne, 1825, p. 229.)

[*Yorkshire*] In Yorkshire, those who are curious to know which of their fellow-parishioners are going to die at an early date, watch in the church porch, on St. Mark's Eve, for an hour on each side of midnight for three successive years. In the third year's watch, they will see the forms of those doomed to die, within the twelvemonth, passing one by one into the church. If the watcher falls asleep during the watch, he will die during the year. An old woman used to keep St. Mark's vigil, about eighty years ago, at St. Mary's, Scarborough. At last, she saw her own apparition passing into the church; she died as a result of the shock. An old man, who died recently at Fishlake, in the West Riding, used to keep these vigils and was an object of dread to his neighbours. (*Notes on the Folk-Lore of the Northern Counties of England and the Borders*, William Henderson, 1879, pp. 50-1.)

Watching the church porch, on St. Mark's Eve, used to be a common practice. Old Peg Doo (Margaret Dove) used to watch, many years ago, in the porch of the Priory Church, Bridlington. (*Folk-Lore of East Yorkshire*, John Nicholson, Driffield, 1890, pp. 84-5.)

In Yorkshire, the old custom of sitting and watching, on the night of St. Mark's Eve, in the porches of churches, from 11 p.m. till 1 a.m., is still kept up. In the third year of its performance, it is supposed that the ghosts of those who are to die, during the next twelve months, pass into the church—P. H., *Westmorland Gazette*, 9th May, 1885. (*Folk-Lore Journal*, vol. 3, 1885, p. 278.)

The church-porch watch, always thrilling and, for those with cardiac weakness, dangerous, is practically forgotten.

St. Mark's Day
25th April

LEAPING THE WELL

[*Northumberland*] At Alnwick, an ancient custom, called "Leaping the Well," used to be celebrated on St. Mark's day, annually, until about the year 1852, by young men eligible to become freemen of the Borough. In the year 1829, thirteen young men became freemen. The custom was celebrated with much display and among its ceremonies was an unpleasant one, that of plunging into and wading through a very dirty and weedy pool of water about twenty yards long.

Those who are to be made free or, as the phrase goes, leap the well, assemble in the Market Place, very early in the morning, on the 25th of April, being St. Mark's day. They attend on horseback, dressed in white, with white night caps, and every man a sword by his side, attended by the four chamberlains and the castle bailiff, mounted and armed in the same manner. They then proceed, led by a band of music, to a large, dirty pool, called Freeman's Well, where they dismount, draw up in a body, then rush into the pool and scramble through the mud as fast as they can. After this, they take a dram, put on dry clothes, remount, gallop round the boundaries of the district and re-enter the town, sword in hand. They are met by women dressed in ribbons, with bells and garlands, dancing and singing; these are called Timbrewaits. On this day, the houses of the new freemen are indicated by a holly-bush to serve as a signal for their friends to come and make merry with them on their return. This custom is peculiar to Alnwick and is founded on a clause in a Charter given by King John, who, travelling this way, floundered in the pool on a dark night and so punished the town in this manner for neglecting to repair their roads. (Printed cutting, dated 1773, in Joseph Haslewood's copy of Brand, 1813 edition, and facing p. 338 of that copy.)

At Alnwick, on the 24th of April, the Eve of St. Mark, the Corporation met to admit the new freemen. All the young men of the town who were entitled by birth or apprenticeship to take up their freedom did so on that day. There might be only two or three, or there might be as many as thirty; in modern times, there were usually about ten. On the following day, 25th April, at 8 a.m., the new freemen assembled in the Market Place, on horseback, each carrying a sword; thence they set out, escorted by the chamberlains of the town, the bailiff of the Duke of Northumberland, two halberdiers and a band of music. The procession was led by the town moorgrieve to Freeman's Well, about 4 m. north of Alnwick. Having arrived at the Well, the young freemen took off their clothes and put on a white dress and a cap ornamented with ribbons. At a given signal, they leaped into the pool and, after an arduous struggle, were assisted out of the pool at its farther end. After the ceremony, the new freemen put on their usual dress. They entered the town, sword in hand, with music playing; paraded the streets, and went to the castle, where a banquet was prepared for them.

Early in the morning of the day, 25th April, the friends of the new freemen placed a holly tree outside the door of each of their houses. This holly tree was a representation of a very ancient symbol—the flowering bough, which appears in the Maypole, the May garland, and many other forms. It is believed to have been originally a fertility charm, imparting its fresh and fruitful qualities to those who wore it or decorated their houses with it.

The ceremony of Freeman's Well is first mentioned in 1645. Tait discovered from *The Itinerary of King John*, that he passed the night of April 24th, 1206, at Alnwick.[1] (*Archæologia Æliana*, 4th series, vol. 1, 1925, pp. 128-31.)

April

POPULAR SAYINGS AND BELIEFS

" A cold April
   The barn will fill."

" A cold April
   Gives bread and wine."

[*Durham*]

" Rain in April, rain in May
   Or Mainsforth farewell corn and hay."

Mainsforth, Durham, stands on dry, gravelly soil and requires frequent rains. (*Denham Tracts*, vol. 1, 1892, p. 85.)

" April showers
   Make May flowers."

" When April blows his horn,
   It is good for hay and corn."

[*Yorkshire, etc.*]

" April comes in, with his hack and his bill,
   And sets a flower on every hill."

—Yorkshire, etc. (*Notes on the Folk-Lore of the Northern Counties of England and the Borders*, William Henderson, 1879, p. 95.)

" An April flood
   Carries away the frog and his brood."

" March borrowed from April
   Three days and they were ill." (*See* p. 168.)

[1] *History of Alnwick*, vol. 2, p. 241.

May-Day Eve

"Plant your taturs when you will,
They won't come up before April."

(*The English Illustrated Magazine*, 1889-90, p. 548.)

[*Hertfordshire*] The first plowing, for barley, is begun in April, for they say:

"Better an April sop than a May clot."

(*The Modern Husbandman*, William Ellis, vol. 8, 1750, p. 308.)

May-Day Eve
30th April

Between the hours of 8 p.m. on the last day of April and 6 a.m. on the first of May, two customs called, respectively, the May Birches and the Mischief-Night customs, were celebrated. These customs lost their popularity during the period 1830-80. A description of them and a few paragraphs on May-day Eve fires, fairies, barring-out and divination will complete this section on May-day Eve.

THE MAY BIRCHES CUSTOM

Those who performed this custom were called May Birchers; they collected small branches of hawthorn and other trees and shrubs, and nettles and other plants suitable for use as May birches. These were fastened over the doors or on other parts of houses or they were laid down before house doors. It was well-understood that these May birches had a symbolical meaning, *e.g.* a branch of hawthorn placed before a house door served to convey a compliment. In some cases, however, the birch selected served to convey an insult and, occasionally, there was a breach of the peace.

COUNTY RECORDS

[*Cheshire*] In Cheshire, May birches were fastened over the doors or on the chimneys, on May-day Eve. Generally, the name of the tree rhymed with the character it symbolized, *e.g.* a branch of alder, colloquially pronounced "owler" signified a scowler. (*A Glossary of Words used in the County of Chester*, Robert Holland, English Dialect Society, 1886, p. 222.)

[*Derbyshire*] It would be, in all probability, a custom borrowed from that of singing carols on Christmas Eve for lads and lasses to do the like on May-day Eve. The next day, the lads went out early with bill-hooks to cut rods of may, which they brought into the villages and left at the doors of good masters, good neighbours and pretty maids. These May songs were sung and these may rods were laid down, as I have heard my mother say, in the early years of the nineteenth century, in Derbyshire. May songs are seldom heard now in the Midland counties.— T. Radcliffe, Worksop. (*N. and Q.*, xi, 1, 1910, p. 446.)

[*Hertfordshire*] At Hitchin, before dawn on May day, it was customary for revellers to place hawthorn branches before their neighbours' doors or, where they wished to express their contempt, elder and nettles were used.

[*Huntingdonshire*] In Huntingdonshire, before dawn on May day, youths laid hawthorn branches at the doors of those to whom they wished to convey a compliment.

[*Lancashire*] May booing or birching used to be customary in Lancashire. A thorn, other than hawthorn, indicated scorn, mountain ash expressed affection, holly represented folly, briar served to indicate a liar, and a plum-tree branch in bloom signified " to be married soon." Salt sprinkled before a door suggested a great insult.—*A History of Leagram*, John Weld. (*Chetham Society's Publications*, new series, no. 72, Manchester, 1913, pp. 128-9.)

[*Northamptonshire*] The birches custom was celebrated, hawthorn conveying a compliment and elder, crab tree, nettle, sloe, and thistle being uncomplimentary. (*Glossary of Northamptonshire Words and Phrases*, Anne Elizabeth Baker, 2 vols., vol. 2, 1854, pp. 426-7.)

MISCHIEF-NIGHT CUSTOMS

[*Scilly Isles*] In the Island of St. Mary, Scilly Isles, early in the morning of May-day or, rather, during the previous night, numbers of youths and girls go into the country and unhang gates, injure fences and otherwise damage property and annoy the inhabitants. (*A View of the Present State of the Scilly Isles*, Rev. George Woodley, 1822, pp. 231-2.)

[*Derbyshire*] In Derbyshire, the last night of April is called " Mischief Night." Then, youths throw bricks down chimneys, pull gates off their hinges, and do all kinds of wanton mischief, but if you hang a brush, shovel, or broom outside your house, the mischief makers will pass by your house and do no harm. (*Household Tales*, Sidney Oldhall Addy, 1895, p. 116.)

[*Lancashire*] At Oldham, the Eve of May day is known as Mischief Night, when it was the custom for people to play tricks on their neighbours. My informant remembers seeing a thatched house, in a village near Oldham, adorned with mops, rakes and brushes, on the tops of which were stuck mugs, tubs, and pails. (*Old English Customs extant at the Present Time*, P. H. Ditchfield, 1896, pp. 104-5.)

On Mischief Night, the young people of Burnley and the surrounding district perpetrate all kinds of mischief. Formerly, shopkeepers' sign-boards were interchanged, *e.g.* " John Smith, Grocer " to " Thomas Jones, Tailor," but the police have stopped these practical jokes. (*Lancashire Folk-Lore*, John Harland and T. T. Wilkinson, 1867, p. 239.)

Mischieve Night is the night of the 30th of April, when boys carry off all mops, tubs, brushes and other articles which may have been left out of doors and place them on the top of a neighbouring hill, on a house top, or in any other place difficult of access. (*A Glossary of Rochdale-with-Rossendale Words and Phrases*, Henry Cunliffe, Manchester, 1886, p. 59.)

[*Yorkshire*] It is still the custom to bring all the gates and carts that can be obtained, on the night of the 30th of April, to Bolton Cross, where they are piled up in a heap for a bonfire. This is said locally to be the work of Lob and Michil, the local elves at Bolton by Bowland, who now confine their labours to erecting the pile, without setting fire to it. (*King Henry's Well and Pudsey's Leap : Ballads founded on Craven Legends*, H. A. Littledale, printed for private circulation, Bolton by Bowland, 1856, p. 33.)

Referring to this custom, a writer, apparently Mildred E. Simeon, Kirklees Park, Brighouse, says : " I believe my Father stopped the gates being taken because that gave trouble with cattle straying ; the carts were carried off to the Cross in 1866 and for some years afterwards, but the custom has gradually died out."

Mischief neet. Boys, thirty years ago, used to go about damaging property, believing that the law allowed them, on this night. The practice is over at Wakefield and the time forgotten. (*A List of Provincial Words and Phrases in use at Wakefield*, William Stott Banks, 1865, p. 47.)

MAY-DAY EVE FIRES

[*Cumberland*] Far into the last century, Beltane fires were lighted all over the country, on the Eve of May day. Boughs of mountain-ash, still called witchwood and supposed to be protective against all evil influences, were carried round these fires and, within my own remembrance, leaves and twigs of the tree were put in keyholes and suspended over doors to prevent witches from working mischief.—A. Craig Gibson on Ancient Customs of Cumberland. (*Trans. Historic Society Lancashire and Cheshire*, vol. 10, 1858, p. 104.)

[*Isle of Man*] In the Isle of Man, on the night of May Eve, elderly people congregated on the mountains, set fire to the gorse, and blew horns, with a view to scaring fairies and witches who were believed to be more numerous than usual, on May Eve. (*An Historical and Statistical Account of the Isle of Man*, Joseph Train, 2 vols., vol. 2, Douglas, 1845, p. 118.)

FAIRIES

" *Fairy*. And I serve the fairy queen,
To dew her orbs upon the green."

(*Midsummer Night's Dream*, Act II, Scene 1.)

When the damsels of old gathered the May dew, for improving their complexions, they left undisturbed such of it as they saw on the fairy rings, being apprehensive that fairies, in revenge, would destroy their beauty ; nor was it considered safe to put the foot within the rings, lest they should be subject to the fairies' power. (*Illustrations of Shakespeare and of Ancient Manners*, Francis Douce, 2 vols., vol. 1, 1807, p. 180.)

[*Herefordshire*] On the Eve of May-day, at Kingstone and Thruxton, folk used to put trays of moss outside their doors for the fairies to dance upon. (*The Folk-Lore of Herefordshire*, Ella Mary Leather, Hereford, 1912, p. 44.)

BARRING-OUT

[*Yorkshire*] At Stannington, the boys bar the schoolmaster out, saying :

" Bay, master, bay, bar for a pin,
If you don't give us a holiday, we won't let you in."

The barring-out took place on May Eve. (*A Glossary of Words used in the Neighbourhood of Sheffield*, Sidney Oldhall Addy, English Dialect Society, 1888, p. 296.)

DIVINATION

[*Lincolnshire*] May Eve is another day for working love charms. A native of a village near Kirton-in-Lindsey, who is now in early middle age, affirms that one of the most successful methods of ascertaining the name of the one you are to marry is to use the first bunch of hawthorn blossom you see in the springtime, especially if you can find it on May Eve. You crag the spray on the bush, that is you break it partly through and then leave it hanging. Afterwards, you go home and at night you ought to see your future husband in your dreams. When the morning comes, you must gather the may and, if you have not already dreamed of him, it is certain that you will see him or his apparition before you enter the house again. (*Folk-Lore*, vol. 12, 1901, p. 167-8.)

May Day

1st May

Many of the popular customs which celebrated the advent of the merry month of May were discontinued many years ago. To-day, it is true, maypoles are dressed, May queens are crowned, maypole dances are performed, and efforts are made to preserve memories of the old English May-day customs in their best forms, but these modern ceremonies are revivals and are rarely fixed for the 1st of May, or even for Old May day, the 13th or, as some say, the 12th of May.

The history of May day as a day of amusement, before the Restoration, was unfortunate. May day lost popularity in 1517, when anti-alien riots were arranged for May day and resulted in the execution of many of the rioters. In consequence of this unfortunate association, May day was called " Ill or Evil May day." In Elizabeth's reign the Puritans began to abuse the maypole and its votaries, from the May queen to the youngest dancer, using language neither moderate nor elegant and sometimes unprintable. Their long-continued hostility culminated in the issue by both Houses, in April, 1644, of an Order to take down all maypoles. It is unlikely that this Order was promptly obeyed in all towns and villages where maypoles happened to stand and it may be asserted that, in the cavalier counties, some maypoles were not taken down. The effect of the Order, however, was inevitable; a very great breach was made in the continuity of the May-day celebration, from which it never fully recovered.

After the Restoration, the erection of maypoles and the performance of the maypole ceremonies were again permitted. Soon, however, the 29th of May began to acquire the popularity of the old English May day and, until about the year 1865, there were towns and villages, Upton-on-Severn, Clent, Offenham and Bromyard are examples, whose inhabitants dressed the maypole for the 29th of May and rarely for May day.

May Day

GOING A-MAYING

This was an eminently rural custom celebrated during the early hours of May day in the fields and woods where May-blossom, in favourable seasons in the south of England, marsh marigold, wood anemone, cowslip and other flowers, and also branches of hawthorn, sycamore, beech, birch and other trees, were collected by the Mayers who, on their return home, used them for decorating their houses. When not employed in collecting the produce of the fields and woods, the Mayers spent their time in horn-blowing, singing, dancing, playing on whistles, flutes and violins, or enjoying light refreshments.

Although several writers criticized the custom in hostile manner, it continued to be celebrated from early times until about the year 1825. It is referred to in Midsummer Night's Dream, Act I, Scene 1, and its popularity in the seventeenth century is shown by the lines:

> " There's not a budding Boy or Girle, this day,
> But is got up and gone to bring in May.
> A deale of youthe, ere this is come
> Back and with White-thorn laden home.
> Some have dispatch'd their Cakes and Cream,
> Before that we have left to dreame.
> .   .   .   .   .
> Then while time serves, and we are but decaying,
> Come, my Corinna, come, let's go a-maying."

(*Hesperides*, *Corinna's going a-Maying*, Robert Herrick, 1648, lines 44-7 and 69-70.)

In ancient times, people of almost every rank went a-Maying, early on May day, and it is especially recorded that Henry VIII and Queen Catherine, in 1511 and in 1515, rode out a-Maying.

RECORDS OF THE CUSTOM

[*Cambridgeshire*] May-day is still observed at Great Gransden, Cambridgeshire, where the young men, farmers' servants, on their return from going a-Maying, leave a hawthorn branch at almost every house in the village, singing what they call the

Night Song. On the evenings of May-day and the 2nd of May, they go round to every house where they had left a branch and sing The May Song. One of the young men, called the May Lord, wears a shirt over his ordinary dress and is decorated with ribbons; another, in girl's clothes, is called the May Lady or Mary and is probably a relic of the Maid Marian of Shakespeare's time; a third has a handkerchief on a stick for use in keeping off the crowd; the rest of the young men have ribbons in their hats. The May Song consists of sixteen verses of a religious type. The money collected is spent in a feast of plum-cake, bread, cheese and tea. (*Time's Telescope* for 1816, p. 130.)

[*Cornwall*] The first of May is inaugurated with much uproar; as soon as the midnight hour is struck, a loud blast of tin trumpets proclaims the advent of May. This is long continued and, at daybreak, young people of both sexes proceed to the country and strip the sycamore trees, called May trees, of their young branches for use in making whistles. This is done by making a peripheral cut through the bark to the wood, a few inches from the lower end of the branch; the bark is wetted and tapped carefully until it is loosened and can be slidden off the wood. The wood is then cut angularly at the end so as to form a mouthpiece and a slit is made in both the bark and the wood so that, when the bark is replaced, a whistle is formed. It was a custom at Penzance and probably many other Cornish towns, when I was a boy, for a number of young people to sit up until midnight and then march round the town, with violins and other musical instruments, and summon their friends to the Maying. When they were assembled, they went into the country and were welcomed at the farm-houses at which they called, with rum and milk, junket and other refreshments. They then gathered the May, which included the branches of any tree in blossom or fresh leaf. (*Popular Romances of the West of England*, Robert Hunt, 1865, p. 170; in the editions of 1881 and 1903, pp. 382-3.)

Another account informs us that, usually, there was dancing at the farm-houses and the refreshments included tea and a heavy country cake made of flour, cream, sugar and currants. (*Bygone*

Days in Devonshire and Cornwall, Mrs. Henry Pennell Whitcombe, 1874, p. 165.)

[*Hertfordshire*] At Hitchin, the Maying parties danced and frolicked during the day in many parts of the town. Two men with black faces were called Mad Moll and her husband; the former carried a birch broom and the latter was dressed in rags, wore a large straw bonnet, and carried a ladle. Next were the Lord and Lady of the company; the Lord was dressed up in ribbons, brightly coloured silk handkerchiefs secured at intervals round his legs and arms, and carried a sword; the Lady was a youth dressed in white muslin and decorated with ribbons. Following these were six or seven couples dressed somewhat like the Lord and Lady, but without swords. Accompanied by violin, clarionet, fife and long drum, the company danced very well indeed.—Letter to Mr. Hone, dated Hitchin, 1st May, 1823. (*The Every-Day Book*, William Hone, vol. 1, 1866, p. 283.)

[*Kent*] On May-day, in the morning, every man would walk into the meadows and woods. Edward Hall hath noted that Henry VIII, in 1511 and 1515, on May-day in the morning, with the Queen and many lords and ladies, rode a-Maying from Greenwich to Shooters Hill and saw there two hundred archers, dressed in green and commanded by a chief called Robin Hood, whose shooting was highly praised. The royal party was interested also in the arrows, which were specially constructed to emit loud, whistling noises when in flight. Finally, the royal party was sumptuously entertained by the company of archers. (*The Survey of London, etc.*, John Stow, 2 vols., 1720 edition, vol. 1, p. 252.)

[*Norfolk*] It was an old custom, in Norfolk, in most farmhouses, for any servant who could bring in a branch of hawthorn, in full bloom, on the 1st of May, to be entitled to receive a dish of cream for breakfast. (*The Norfolk Garland*, John Glyde, junr., [1872], p. 113.)

[*Northern Counties*] On May-day, the juvenile part of both sexes are wont to rise a little after midnight and walk to some neighbouring wood, accompanied with music and the blowing of horns. They break down branches from the trees and adorn themselves with flowers. When this is done, they return homewards with their booty, about the rising of the sun, and decorate their doors and windows with branches and flowers. (*The Antiquities of the Common People*, Henry Bourne, Newcastle, 1725, p. 200.)

[*Northumberland*] The young people of both sexes go out early in the morning of May day to gather the dew of the grass and also hawthorn, which they bring home with music and shouting, and having dressed a pole on the town green with garlands, dance round it. (*A View of Northumberland*, William Hutchinson, 2 vols., vol. 2, Newcastle, 1778, p. 13, Append.)

It is still customary for young people to rise early on May day every year to fetch May or green branches to deck their doors and mantelpieces, but they do not now, as in Bourne's time, go into the woods a little after midnight, Maying and blowing horns. (*A View of the County of Northumberland*, E. Mackenzie, 2 vols., vol. 1, Newcastle, 1825, p. 217.)

HORN-BLOWING

It was a common custom to blow horns on many festive occasions; they were much used on May-day Eve and during the early hours of May day, when celebrating the advent of the month of May, the forerunner of summer. The horns used were usually suitable for the emission of musical notes but many youths delighted in blowing large cows' horns adapted for making loud and not necessarily soothing sounds. Aubrey informs us that, at Oxford, the boys used to blow cows' horns all night. A writer, in *The Journ. British Archæol. Assoc.*, vol. 46, 1890, p. 233, says that the May-horns that welcome summer probably are the welcome whereby the Britons, Armoricans and Gauls of old greeted Turau or Taracno, the Lord of Summer, in the days of Julius Caesar.

RECORDS OF THE CUSTOM

[*Cornwall*] This year, 1884, the May-horns were as noisy as ever in Newlyn West and the west of Penzance. I do not think the horns have anything to do with Diana or with Flora but with the summer god of the ancient Celts who was honoured by horn-blowing in the spring.—W. S. L. S. (*Western Antiquary*, vol. 4, Plymouth, 1885, p. 50.)

At Penzance, the boys assemble at daybreak, on May-day and perambulate the town, blowing large tin horns and collecting money for a feast. (*Old English Customs extant at the Present Time*, P. H. Ditchfield, 1896, p. 105.)

[*Norfolk*] The ushering in of May by the blowing of horns, a custom almost peculiar to Lynn, seems to be of pagan origin. It is still tenaciously kept up in this town by the youths and children, though nobody pretends to know its meaning or its origin. Since May day is known to have been one of the most notable days of the year among our heathen ancestors, the said custom may be safely concluded to have originated from them. (*The History of Lynn*, William Richards, 2 vols., vol. 1, Lynn, 1812, p. 262.)

[*Oxfordshire*] On the first of May, the custom of blowing with and drinking from horns was common and, though generally disused, the custom of blowing horns prevails at that season, even to this day, at Oxford. (*Preface to Robert of Gloucester's Chronicle*, Thomas Hearne, 1724, p. xviii.)

MAY DEW

There is a section of the literature relating to English calendar customs which savours of antiquity, is associated with fairy-lore, and presents a claim to having been derived from customs of early Celtic times. That May dew, collected before sunrise on the first of May, from grass, hawthorn bushes and various flowers, and rubbed on the skin, would cure an affected part of the body, or improve the complexion, has been believed and acted upon for ages. It has long been said :

> " The fair maid who, the first of May,
> Goes to the fields at break of day
> And washes in dew from the hawthorn tree,
> Will ever after handsome be."

In the absence of a poetic advertisement of the use of May dew as a cure of disease, it may be said that the popular belief in its curative qualities was strong.

COUNTY RECORDS

[*Berkshire*] May dew. Vale of White Horse, Berkshire. All the girls were most anxious to get up early on May day to wash their faces in May dew to ensure beauty. (Mrs. Helen G. Longcroft, Havant, 10th June, 1913.)

[*Cornwall*] On this very May morning, 1884, my children have been out getting that still-famed cosmetic, May dew (as did Mrs. Pepys and party more than two hundred years ago), and bringing home the flowering branches of whitethorn.—Cornwall. (T. Q. Couch in *Western Antiquary*, vol. 4, Plymouth, 1885, p. 1.)

In Launceston, poor people say that a swelling in the neck may be cured by the patient, if a woman, going before sunrise, on the first of May, to the grave of the young man last buried in the churchyard, collecting therefrom the dew by passing the hand three times from the head to the foot of the grave, and applying the dew to the part affected. If the patient be a man, the grave chosen must be that of the last young woman buried in the churchyard. In the Launceston district, belief in the efficacy of May dew in improving the complexion prevails extensively. (*N. and Q.*, i, 2, 1850, pp. 474-5.)

[*Derbyshire*] Many customs of the ancient Druids still remain amongst the villagers of Eyam, Derbyshire. One of the proceedings at their festivals was to bathe the forehead with May dew, which was probably gathered at daybreak. Hence the prevailing custom of applying May dew to children. (*The Notts and Derbyshire Notes and Queries*, vol. 3, Nottingham and Derby, 1895, p. 63.)

[*Devon*] May dew, collected before or close upon sunrise, is looked upon as an infallible beautifier of the complexion. Young girls rose early to wash their faces in May dew. (*Nummits and Crummits*, Sarah Hewett, 1900, p. 90.)

At Morchard Bishop, in north Devon, a cup of dew collected in the churchyard on May morn was formerly thought to be good for a person in consumption. (*Church Folklore*, James Edward Vaux, 2nd edition, 1902, p. 398.)

[*Gloucestershire*] Belief in the virtues of May dew has not quite died out. In 1906, I overheard this conversation between two Minchinhampton girls : " They do say that if you wash your face in May dew, early in the morning, you'll have a good complexion." " Oh, you silly, they only tell you that to make you get up early ! " (*Folk-Lore*, vol. 23, 1912, p. 451.)

[*Herefordshire*] May dew gathered from beneath an oak tree is thought to be more beautifying than any other and was formerly gathered by girls for application to their faces. (*The Folk-Lore of Herefordshire*, Ella Mary Leather, Hereford, 1912, p. 20.)

[*Lancashire*] 1905. May-dewing or washing the face in dew early on the first Sunday in May, to ensure lasting beauty, is still indulged in, at Blackburn. (Author's MSS. Notes.)

[*London*] Yesterday, according to annual custom, a number of persons went into the fields and bathed their faces with the dew on the grass (May dew), under the idea that it would render them beautiful. (*The Morning Post*, 2nd May, 1791.)

[*Northumberland*] On the first of May, young people go out into the fields, before breakfast, to wash their faces in May dew. (*Northumberland Words*, Richard Oliver Heslop, Eng. Dial. Soc., 1892-4, p. 470.)

In Hawick, a few of the young people still go a-Maying, and rub their faces in May dew but, year by year, the number of those who do so becomes less. (*Old English Customs extant at the Present Time*, P. H. Ditchfield, 1896, p. 103.)

[*Shropshire*] Washing in May dew was (and no doubt still is) supposed, in Edgemond, to strengthen the joints and muscles. I know a little boy whose mother, believing that his inability to walk was due to spinal weakness, took him into the fields on nine consecutive mornings to rub his back with May dew. (*Shropshire Folk-Lore*, Charlotte Sophia Burne, 1883, p. 190.)

MAGDALEN TOWER CUSTOM

[*Oxfordshire*] It has long been a custom, on May day, for choristers to ascend the Tower of Magdalen College, Oxford, and sing a hymn of thanksgiving and praise beginning with the words : " Te Deum Patrem colimus." Although celebrated very early in the day, 5 a.m. formerly and 6 a.m. in recent times, several hundred spectators assemble to witness the proceedings.

The custom has been observed regularly but its celebration was in abeyance, during the War, for two if not more years. The annual cost of the celebration is paid for out of a sum of £10 reserved from the annual stipend of the Rector of Slimbridge Church, Gloucestershire, the advowson of which belonged, and may still belong, to the College.

RECORDS OF THE CUSTOM

The ceremony lasted about two hours and concluded with the ringing of the bells. The clerks, choristers and the rest of the performers, are allowed a side of lamb for their breakfast. (*Time's Telescope* for 1826, pp. 117-8.)

At six o'clock to-morrow morning the choir of Magdalen, now restored to the strength it had before the War, will ascend the 145 steps of the Tower and there sing the *Hymnus Eucharisticus* by way of greeting to the May-day sun. The Latin hymn now used was written, about 1660, by Dr. Thomas Smith, but was not used for the purpose until the end of the eighteenth century. (*Westminster Gazette*, 30th April, 1920.)

I have come to the conclusion that the hymn was composed by Dr. Thomas Smith, Fellow of Magdalen, soon after the Restoration, and that it was not sung, on the top of Magdalen Tower, till about the middle of the eighteenth century. I believe that this was the opinion of the late venerable President of Magdalen, Dr. Routh.—Magdalenensis. (*N. and Q.*, ii, 7, 1859, p. 446.)

Some years ago, a prospectus was issued announcing, as in preparation, a work entitled *The Maudeleyne Grace, including the Hymnus Eucharisticus*, with the music by Dr. Rogers, as sung every year, on May morning, on the Magdalen Tower, in Latin and English. I am inclined to think that this work was not published but, in the Library of Christ Church, Oxford, I accidentally met with what appears to me to be the first draft of the Grace in question. It commences *Te Deum Patrem colimus* and has the following note : " This hymn is sung every day in Magdalen College Hall, Oxon, dinner and supper throughout the year for the after grace, by the chaplains, clarkes and choristers there. Composed by Benjamin Rogers, Doctor of

Musique of the University of Oxon, 1685." It is entered in a folio volume, with this title on the fly-leaf: " Ben Rogers, his book, Aug. 18, 1673, and presented to me by Mr. John Playford, Stationer in the Temple, London."—Edward F. Rimbault. (*N. and Q.*, i, 1, 1850, p. 437.)

Before the Reformation, a requiem for the soul of Henry VII was performed early on May day, annually, on the top of Magdalen Tower. It has been said that the Magdalen Tower custom was, in effect, a substitute for the older custom.

MAY-DAY BELL-RINGING

This ancient custom survived until early in the eighteenth century.

[*Lincolnshire*] All Saints' Church, Stamford.

" 1707. Expended on the ringers on May Day. 5s. od." (*Church Bells of Lincolnshire*, Thomas North, Leicester, 1882, p. 236.)

[*Staffordshire*] St. Peter's Church, Wolverhampton.

" 1665. For ye gathering of ye may, may poles, and for ringers, as usual. 15s. 9d."

" 1671-2. For ringing and for music on May Day. 12s. 6d."

St. Leonard's Church, Bilston.

" 1702. For a maypole and for ringers. 4s. 6d." (*Midland Weekly News*, 13th May, 1893.)

MAY-DAY GUN-FIRING

[*Dorset*] Our ancestors gave way to manifestations of joy and had recourse to the following mode of expressing it :

" Wm. Tudbold, Mayor of Lyme, 1551. Item paid to Robert Willynes to chute the gones on May-day, 4d." (*The Social History of the People of the Southern Counties of England*, George Roberts, 1856, p. 386.)

DECORATING HOUSES, CHURCHES AND CROSSES

The custom of decorating doorways, porches, pillars, crosses, and other structures with hawthorn and other branches and with flowers, on May day, was celebrated almost universally in England in ancient times. *The Shepeardes Calendar* of Edmund Spenser, 1552-99, reads:

> " Youthes folke now flocken in every where
> To gather May bus-kets[1] and smelling brere,
> And home they hasten the postes to dight,
> And all the Kirke pillours eare day light,
> With Hawthorne buds and swete Eglantine
> And girlonds of roses and Sopps-in-wine."

Many years later, after commenting on the customs and amusements of May day, it was written : " How few relics of even these are now in use! In some parts of the country, the villagers spread the steps before their doors with daisies and other simple flowers." (*Time's Telescope* for 1831, p. 90.) A great deal of the decorative work was done by the Mayers on their return from the fields and woods.

COUNTY RECORDS

[*Cornwall*] On May day, in Cornwall, the Maying party returned between 5 and 6 o'clock in the morning, and decked the houses and porches with green boughs of the hawthorn and sycamore. (*Bygone Days in Devon and Cornwall*, Mrs. Henry Pennell Whitcombe, 1874, pp. 165-6.)

[*Derbyshire*] Mrs. George Middleton, of Smalldale, aged 43 years, said that she was born at Abney, two miles from Bradwell. When she was young, every house in Abney had a garland hung above its door on the first day of May. She had helped to make these garlands ; they were round, like hoops, and made of bits of green things, primroses, Mary blobs,[2] and so on. People would plod through snow to get flowers for them. The garlands were about a foot in diameter and were left hanging over doors till the flowers were withered. She thought they were intended to welcome the spring. (*Folk-Lore*, vol. 12, 1901, p. 426.)

[1] Busket = a little branch.
[2] Evidently May blobs, probably compact masses of flowers. " Blob " is a word sometimes used to denote a small mass, *e.g.* a blob of mud or of putty.

[*Herefordshire*] Whether or no the custom of decking houses with green boughs on the first of May is gone out of use during the last few years, I do not know, but when, as a boy, I lived at Kington, no house was without its bough of green birch in the doorway. (*Trans. Woolhope Naturalists' Field Club*, 1877-80, Hereford, 1887, p. 26.)

[*Leicestershire, etc.*] It hath been a custom, time out of mind, for children to scatter flowers before people's doors in towns, on May day. (*County F.L.*, vol. 1 (3), *Leicestershire and Rutland*, Charles James Billson, 1895, p. 102.)

[*Lincolnshire*] A woman from the extreme north of Lincolnshire, who died a few years since at more than 80 years of age, said that when she was a girl at Winteringham, she and other girls always dressed the lugs (ears or handles) of their milk-kits with leaves, on May-day morning. (*Folk-Lore*, vol. 9, 1898, p. 365.)

[*Northamptonshire*] Formerly, it was customary in the northern part of Northamptonshire to place a large branch of hawthorn at the doors of most of the houses. At Fotheringay, the May bush was a large one put into a hole in the ground before the front door. Flowers were then thrown over the bush and around it and also strewn before the door. (*Glossary of Northamptonshire Words and Phrases*, Anne Elizabeth Baker, 2 vols., vol. 2, 1854, pp. 426-7.)

[*Oxfordshire*] A wooden cross which stands on the roodscreen at Charlton-on-Otmoor has long been, and, apparently, continues to be, taken down, decorated with flowers, and replaced on the screen, on May day, annually. Formerly, until about the year 1860, it was customary for two men, accompanied by a troupe of morris dancers, to carry the decorated cross or garland about the village and its neighbourhood and obtain money.

[*Shropshire*] The hawthorn is seldom in full flower in Shropshire till the middle of May; with us the marsh marigold takes its place and is even known as the " Mayflower." On May day, as late as 1876, every house in Edgmond used to be adorned with a bunch of these flowers hung, stalk uppermost, on the doorpost, where they remained withering for two or three days. The custom is still in use at Meole Brace, Shrewsbury, and several bunches of mayflowers were noticed in Coleham, a suburb of Shrewsbury, on May day, 1878. (*Shropshire Folk-Lore*, Charlotte Sophia Burne, 1883, p. 356.)

[*Staffordshire*] I saw a bunch of mayflowers on the doorpost of the Crown Inn, Eccleshall, on May day, 1878. (*Shropshire Folk-Lore*, Charlotte Sophia Burne, 1883, p. 356, footnote.)

[*Worcestershire*] On May day, branches of silver birch, hung with cowslip balls, are fastened to the sides of the doorways; over the doorways hang garlands of evergreen, tinsel and paper flowers. (*Glossary of West Worcestershire Words*, E. L. Chamberlain, 1882, p. xii.)

HORSE DECORATIONS

The custom of decorating horses on May day is one of the few calendar customs to survive, although on a small scale. On May Day, 1936, in Holborn and the City, I saw seven horses, out of a large number, with ribbon decorations on bridle or forelock. There were two other horses which were not decorated, but the driver of one of them had a whip adorned with ribbon and the driver of the other horse had a whip decorated with red and white artificial flowers. In Watford, the custom is rarely kept up and the same is true of many other towns.

[*Cheshire*] Even the trifling observance of May day by the carters of Chester seems to have fallen into disuse. (*Bye-Gones relating to Wales and the Border Counties*, Oswestry and Wrexham, 1884-5, p. 76.)

[*Lancashire*] In most of the Lancashire towns, the carters decorate their horses with ribbons, rosettes, and flowers on May day, and parade them through the chief streets of the towns. (*Old English Customs extant at the Present Time*, P. H. Ditchfield, 1896, p. 105.)

At Manchester, in the old coaching days, many of the coaches were painted anew for the May-day parade, and the horses were provided with new harness and were decorated with cockades and nosegays about their heads and ears. The May-day cavalcade was a pretty sight on a fine May-day morning. (*Lancashire Folk-Lore*, John Harland and T. T. Wilkinson, 1867, p. 245.)

[*Staffordshire*] The decoration of horses is the only way in which May day is now marked here.—Stone. (*Notes on the Folk-Lore of North Staffordshire*, [W.] Wells Bladen ... p. 28.)

[*Yorkshire*] May day fêtes, as " Spring gratulations," seem to be more regarded in inland places than in those by the sea-coast. They are here no otherwise observed than by the stable-boys and draymen garnishing their horses' heads with ribbons, which are usually begged at the shops, hence the name " Horse-ribbon day."—Whitby. (*A Glossary of Words and Phrases used in, etc., Whitby*, Francis Kildare Robinson, 1876, p. 121.)

MAY GARLAND AND MAY DOLL CUSTOMS

These pretty customs, celebrated chiefly by young children, have become evanescent only during the last few years. They are very closely related; either of them passes by almost imperceptible gradations into the other and, mainly for this reason, they are considered here under the same heading. Such relationship does not end with a comparison between these two customs; it extends, *e.g.* to the maypole and the May queen, but these can be described, without difficulty, under separate headings. Incidentally, the method of classification adopted in this section is in conformity with the view commonly held, that such customs have been derived from the same source, *viz.* the very ancient rites and ceremonies of tree worship.

The May garland is made so as to display a rich and varied profusion of flowers, ranging from cowslips to Crown Imperial lilies, built up on a simple framework. This may be spheroidal, being made of crossed hoops, or pyramidal and made of parallel hoops secured to three uprights so as to keep the hoops at suitable distances apart; a third and less common form, the coronal or bower type, is made of half-hoops secured to a circular hoop or base. The spheroidal form was often used in Bedfordshire, Cambridgeshire, Hertfordshire, Norfolk, Northamptonshire, and Staffordshire; the pyramidal form was commonly used in Huntingdonshire and Rutland; the coronal form has been used in Lincolnshire and Oxfordshire. A garland secured to the top of a pole was used at Dagenham in Essex, Combe in Oxfordshire, Uttoxeter in Staffordshire, and Evesham and neighbouring villages in Worcestershire. This last form was called by the children, at their option, a May garland or a maypole. In some counties, the children sang May songs or carols from door to door.

COUNTY RECORDS

[*Bedfordshire*] May-day customs are dying slowly, but the singing of children from door to door is still heard in the county. It is recorded this year of one north-country visitor to Bedfordshire that he told his hosts he had never heard Christmas carols, at this time of the year, in any other part of the country. (*The Bedford Record*, 12th May, 1931.)

[*Buckinghamshire*] At Amersham, on May day, I saw children carrying bunches of flowers and singing like carol singers at the doors of houses. (*Daily News*, 6th May, 1930.)

[*Hertfordshire*] At 10.15 a.m. on the 1st of May, 1931, I saw a party of six children and a conductress in Alexandra Road, Watford. The children, four girls and two boys, about 6 to 9 years old, were gaily dressed and two of them carried a large hoop decorated with flowers and ribbons. The children sang a May song at the houses visited. This appears to have been the last of the custom in Watford. In earlier years it was usual to see several parties of children decorated with flowers and ribbons and carrying crossed-hoop garlands, each with a ribbon rosette above and streamers below.

[*Huntingdonshire*] At Kimbolton, several school children went from house to house with May garlands on May Day, 1931. This is one of the few May-day customs which have survived. (*The Bedfordshire Times and Independent*, 8th May, 1931.)

[*Oxfordshire*] At Bampton, until forty or fifty years ago, children dressed in white, with red, white, and blue ribbons, went about annually on May day. A boy, called the "Lord," carried a collecting-box and a stick adorned with ribbons and flowers. Two girls called, respectively, the "Lady" and her

"Maid," carried a crossed-hoop garland. The Lord and the Lady were accompanied by a Jack-in-the-Green. (*Old English Customs extant at the Present Time*, P. H. Ditchfield, 1896, p. 99.)

At Headington, on May day, a dozen or more parties of children, gaily dressed, carry about as many garlands of the coronal type. Each garland is attended by four children, two to carry the garland by means of a stick, and two, the Lord and the Lady, dressed very daintily and officiating as pursers. (*Brand*, i, p. 233.)

[*Rutland*] At Tinwell, my wife took part in the May-day custom, about 1910-15, and remembers it fairly well. On the 30th of April, the children were sent from the school in the afternoon to pick flowers, which were tied in bundles and placed in tubs of water to keep fresh. Early on May day adult villagers made up the garlands, originally of two kinds, one for the girls and the other for the boys. The boys' separate garland fell out of use about the year 1910, as the school became smaller, and the boys and girls all joined together. The custom was always celebrated and, if possible, always on May day.

The girls' garland was pyramidal and its framework consisted of three circular hoops secured to three broomsticks or poles; bunches of wild flowers were tied to the hoops and poles and a bunch of Crown Imperials always surmounted the garland. Slung on a long pole, the garland could be carried by two children. The boys' garland was spheroidal and was secured to the top of a pole or broomstick, called the "Maypole"; the two crossed hoops were covered with flowers tied to them and there was a bunch of Crown Imperials on the top.

The making of the garlands was done from about 5 a.m. onwards and the carrying of the garlands began at 8 a.m. to 8·30 a.m., the girls leading and the boys following in a separate group. The procession went to each house in the village, first the girls and then the boys, so that each house was sung to twice, beginning with the traditional Garland Song:

" Good morning, lords and ladies, it is the first of May.
We hope you'll view our garland, it is so very gay.

The cuckoo sings in April; the cuckoo sings in May,
The cuckoo sings in June; in July she flies away."

The tune was somewhat like that of the hymn, " All things bright and beautiful." Then followed other popular country songs; the boys' selection always included " The Farmer's Boy." The day was taken as a general holiday, the custom was very popular, and generous donations were made to the children. (Mr. John H. Harvey, formerly of Tinwell.)

[*Worcestershire*] At Evesham and neighbourhood, during the period 1927-33, parties of children carried about, on May day, what they called " maypoles," which had been made carefully, usually with the aid of their parents. These " maypoles " were stout sticks adorned at their upper ends by garlands and ribbons.

[*Staffordshire*] At Uttoxeter, on the 1st of May, groups of children carry garlands about the town. The garlands are of the spheroidal type, decorated with flowers and evergreens and surmounted by a bunch of flowers. An orange and flowers are suspended at the centre of the garland. Sometimes the children carry a little pole or stick with a bunch of flowers attached to the top of the pole. (*The Customs, Superstitions and Legends of the County of Stafford*, Charles Henry Poole, [later than 1875], p. 26.)

[*Lincolnshire*] We watched for the village children with their garlands, pretty, fragrant, beflowered structures of the bower type which they carried about, covered with a cloth, and were proud to show at a half-penny a peep.—Massingham. *Grantham Journal*, 29th June, 1878. (*County F.L.*, vol. 5, *Lincolnshire*, Mrs. Gutch and Mabel Peacock, 1908, p. 195.)

[*Northamptonshire*] Many dolls are still seen in Northampton. One, two or three dolls, according to the size of the garland, are placed in the centre of a spheroidal garland, which is carried from house to house concealed from view by a large handkerchief. The girls from the adjacent villages bring in their garlands and perambulate the streets. In some villages, it is customary to ask whether the inmates of a house wish to see the Queen of May. (*Glossary of Northamptonshire Words and Phrases*, Anne Elizabeth Baker, 2 vols., vol. 2, 1854, pp. 421-2.)

[*Gloucestershire*] Being lately on a visit to Bourton-on-the-

Hill, Gloucestershire, I remarked how extensively the observance of May day is still carried on in that neighbourhood. The children, dressed out with flowers and ribbons, go from house to house, each party of children carrying a doll seated in a kind of cage composed of flowers. (*N. and Q.*, iii, 7, 1865, p. 449.)

[*Huntingdonshire, etc.*] In Huntingdonshire, the garland was usually of a pyramidal type and on it, in a convenient position, a doll was displayed. At Edlesborough, Buckinghamshire, the doll, dressed up with flowers and ribbons, was carried about in a small chair. In Northamptonshire, at Polebrooke, the children formed a procession headed by a May queen and two of the girls carried dolls placed in a garland of flowers. In Devonshire, the May doll custom was celebrated with much ceremony.

[*Devonshire*] Annually, on May-day Eve, the owners of flower gardens in the Torquay district receive a succession of visits by young girls who beg flowers for the May doll. After 9 a.m. on May day, these girls go about carrying their boxes, about eighteen inches long, neatly covered by a white napkin. Each girl visits houses in the town and its neighbourhood, and stops people in the streets, at the same time asking " Will you please to see a May doll? " Suiting the action to the question, she removes the napkin and displays a prettily dressed doll lying on a bed of gay flowers tastefully arranged. If she receives a donation, she is quite satisfied. (*Trans. Devon. Assoc.*, vol. 6, Plymouth, 1874, p. 269.)

In the parishes of Tor and Upton, a carefully dressed doll is laid on a toy bed and pillow, in a cardboard box, and is nearly hidden by flowers. The girl carrying the box is accompanied by about six little friends, carefully dressed. The money obtained is kept in a little bag and shared out at the end of the day. (*Trans. Devon. Assoc.*, vol. 8, Plymouth, 1876, p. 50.)

THE MAYPOLE

The maypole, painted in spirals or horizontal rings of different colours, provided with a crown, garland, cross, or wind vane on its summit, and decorated with flowers, ribbons and streamers, was commonly seen throughout England, except during the period 1644-60. After the year 1660, it recovered much of its former popularity. Soon, however, there was an increasing tendency, especially in cavalier counties, towns, or villages, to dress the maypole for Restoration day and not for May day. To-day the maypole is rarely dressed for either day. This may be illustrated by the course of events at Offenham, near Evesham, where the maypole, renewed when necessary, was dressed for May day and after the year 1660 was dressed for Restoration day, until about the year 1880, when the custom ceased.

Many maypoles were more than sixty feet high; they were made from carefully selected pine, larch, ash, or other long, straight stems. After service as maypoles, they were used in making ladders, house beams, baulks for building into masonry and, occasionally, as a support for a heavy reflecting telescope.

[*Lancashire*] A very early maypole reference is given in a long account of a charter of the time of King John granting land to Cokersand Abbey. One section of this account relates to a free transfer (*donatio*) of land delimited by a line starting from the Lostock maypole, about three miles west from Bolton, that is to say, from the Lostock maypole, where a cross was situated, along a straight line extending in a southerly direction all the way to the cross beyond le Tunge.[1] (*Monasticon Anglicanum*, Sir William Dugdale, vol. 6, part 2, 1846, p. 907, 2nd col., lines 81-3.)

An early reference to the maypole is given in *Midsummer Night's Dream*, Act III, Scene 2, where Hermia calls the tall Helen " a painted Maypole." Pasquil calls the maypole " the rod of peace." (*Palinodia, or His Progresse to the Taverne*, 1619, p. B$_3$, line 12.)

MAYPOLE RECORDS

[*Bedfordshire*] The gaily painted, tall, and stout maypole at Ickwell, Bedfordshire, is shown in Plate VIII, as it appeared on the 14th May, 1936.

[*Berkshire*] On a visit this day to Aldermaston, Berkshire, I was struck by its lofty maypole, standing in a commanding

---

[1] *Scilicet de Lostock mepul, ubi crux sita fuit, recta linea extensa in austro, usque ad crucem super le Tunge.*

PLATE VIII

MAY REVELS AT ICKWELL, BEDFORDSHIRE, 1936

The Times.

position at the top of the street; it is about seventy-five feet high and is surmounted by a wind vane and a crown. (*N. and Q.*, ii, 12, 1861, p. 11.)

[*Cornwall*] The erection, on May day, of a lofty maypole adorned with garlands of flowers, was customary at Bay-tree Hill. The custom was abandoned early in the nineteenth century. (*History of the Borough of Liskeard*, John Allen, 1856, pp. 346-7.)

In Cornwall, once the home of the Mayers, the maypole no longer exists. (*Old English Customs extant at the Present Time*, P. H. Ditchfield, 1896, p. 105.)

[*Dorset*] At Buckland Newton, the maypole was set up on the rising ground in the midst of the village. At Cerne Abbas, the maypole celebration used to be a great event. In the Churchwardens' Accounts for Cerne Abbas is an entry:

"1635. Paid Anth. Thorne and others for taking down ye maypole and making a town ladder of it. 3s. 10d."

Childs, the former sexton, remembers a maypole at Cerne; it used to be set up a long way from the village, in the ring just above the Giant, a large figure sculptured in the turf on the western side of Trendle Hill. The maypole was made of a fir bole and was renewed every year. It was raised in the night, decorated with garlands, and the villagers went to the hill and danced round the maypole on the 1st of May. (*Folk-Lore*, vol. 10, 1899, p. 481.)

[*Gloucestershire*] A new maypole was erected at Bream, Gloucestershire. (*Folk-Lore Journal*, vol. 2, 1884, p. 191.)

[*Hampshire*] The survival of one maypole in Hampshire, at the present time, shows that the ancient May games were long continued. (*A History of Hampshire*, T. W. Shore, 1892, p. 31.)

[*Lincolnshire*] Hemswell is our only village which claims to have a maypole still in position. The ladder up to the belfry in Castle Bytham Church has this inscription: "This ware the May Poul, 1660." At the Reformation, there was at Waddingham St. Peter " one sacringe bell wich honge at a maypole top." This suggests that the maypole was close to the church, if not actually in the churchyard.—Mrs. E. H. Rudkin. (*The Lincolnshire Magazine*, vol. 2, no. 5, May-June, 1935.)

[*London*] The most famous maypole in England was the maypole in the Strand erected in 1661 and referred to in the *Dunciad*, II, ll, 27-31 :

> " Amid that area wide, they took their stand,
> Where the tall Maypole once o'erlooked the Strand
> But now, so Anne and Piety ordain,
> A church collects the saints of Drury Lane."

The site of the maypole was on or near the area now occupied by the Church of St. Mary le Strand, which was built during the years 1714-7. Apparently, the maypole stood for about half a century, quite a long time for a maypole for, mainly because of decay of its foot, the life of the ordinary maypole rarely exceeds fifteen years.[1]

The plan which Anthony van den Wyngaerde issued in 1543 shows a maypole in front of the old Church of St. Mary le Strand, which was demolished in 1549 ; this, apparently, would be on the site of the present church. In ancient times, a stone cross stood on this site and *The Calendar of Patent Rolls*, under date 27th January, 1242, refers to the " Stone Cross of la Straund." When this cross was demolished, or when the first maypole was erected on its site, is not known, but the last maypole erected on the site was probably the famous maypole of 1661. This was 134 feet high and very carefully made of two parts bound together by iron bands. After conveyance to Scotland Yard, it was carried in solemn procession to the Strand, 14th April, 1661. In *The Citie's Loyalty Displayed*, 1661, it is said that the maypole was carried with a streamer flourishing before it, drums beating all the way. The maypole was considered so long and heavy that landsmen could not raise it. However, Prince James, Lord High Admiral, commanded twelve seamen off aboard to go to the Strand and complete the task. A crown, a vane, and the King's Arms, richly gilded, were placed on the head of the pole and a

---

[1] The lines : " What's not destroyed by Time's devouring hand ? Where's Troy and where's the Maypole in the Strand ? " are well-known.

large top, like a balcony, was constructed about the middle of it. After four hours' work, drums beating and trumpets sounding merrily the while, the great maypole was raised and its foot was firmly embedded in the ground. Morris dancers then circled round it and afterwards went the rounds of the Duchy of Lancaster. The maypole was erected, as near as could be determined, on the same site as that of the last preceding maypole. In course of time, the maypole was taken down and, it is said, was obtained by Sir Isaac Newton, in 1717, for use in supporting Mr. Huygens' reflecting telescope. (*The Annals of the Strand*, E. Beresford Chancellor, 1912, pp. 80-3.)

In ancient times, in Aldgate, a famous maypole was set up before the south door of St. Andrew Undershaft Church, so called because this tall maypole overshadowed the church. When not in use, the maypole was placed on a row of hooks over the house doors of Shaft Alley. After Evil May day, 1517, it was not used again but, thirty-two years later, the people of Shaft Alley, influenced by the admonition of a preacher at Paul's Cross that they were making an idol of the maypole, removed it from the hooks, sawed it into lengths and burnt these. Until 1795, a maypole stood opposite the Black Prince, at Kensington, and milk-maids thronged about it on May day morning. (*The Morning Post*, 1st May, 1912.)

[*Nottinghamshire*] Passing through Wellow, Notts, a few days ago, I saw a maypole in the centre of the village. It was about sixty feet high and had three cross-pieces near the top, at intervals apart. I found that it was a real maypole and had been standing about a quarter of a century; it had replaced an old one which had become rotten and tottering. Many of the people remember when dancing round the maypole, climbing it when greased, and other games were in full vigour. (*Folk-Lore Journal*, vol. 2, 1884, pp. 317-8.)

[*Oxfordshire*] A few of the old inhabitants remember the last hoisting of the maypole at Chalgrove. The maypole itself, engraved with a large " M," is still to be seen built in among the rafters of an old barn. Dancing round the maypole ceased in the year 1805 or 1806.—*Chalgrove: A Sketch*, Laura M. R.

Gammon of Chalgrove. (*The Pelican*, vol. 5, February, 1883, pp. 7-8.)

At the entrance from the London side is a tall maypole. —Nettlebed, Oxon. (*The Beauties of England and Wales*, vol. 12, part 2, *Oxfordshire*, 1813, p. 367.)

[*Scilly Isles*] At High Town, St. Mary's Isle, a maypole is erected and dressed, annually, and the girls dance round it. (*Old English Customs extant at the Present Time*, P. H. Ditchfield, 1896, p. 105.)

[*Wiltshire*] A maypole surmounted by a wind vane stands in the village of Dean, near Salisbury. (*N. and Q.*, ii, 12, 1861, p. 338.)

[*Worcestershire*] For many years maypoles stood at Berrow, Clent, Offenham, Upton-on-Severn, Bayton, and many other places. At Offenham a maypole has stood on the green from time immemorial. The present one, rather new in 1931, was erected in place of an old one which stood on the same spot for many years. At Clent, eight miles westwards of Birmingham, the maypole was dressed regularly for Oak-apple Day, 29th May. This custom was very popular there as late as 1860. It was the almost universal custom, in Worcestershire, to dress the maypoles for Oak-apple day.

The maypole was raised, with its floral wreath, within my remembrance, not far from Worcester, but for some time I have lost sight of it. (*The Affinities of Plants*, etc., A Lecture delivered before the *Worcestershire Field Naturalists' Club*, 26th November, 1833, Edwin Lees, 1834, p. 28.)

The village of Bayton, near the Shropshire county boundary, has a maypole which has been carefully preserved for many years by the rural authorities and decorated with garlands. (*N. and Q.*, ii, 12, 1861, p. 78.)

[*Yorkshire*] In most parts of Yorkshire, maypoles and their associated games were popular. Among many examples, the maypoles of Carlton in Cleveland, Thoralby, Upper Poppleton, Slingsby, Aysgarth, Ovington, Barwick, and Naburn may be mentioned. The Carlton maypole was in use later than 1859 and the Thoralby, made of two tall larches, was erected about the year 1842.

May Day

In August, 1893, the stump of the old maypole at Upper Poppleton, taken down almost thirty years before, was unearthed and a new one, eighty feet high, set up on the spot.—*The York Herald*, 8th August, 1893. (*County F.L.*, vol. 2, *North Riding of Yorkshire, York and the Ainsty*, Mrs. Gutch, 1901, p. 55.)

Besides a maypole at Aysgarth, in Wensleydale, there is a noble specimen at Ovington, on the banks of the Tees. The pole, sixty-three feet high, was taken down, repainted, decked with garlands, and raised on the green ready for the May-day games and dances. (*N. and Q.*, ii, 12, 1861, p. 219.)

A fine, new pole, sixty-six feet out of the ground, was set up in 1829, at Slingsby, North Riding of Yorkshire, to replace an old one, erected in 1815; the new pole was set up on the village feast-day, the 12th of May. (*N. and Q.*, ii, 12, 1861, p. 403.)

At Naburn, four miles from York, is a maypole erected lately on the site of an old one. A wind vane is fixed on the top and the pole is painted green and white. I am not aware that it was ever decorated with garlands.—J. H. Steward. (*N. and Q.*, ii, 12, 1861, p. 275.)

In the village of Barwick, seven miles from Leeds, a maypole stands near the remains of an old cross; it is taken down, repainted, and repaired every third year, or renewed, if necessary. This maypole is dressed for Whitsuntide and no longer for May day, as was the custom. (*N. and Q.*, ii, 12, 1861, p. 446.)

MAY-QUEEN AND MAYPOLE CEREMONIES

Many of the following descriptions relate to revivals of customs celebrated in times of which it was said :[1]

> " Happy the age and harmless were the days,
> For then true love and amity was found,
> When every village did a maypole raise
> And Whit-sun ales [2] and May games did abound."

The modern revivals illustrate these customs at their best, the procession to the village green, the crowning of the May Queen,

---

[1] Pasquil's *Palinodia*, 1619, p. B₂, ll. 17-20.
[2] Whit-sun ales were often held in May.

her dress, crown, and sceptre, her maids of honour and other members of her retinue, their dress, sometimes of the seventeenth or eighteenth century style, and the maypole and other dancing.

COUNTY RECORDS

[*Bedfordshire*] Elstow. This village, Bunyan's birthplace, is steeped in tradition and famous for its May Festival. This year, 1931, it was held on Thursday, 7th May, on the Green. The main street was bright with gaily coloured streamers, bunting and flags. The procession to the Green was headed by the Maypole carried by boys; then followed gaily dressed boys and girls bearing the coloured streamers. The crown-bearer came next, followed by several former May Queens. The May Queen elect, in a brightly decorated car, was drawn by boys directed by a scarlet-coated coachman who was also the Queen's herald. There were about thirty maids of honour. Following were the dove carriers, a fiddler in his smock, the Queen's jester in motley dress and carrying a joy-stick with balloon, and, finally, many children carrying sprays of flowers. The May Queen was crowned after arrival at the Green; according to custom, she had been elected mainly by the school children. By her command, after the crowning ceremony, the doves of peace were released. In the revels which followed, " Gathering Peascods " was the favourite dance. (*The Bedford Record*, 12th May, 1931.)

Elstow is keeping May Day in ceremonial manner and is electing its May Queen. (*The Bedfordshire Times and Independent*, Friday, 1st May, 1936.) The May Festival at Elstow was celebrated on Thursday, 7th May, 1936.

Ickwell. The Ickwell May Festival was celebrated on Thursday, 14th May, 1931. Girls bedecked with flowers and carrying floral hoops preceded the decorated cart carrying the May Queen and her attendants. The girls were dressed in quaint old English costumes. On arrival at Ickwell Green, the Queen was crowned and this ceremony was followed by maypole and country dances. (*The Bedfordshire Times and Independent*, 15th May, 1931.)

On Thursday, 14th May, 1936, at Ickwell, the May festival was held; *see* Plate VIII. In bright sunshine, the procession to the Green, the crowning of the May Queen, and maypole and country dancing took place. (*The Times*, Friday, 15th May, 1936, p. 20.)

Eaton Socon. The May festival at Eaton Socon was discontinued years ago. (*The Bedford Record*, 12th May, 1893.)

[*Cheshire*] Knutsford. The old custom of crowning the May Queen was performed at Knutsford in the presence of thousands of spectators. The prettiest child in the village was crowned Queen of the May. A letter from Lord Tennyson to Mr. Lever expressed a hope that the people of Knutsford might long continue the observance of their time-honoured festival. (*Folk-Lore Journal*, vol. 2, 1884, p. 191.)

Early in the morning of May day, at Knutsford, the streets are sanded with brown and white sand in preparation for the procession, which starts from the Town Hall and is nearly a mile long ; at the end is the May Queen elect. Circuiting the town, the procession goes to the Heath, where the ceremony of crowning takes place, followed by games, morris dances, and the usual festivities, all of which are performed before the throne, an imposing structure. A distinctive feature of the festivities at Knutsford is the morris dance. (*The Origin of Popular Superstitions and Customs*, T. Sharper Knowlson, 1910, pp. 38-9.)

[*Huntingdonshire*] For the last three May days, I have been in Huntingdonshire and have made sketches of the May Queen and her attendants, the May garland, and the after sport of throwing at the garland. On referring to my sketches of the pyramidal garland, I find that its crown is composed of tulips, anemones, cowslips, king-cups, lilacs, laburnums, meadow-orchis, wallflowers, primroses, crown imperials, and as many roses as can be obtained. These, together with green boughs, are made into a huge pyramidal nosegay, from the front of which a gaily dressed doll (called " Madame Flora ") stares vacantly. From the base of the nosegay hang ribbons, pieces of silk, handkerchiefs, and any other gay-coloured fabric that can be borrowed. Annually on May-day morning, the May Queen is chosen by her schoolfellows. She wears a white frock, white gloves, a white veil, and a crown of flowers round her bonnet ;

she carries a handkerchief bag and a parasol. The garland is carried by her two maids of honour. Followed by her maids of honour and other attendants, male and female, she makes a tour of the village or town and before some of the houses the company sing and collect money to pay for the Coronation Banquet; this is usually held in the schoolroom and commences about three in the afternoon. After its conclusion, a rope is drawn from chimney to chimney or from tree to tree across the main street, and the garland is suspended from the centre of the rope. Provided with a number of balls, the children throw them backwards and forwards over the rope and garland. Games also are played, *e.g.* " I spy "; " Tick "; " Here we go round the mulberry bush "; " Thread the needle "; " What have I apprenticed my son to? ; " " Blind-man's buff." Accompanied by flute or violin, these sports may be concluded with a dance.—Cuthbert Bede. (*N. and Q.*, i, 10, 1854, pp. 91-2.)

In *N. and Q.*, i, 10, 1854, pp. 91-2, I described the May-day customs, as then existing, in Huntingdonshire. That description would stand for an account of the May-day customs in 1865, at Glatton, Stilton, Denton, Caldicot, Folksworth and other villages in the county. On May Day, 1865, a traditional May-day song was sung by the Mayers at Denton and Caldicot when they went round with their garland.—Cuthbert Bede. (*N. and Q.*, iii, 7, 1865, p. 373.)

A singular May-day custom in Huntingdonshire is that of suspending from a rope hung across the road of every village a doll with pieces of gay-coloured silk and ribbon, and no matter what attached to it; spoons, forks, candlesticks and snuffers were some of those I saw the other day in Summersham, St. Ives, and other places.—Henrietta M. Cole. (*N. and Q.*, i, 9, 1854, p. 516.)

[*Lancashire*] On the first of May, the maypole was drawn to the village green by several oxen, whose horns were decorated with bunches of flowers. After its erection on the accustomed spot, the joyous band of revellers held their jubilee of feasting and dancing round the maypole. This was covered with floral garlands and streamed with flags and handkerchiefs from its summit.

A Lord and a Lady or Queen of May were elected to preside over the ceremonies; their costumes were liberally adorned with scarfs and ribbons. The morris dance was an important feature of the festival and the performers wore richly decorated clothes on to which were fastened small bells, varying in tone. (*History of the Fylde of Lancashire*, John Porter, Fleetwood and Blackpool, 1876, pp. 96-7.)

The first of May was formerly observed here in the orthodox style. There were dancing round the maypole, the election of a Queen of May, and mummers. A scrap of an old song tells us that amongst the maskers:

> " There was Babel with his wooden tool,
> Too scant of wit to be a fool."

This wooden tool was a ladle whose bowl was well covered with chalk, so that Babel left his mark wherever he struck. (*The History of the Parish of Kirkham, Lancs*, Henry Fishwick, 1874, pp. 206-7.)

[*London*] May-day Festival was observed with impressive enthusiasm by the junior members of the Guild of Merrie England, in the Morris Hall, Miles Street, on Saturday. This was the third year of the performance and the proceeds were for St. Dunstan's Fund. The procession of the May Queens and the crowning of the new May Queen were very well done. There were morris dances, country dances, the dance round the maypole, and old English songs. A representation of the old English custom of little girls going from house to house carrying garlands and asking for gifts for Our Lady was very effective not only in its performance but also in aiding the Fund.—St. Peter's, Vauxhall. (*Brixton Free Press*, 10th May, 1917.)

[*Middlesex, etc.*] May Day, 1931, was celebrated on the Green, West Drayton, Middlesex, on Friday, 1st May, when scholars of the local school crowned the May Queen, danced round the maypole and sang " The Barley Mow," " Come Lasses and Lads," and other country songs. (*The Middlesex Advertiser and County Gazette*, 8th May, 1931.)

At Hayes Common the May Queen was crowned at the 25th

annual festival on Saturday, 2nd May. (*The Observer*, 3rd May, 1931.) Similar celebrations took place at Walworth, 1st May, 1920 ; Hayes Common, 1st May, 1920 ; Fulham, 1st May, 1929.

[*Norfolk*] At the first May carnival at Sedgford, Norfolk, on May Day, 1905, the girls danced round the maypole. The inhabitants considered it good fun ; the girls were pleased because they were the first children in Norfolk to be taught Morris Dancing, a teacher from London having taught them. The boys also became cockier, though teacher told them to hold their clappers and not talk swank. It was great fun and we were soon able to do the Bean-setting, the Handkerchief Dance, Blue-eyed Stranger, Riggs o' Marlow, Trumbles, and so on. By the kindness of Mr. and Mrs. Ingleby, we were provided with print dresses, fichus, aprons and poke bonnets and we had bells on our ankles and arms. Thus dressed, we performed at the Carnival of May, 1908.—Account by one of the Morris Dancers. (*The Charm of a Village, Sedgford*, Mr. Holcombe Ingleby, *n.d.* pp. 109-112.)

A dance recorded as a source of profit to St. Edmund's, Sarum, was the Maypole Dance of the children. The first definite mention of this dance is in the 1490 roll of expenses and receipts :

" 1490. To Willm. Belrynger for clensinge of the Church at ye Dawnse of Powles ... 8d."

From this it is clear that this dance took place within the church, almost certainly in the nave. The last reference to this dance is in 1594, when the " children's daunce " produced 20s. 1d. towards the church funds, (*Churchwardens' Accounts from* 1400-1700, Rev. J. Charles Cox, 1913, p. 66.)

A representation of the maypole custom for the 14th of May, or one day after Old May day, is shown on Plate VIII. It may also be of interest to record that a view of the May-day maypole custom and some of the May games is shown by the frontispiece of *The Merrie Days of England*, Edward MacDermott, 1859.

THE MORRIS DANCE

This is a rustic dance performed by dancers who, sometimes attired in fancy dress and wearing gaily-coloured scarfs and sashes, execute various picturesque figures by movements which synchronize with the notes of drum and pipes or flute and with the clack, clack, of wooden staves sometimes carried by the dancers; swords are sometimes used instead of staves, especially in Yorkshire, Durham and Northumberland. The displays of colour effected by means of the scarfs and sashes are very attractive.

In earlier times, the troupes of Morris dancers included any of the following characters, the Fool or Clown, Maid Marian, the Friar, Robin Hood, and the Hobby Horse, a character of great antiquity. The carrying of bells yielding different notes and attached to the dress of the performers was almost a characteristic feature of the morris dance, but sometimes bells were not used, and I remember a troupe touring the west Midlands about the year 1868 in which there was only one bell, carried by the Clown, who thus advertised his presence and that of his inflated bladder. The number of dancers in a troupe ranged from six to more than twenty; at the Wirksworth Well-dressing, 3rd June, 1914, the number was twenty-four.

Introduced at some time in the fifteenth century, probably from Spain, France, or Flanders, the morris dance, of which little seems to have been recorded before the reign of Henry VII, became very popular during the reign of Henry VIII and was an important item in the celebration of May day, Whitsun ales, and parish festivities in general. There were numerous performances by morris dancers on May day, yet there are few accounts of their dress and performance; in fact, the best accounts known to me relate to the performances of the Christmas season. The following items are from the Churchwardens' Accounts of several churches.

St. Mary's Church, Reading.

" 1557. Item Paid to them [the morris dancers and minstrels] the Sunday after May day ... 20d."

St. Laurence's Church, Reading.

" 1529. For bells for the Morece dauncers . . . 6d."

All Saints' Church, Great Marlow.

" 1612. Received of the churchwardens of Bysham, loane of Morris coats and bells . . . 2s. 6d."

All Saints' Church, Kingston upon Thames.

" 1508. For 4 plyts and ¼ of laun for the Mores garments . . . 2s. 11d."

" 1509. For silver paper for the Mores daunsars . . . 7d."

" 1520. Shoes for the Mores daunsars, the frere, and Mayde Maryan at 7d. a peyre . . . 5s. 4d."

" 1522. Eight yerds of fustyan for the Mores daunsars coats . . . 16s."

There are also entries showing that the morris dancers' coats were painted.

St. Helen's Church, Abingdon.

" 1560. For two dossin of Morrice bells."

ROBIN HOOD PLAYS AND BALLADS AND THE MAY GAMES

Many of the old English ballads, made known from town to town and from village to village by wandering minstrels, introduced the name of the legendary hero[1] Robin Hood. One of the best of these ballads, entitled *Robin Hood and the Monk*, is said to be as ancient as the reign of Edward II, 1307-27, but the earliest reference in English literature which indicates the date of the reference itself is said to be in the 2nd edition of *Piers Plowman*, about 1377, where Sloth admits that his citation of his Paternoster is defective but he can rhyme about Robin Hood and Randulf, Earl of Chester.

[*Nottinghamshire, etc.*] During the fifteenth and sixteenth centuries, the Robin Hood plays and ballads were especially popular; the people were pleased to be entertained by stories and songs of the outlaw, the forest, and the chase, and were often

[1] In the years 1890 to 1910, Robin Hood was a real personage for many in the Mansfield and Chesterfield district.

heard to say that they preferred the Robin Hood plays to any other. About the year 1500 morris dancers became associated, in a subordinate way, with the Robin Hood companies.

Robin Hood was an imposing character in Kendal-green and equipped as an archer. Maid Marian, almost always impersonated by a youth, wore a skirt of coarse woollen cloth and sometimes a loose bodice of Kendal-green provided with a hood. Friar Tuck wore a russet gown and a girdle. The Fool or Clown wore the usual Fool's head-dress and was especially conspicuous by wearing a yellow stocking (say) on his left leg and a red one on his right leg. Then there were Little John and Will Scarlet, whose dress is rarely referred to in the Churchwardens' Accounts.

In the May games, Robin Hood often appeared as the King or Lord of the revels and Maid Marian as the Queen or Lady. These revels were held throughout May and part of June but although thus celebrated in June they were still called May games. They included archery, sword and other martial exercises, maypole and country dancing, swings and roundabouts, conjuring and sleight of hand tricks, bowls, rope tying-up and releasing performances, climbing the greased pole, cock-shying, racing, boxing, wrestling and other gymnastic displays, dropping the handkerchief, threading the needle, called also " duck under water," and other juvenile games.

CHURCHWARDENS' ACCOUNTS

Croscombe Parish Church, Somerset.

" 1476. Comes Thomas Blowre and John Hill and presents in of Robin Hod's recones."

All Saints' Church, Kingston upon Thames.

" 1508. For paynting a bannar for Robin-hode ... 3d."

" 1509. For Kendall for Robyn-hode's cotes ... 1s. 3d."

"   „   For 4 yerds of Kendall for Mayd Marian's huke [bodice] ... 3s. 4d."

" 1525. Payd for 6 yerds ¼ of satyn for Robyn hode's cotys ... 12s. 6d."

" 1525. For 3 ells of locram [a linen fabric] ... 1s. 6d."

"1537. 4 yerds of cloth for the fole's cote ... 2s. od."
" ,, 2 ells of worstede for Maid Maryan's kyrtle ... 6s. 8d."

St. Laurence's Church, Reading.

"1501-2. It. rec. of the May play called Roby hod on the fayre day ... 6s." [A fair has been long held at Reading on the 1st of May.]

"1504. Rec. of the gaderyng of the said Roby Hod, in money ... 49s."

"1531. It. for 5 ells of canvas for a cote for Made Marion ... 17d."

Town Warden's Accounts of Melton Mowbray, extract from the original MSS.: "1564-5. Recd, of John Downe the rest of Robin Hood's money ... 14s. 1d."

PADSTOW HOBBY HORSE

[*Cornwall*] If anything is certain in an uncertain world, it is that to-day, the 1st of May, 1936, the Hobby Horse will emerge from the Red Lion and bring " the Summer and the May " into every house and cottage of Padstow. In most parts, the Hobby Horse, so popular in the Middle Ages, is forgotten more completely even than in Shakespeare's time. On May Day, however, Padstow is faithful to his memory.

The rider is enveloped in a hoop-shaped frame covered with black tarpaulin. Convention dictates that this frame shall have a little horse's head in front but the monster's true head is the fantastic mask with baleful eyes, cruel beak, and tufts of fur which conceals the features of the one who happens to carry it. Above the mask is a tall, black and white dunce's cap, with a mysterious inscription " O.B." which, no doubt, is a simplified spelling of " Obby." Issuing from the low parlour of the Red Lion, the 'Oss is accompanied by the clubman or teazer, armed with a cardboard club, *see* Plate IX, a man dressed as a woman called " All Sorts," a sailor, and two musicians. With his head cocked on one side, the 'Oss dances a burlesque rigadoon with the clubman and then sets off round the town with his retinue. The narrow streets resound with the strains of the " Night Song,"

PLATE IX

THE PADSTOW HOBBY HORSE, WITH THE TEAZER

one of the loveliest tunes of English folk-song with words not unworthy of it :

> " Unite, unite, let us all unite,
>   For Summer is acome unto day [a-comin' in to-day].
> And whither we are going we will all unite
>   On the merry morning of May.
> The young men of Padstow, they might if they would,
>   For Summer is acome unto day.
> They might have built a ship and gilded her with gold,
>   On the merry morning of May.
> The maidens of Padstow, they might if they would,
>   For Summer is acome unto day.
> They might have made a garland of the white rose and the red,
>   On the merry morning of May."

With the curious and unexplained cry of " 'Oss, 'Oss, we 'Oss," the crowd incite the 'Oss to charge and he is not slow to respond to the challenge. Picking out a pretty girl, he corners her against a wall and, heedless of her shrieks, capes her, that is to say, turns his back, lifts his hood, and brings it down over her head. Within living memory, the inside of the hood was smeared with blacklead, which left its mark and brought good luck and a husband within the year.

At intervals, the tune changes to the slower and no less beautiful " Day Song," the words of which, unfortunately, have lost any sense they may once have had :

> " Oh, where is King George, oh where is he, oh?
>   He's down in his long boat, all on the salt sea, oh.
>   Up flies the kite, and down falls the lark.
>   There was an old woman, she had an old yow [ewe],
>   But she died in her own park, oh."

While this is being sung, the 'Oss sinks down as though expiring and the teazer pats him caressingly with his club. Then, with a sudden bound, he is on his feet again and dancing madly as the " Night Song " bursts out once more :

"Up Merry Spring, and up the merry ring,
For Summer is acome unto day.
How happy are those little birds that merrily do sing
On the merry morning of May."

All through the day, the 'Oss gambols through the town, capes the girls, and money is collected. After lunch a rival " horse " appears and, in the evening, the two dance round the maypole, each with his own teazer. This second horse is a recent innovation and makes up for features of the ceremony which have dropped out, such as, for example, the dawn procession to the woods and back with greenery, the blacking of the girls, the twelve little girls all in white who used to accompany the 'Oss, and his visit to Treator Pool, to drink, and his splashing, so curiously suggestive of rain-making magic.—Mr. Rodney Gallop. (*The Times*, 1st May, 1936, p. 19, *f.*)

The following tunes for the Night Song and the Day Song collected by Mr. Rodney Gallop have not been printed before, to the best of his knowledge. They are of great folk-lore interest.

At Padstow, on the 1st of May, at 11 a.m., the members of the company meet at the Red Lion and " carry out the Hoss." The company includes the Teaser, the Hoss, a man in a dress and bonnet, called " All Sorts," two or three other men in sailors' dress, and musicians. The Teaser dances in front of the Hoss, making graceful passes with his club. Occasionally, at one particular part of the Day Song, the Hoss squats down and the Teaser beside him; then children pat him and girls stroke him. At the correct line of an interpolated verse of the Night Song, the Hoss leaps up, both feet off the ground. He runs after women and girls, catches them under his cloak—his round body part—and pinches them. To one visitor he caught he said : " Don't be frightened ; it's very lucky."—1935. The company has not gone to Treator Pool since 1930. Girls, who should be in white, go in front and sing both Day and Night Songs and, when the Hoss runs about, they say softly " Hoss, hoss, we hoss," meaning " to we." (Violet Alford, October 18, 1937.)

May Day

Andante

U-nite, u-nite, let us all u-nite For Sum-mer is a-come un-to day And whi-ther we are go-ing ___ let us all u-nite on the mer-ry morn-ing of May.

Adagio rubato

Oh where is King George oh where is he oh? He's down in his long boat All on the salt sea oh Up flies the kite and down falls the lark There was an old wo-man she had an old yow But she died in her own park oh.

THE MINEHEAD HOBBY HORSE

[*Somerset*] On the 1st day of May, the Hobby Horse and his attendants still parade the streets of Minehead and Dunster. The frame of the Horse is made of pasteboard and is covered by streamers of coloured paper, imitating coloured ribbons; within it is a young man who makes it jump about in all directions. A ladle ornamented by a ribbon used to be, and still may be, stuck in its mouth for collecting money. A number of men and youths, dressed in gay costume, accompany the Horse and, at intervals, execute a dance. The Hobby Horse is much more ancient than the Morris dance, which was introduced into the May Games centuries ago. Before the introduction of the Morris, a king and a queen of May were elected and were two lads gaily dressed; they, perhaps, are represented by some of the characters that accompany the Hobby Horse at Minehead. (*History, etc., of Minehead*, Frederick Hancock, Taunton, 1903, p. 403.)

The following is a very brief account of what I learned at Minehead from the Hobby-horse man and his wife in 1935, and at the ceremony in the Albert Hall, at the International Folk Dance Festival, in the same year, when the Minehead company came up to London.

The Minehead Hobby Horse is called the " Sailors' Horse "; there is a " Town Horse," but the Sailors' is the proper one. It is covered entirely with scraps of ribbon and silk fabric, like a rag mat, *see* Plate X; no horse-head, but a cowtail beard, and a long rope for a tail. The man's head is in a high cap and his face is hidden under a painted tin mask. Six men form the company; they go out at six p.m. on 30th of April and all day on 1st of May. They used to catch women but now they catch men and lift them up by their arms and legs, while the Horse winds his tail round them and lashes them with it. Women in sunbonnets and clean aprons should go with them, but Mrs. Martin is the only one left. A charming traditional tune is played on an accordion. (Violet Alford, 18th October, 1937.)

PLATE X

THE MINEHEAD HOBBY HORSE

Fox Photos.

May Day

THE MILKMAID'S CUSTOM

It was customary, until the earlier years of the nineteenth century, for milkmaids to dress in their best attire on May-day morning and decorate their milk pails with ribbons, flowers and also silver and pewter articles, such as, for example, cups, dishes and tankards, borrowed from their customers. The pyramidal pile thus formed, called the " Milkmaid's Garland," was carried by the milkmaid on her head. She visited the houses of her customers and, accompanied by a fiddler, danced in order to obtain money. The custom was very popular, especially in London, and the gifts received ranged from small sums to half-guineas. In some cases, where the borrowed articles were heavy, a man acted as a carrier, with or without the aid of a barrow.

RECORDS OF THE CUSTOM

[*Devonshire*] May day is still celebrated in the west of England though not so gaily as it used to be some years ago, when I have heard my husband say that the milkmaids of Tavistock would borrow plate from the gentry to hang upon their milk pails, intermixed with bunches of ribbons and crowns of flowers.—9th June 1832. (*The Borders of the Tamar and the Tavy*, Anna Eliza Stothard, afterwards Bray, 1879, vol. 1, pp. 282-3.)

[*London*] The London milkmaids' custom seems to have been discontinued before the middle of the nineteenth century but, like the sweeps' May-day custom, showed much vitality before becoming evanescent.

On May day, the milkmaids who serve the Court danced minuets and rigadoons before the Royal Family, at St. James's, and were much applauded.—*Read's Weekly Journal*, 5th May, 1733. (*N. and Q.*, i, 3, 1851, p. 367.)

May 1st. I was looking out of the parlour window this morning and receiving the honours which Margery, the milkmaid to our lane, was doing me by dancing before my door with the plate of half her customers on her head.—*The Tatler* for 2nd May, 1710. (*N. and Q.*, i, 4, 1851, p. 73.)

The Merry Milkmaid. This is the title of a Plate, apparently of date 1685-8, M. Lauron, *del.*, representing a pretty and sprightly London milkmaid, Kate Smith, dancing with her milk pail on her head. The pail is shown with cups, tankards, porringers, and other articles of borrowed plate hung around it. She is dressed in a white hood, over which is a narrow-brimmed black hat. On each shoulder is a knot and she holds a white handkerchief in her right hand. (*A Biographical History of England*, Rev. J. Granger, 5th edition, 6 vols., vol. 6, 1824, p. 173.)

THE SWEEPS AND JACK-IN-THE-GREEN

May day was the chimney-sweeps' holiday. In holiday attire, with blackened faces, and adorned chiefly by ribbons and tinsel, they went along the streets, dancing and attracting attention by banging brushes and fire shovels. In the sweeps' procession was Jack-in-the-Bush, or -Green, a man carrying a framework covered by a thick mass of leaves secured to it so as to form a tall verdant pyramid or cone having an aperture through which Jack could see external objects and thus be enabled to dance freely with the rest of the company.

COUNTY RECORDS

[*Cheshire*] The sweeps of Boughton, a suburb of Chester, used to deck themselves in their holiday garb on the 1st of May and, adorned with ribbons, like Morris dancers, paraded the streets. (*Cheshire Sheaf*, vol. 1, Chester, 1880, p. 2.)

[*Devonshire*] Of late years maypoles have experienced some change; in former times they were often stationary but now we generally see only the verdant pyramid crowned with flowers. This pyramid joins the procession and sometimes the dance; it receives its motion from having concealed within it a good, stout fellow, strong and tall enough to perform the part for the day. Jack-in-the-Bush is his name and he has existed, so I am told, as long as the maypole itself.—June 9th, 1832. (*The Borders of the Tamar and the Tavy*, Anna Eliza Stothard, afterwards Bray, 1879, vol. 1, p. 283.)

[*Gloucestershire*] Last year, [1892], May day fell on a Sunday and the sweeps' display took place on 2nd of May at Cheltenham. The Bush or Green was an imposing structure, conical, and about six feet high. Three young men, respectively dressed in three different colours, red, blue and yellow, danced round the Bush; their faces were blackened and they wore caps made of flowers and leaves. There were also four others, serving as musicians and collectors, and a clown, dressed fantastically and wearing a top-hat having a loose, flapping crown.—W. H. D. Rouse. (*Folk-Lore*, vol. 4, 1893, pp. 50-4.)

May day, 1894, at Lewisham. In the High Street, at the inn near St. Mary's Church, we saw a Jack with a Queen of the May, two maidens-proper, one man dressed as a woman, and a man with a piano-organ. The organ was playing a quick tune and the Queen and the maidens danced round the Jack with a kind of " barn-dance " step, the Jack turning the other way. The man-woman sometimes danced with the maidens, turned wheels, and collected pence. The Jack was a bottle-shaped case covered with ivy leaves and surmounted by a crown of paper roses. The Queen wore a light-blue dress and had a crown similar to the Jack's. The senior maiden wore a red skirt and a black body; the junior wore a white dress; each wore a wreath of roses. The man-woman wore a holland dress and over it a short, sleeveless jacket; his face was blackened, and he had a Zulu hat trimmed with red, the brim being turned up. The man-proper [apparently the one with the piano-organ] wore dark grey gaiters (long ones), a dark suit with ribbons on it, and a grey night-cap, with red, blue and green ribbons; his face was blued all over. (Witnessed by Mr. Frank Lewis, who made notes carefully, as he had never seen anything of this kind before, and communicated the same to his cousin, Mr. Leland L. Duncan.)

[*London*] I happened to be going along South Audley Street about a fortnight ago whilst some chimney-sweeps were dancing before Lord Bute's door and beating time, as usual, with their shovels and brushes. This motley band was decked with all their May-day finery; heads covered with enormous periwigs, clothes laced with paper, and faces marked with chalk. After the dance they asked for a contribution; this was refused, the sweeps were very angry and, so it is said, joined the Opposition. (Printed cutting, marked *Whitehall Ev. Post*, 26 of May, 1763,

240   *Calendar Customs*

inserted between pp. 178 and 179 in Joseph Haslewood's copy of *Brand*, 1813 edition.)

To-day, almost the only followers of May sports are the poor chimney-sweepers, with their soot, shovels, brushes and finery. To them the first of May is still a gaudy day; they are now the sole lords of holiday, the only sporters and revellers in the spring. They are, indeed, splendid instances of gaiety. They have crowns, and garlands, and merry looks, and even pyramids of flowers. They come forth in the morning decked out in all the paraphernalia of their order, while their faces are of an indisputable black. This sombre colour is relieved by a liberal use of the brightest rouge and glitters with tinsel that might look becoming on the boards of our great theatres. Yet, we think that even the chimney-sweeps begin to feel the influence of the times. Yes, it is certainly so. (*Time's Telescope* for 1821, pp. 135-6.)

This being the first day of May, Mrs. Montague will give the annual entertainment of roast beef and plum pudding to the chimney-sweeps of London, in the court-yard of her house in Portman Square, in commemoration of discovering her child among them, long after it had been enticed away. (*The Times*, Wednesday, 1st May, 1799, p. 3, col. 4.)

[*Yorkshire*] For the last twenty years or more, thanks to Montgomery the poet and others, it has been customary to give the climbing-boys of Sheffield an annual dinner on the 1st of May. About twenty-five chimney-sweeps attended. (*Time's Telescope* for 1828, p. 108.)

DIPPY DAY

[*Cornwall, etc.*] On May day, the boys of many towns and villages in Cornwall and Devon used to parade the streets and exercise what they considered their right to throw water over those they met who were not wearing hawthorn in their hats or button-holes. The boys used all kinds of containers for the water, *e.g.* cans, buckets, or cows' horns. The day, 1st May, was called Dippy-day and sometimes Ducking-day. The celebration of the custom was not free from causing serious results.

[*Devonshire*] In the village of Loddiswell, May day is called

"Ducking day," from the custom observed, on that day, of throwing water at people who wore no hawthorn twigs or leaves. On May day, 1894, two boys threw a bucket of water at Dr. Twining as he was driving through the village; his horse bolted, he was thrown out and received fatal injuries. (*The Globe*, 18th May, 1894.)

MAY FIRES

The lighting of fires on May day was a common event in many parts of England, especially in the north, and this May-day custom was of very ancient origin. In Scotland on the 1st of May the herdsmen of every village held their Beltein, a rural sacrifice.

[*Cornwall, etc.*] In Cornwall and Devon May fires were long numbered among the sports of May, though I believe that they are quite forgotten in Devon.—9th June, 1832. (*The Borders of the Tamar and the Tavy*, Anna Eliza Stothard, afterwards Bray, 1879, vol. 1, p. 281.)

[*The Lake District*] In the Lake District May-day fires were lighted, especially before the middle of last century.

PROTECTION AGAINST WITCHES

[*Monmouthshire*] On May day it was the custom, and this custom still lingers, to put a cross, made of whitethorn or birch, above the house door and also above the stable door, to keep out the witches and their spells. I mentioned this to an old woman and she said: "Yes, my father used to do that and also put some May-tree twigs in each seed-bed to make null and void the witches' spells."—The Rev. T. A. Davies, Chepstow. (*South Wales Argus*, 10th March, 1928.)

PACK-RAG DAY

[*Lincolnshire*] This generic name denoted the day on which farm and sometimes domestic servants hired by the year packed or pagged up their clothes and other effects in a bundle ready for being carried away on the back, preparatory for spending a week at home or entering, at once, the service of a new employer. In Lincolnshire the said day was almost always Old May day. In Yorkshire the day was, in many cases, Martinmas, and in Norfolk, Old Michaelmas day.

MAY GESLINS

[*The Lake District*] The custom of making May geslins or goslings on the 1st of May still seems to be celebrated. Mr. Edward M. Wilson, Cambridge, says that a distinction between a May geslin and an April noddy, *see* p. 172, is that the May geslin has to look towards or for something that is not there. This distinction is still made in Crosthwaite and Windermere and seems to be general all over South Westmorland and North Lancashire. (Letter from Mr. Wilson, dated 7th November, 1936.)

DIVINATIONS

" Last May-day fair, I searched to find a snail
That might my secret lover's name reveal;
Upon a gooseberry bush a snail I found,
For always snails near sweetest fruit abound.
I seized the vermin; home I quickly sped
And on the hearth the milk-white embers spread.
Slow crawled the snail and, if I right can spell,
In the soft ashes marked a curious L.
O! may this wondrous omen lucky prove,
For L is found in Lubberkin and Love! "

(*The Shepherd's Week*, Thursday, John Gay, ll. 49-58.)

[*Cornwall*] At Madron Well, divination is performed on May morning by rustic maidens. Two pieces of straw about one inch long are crossed and transfixed with a pin. This, floated on the waters, elicits bubbles the number of which, carefully counted, denotes the years before the wedding day. (*Ancient and Holy Wells of Cornwall*, M. and L. Quiller Couch, 1894, p. 132.)

[*Northamptonshire, etc.*]

" Richard," she said and laugh'd, " the moon is new
And I will try if that old tale is true,

May Day

Which gossips tell, who say that if as soon
As anyone beholds the new May moon,
They o'er their eyes a silken kerchief fling
That has been slided through a wedding ring,
As many years as they shall single be,
As many moons they through that veil will see."

(*The Shepherd's Calendar*, John Clare, 1827, pp. 159-60.)

POPULAR SAYINGS AND BELIEFS

" The yellow-hammer drinks one or more drops of the Devil's blood on May morning." Influenced by this saying, boys used to destroy this bird's nest and its young.

" If the dew falls on May-day morning it foreshadows a good butter year." (*Weather Wisdom from January to December*, compiled by Wilfrid Allan, [1889], p. 28.)

[*Cornwall*] The youth or girl who, on May day, brought a frond of a lady fern (*Aplenium filix fœmina*, Bernh.) long enough to cover a cream-scalding pan was entitled to a dish of cream and was believed to have brought luck to the dairy.—West Cornwall as late as 1880. (MS. note, 13th July, 1912, from Redruth.)

[*Gloucestershire*] A Nailsworth lady says : " A friend of ours used always to bring us a spray of young beech leaves, for luck, on May day." (Miss J. B. Partridge.)

[*Shropshire*] " May flowers (marsh-marigolds) are very unlucky if brought into the house before the 1st of May." (*Folk-Lore of Shropshire*, Charlotte Sophia Burne, 1883, p. 253.)

FAIRS

In olden times there were many May-day fairs, some of which degenerated into boisterous revels and were suppressed. To-day there are important fairs at Reading, Stockport, Poole, Lancaster, Ludlow, Bridgnorth, Tenbury Wells and other places, on May day.

[*Shropshire*] A good deal of hiring is still done at Bridgnorth Mop, on the 1st of May; hiring goes on also at Ludlow, on the 1st of May, and those who are not suited go to Much Wenlock on the 12th or to Church Stretton on the 14th of May. (*Shropshire Folk-Lore*, Charlotte Sophia Burne, 1883, p. 461-3.)

244   *Calendar Customs*

[*Staffordshire, etc.*] A typed note, undated, from Mr. Nicholls to Miss C. S. Burne, reads: " Between Wolverhampton and Bridgnorth, on 1st May. This side Wolverhampton, *i.e.* Wednesfield and Walsall, at Christmas." This means that the custom was for servants to change their places of service, in the two districts indicated, on the 1st of May and at Christmas, respectively.

[*London*] Mayfair. Near Piccadilly, in a part of the area between Bond Street and Park Lane, was held a fair, distinguished for its revelry, from the time of Charles II to the end of the eighteenth century, when the fair was suppressed. The fair commenced on the 1st of May and continued for fifteen days, by Charter of James II.

March 6th, 1816. Fifty years have passed away since this place of amusement was at its height of attraction. The spot where the fair was held still retains the name Mayfair and exists in much the same state as at that period. The Market House consisted of two stories; the first story a long and cross aisle for butchers' shops and externally other shops, chiefly those connected with culinary operations; the second story served as a theatre, for use in fair time. Below the butchers' shops were toy sellers and gingerbread makers. At the present time, the Market House is in a deplorable state, some of its lower part being occupied by needy dealers in smallwares. In the areas about the Market buildings were booths for jugglers, prize-fighters, backsword and cudgel play, and wild beasts; those not under cover were mountebanks, fire-eaters, merry-go-rounds, ass races, bull-baiting, hasty-pudding eaters, and eel divers.

I was born and spent my youth near Piccadilly and well remember the Ducking Pond, used for the sport of hunting ducks by means of dogs; Charles II favoured this sport. Another feature was the Mountebank Stage, opposite the Three Jolly Butchers, now the King's Arms. Beheading the Puppets was a star turn; a shutter was fixed horizontally, a puppet bowed in acknowledging the justice of his fate, laid his head on the edge of the shutter, and was at once beheaded by another puppet, using an axe. There were the Strong Women and, finally, Tiddy Doll, a famous gingerbread maker who recommended his goods in a long song or speech in which " Tiddy Doll " occurred frequently. He was very successful in his business, dressed very stylishly, and was an adornment of the Mayfair of his time.—Mr. Carter, Antiquary. (*Gentleman's Magazine*, vol. 86, January to June, 1816, pp. 228-30.)

2nd May

This is the Eve of the Invention of the Cross and is associated with the popular belief that branches and twigs collected on this day from the mountain ash, rowan or witchen tree are protective against the evil influences of witches and others.

PROTECTION AGAINST EVIL INFLUENCES

I have seen a twig of rowan tree, witchwood, or mountain ash, which had been gathered on the 2nd of May, wound round with dozens of yards of " reed threed," *i.e.* red thread, placed visibly in the window, as a protection against the influence of witches and boggleboes. (*Denham Tracts*, vol. 2, 1895, p. 83.)

In Cleveland, on the 2nd of May, which is Rowan-tree day or Rowan-tree Witch-day, the method of procedure is for a member of the family to go first thing in the morning and proceed until some rowan tree, not known of before, is met with by chance. The return home, after cutting branches from this tree, is made by a route quite different from that followed before. Finally, twigs cut or broken from the branches carried home are stuck over every door of every house in the homestead, and left there till they fall away. (*Glossary of the Cleveland Dialect*, Rev. J. C. Atkinson, 1868, p. 417.)

HURLING MATCHES, CORNWALL

[*Cornwall*] These matches, in which cork and other light balls, sometimes silvered, were employed, were commonly played in the spring, at many places, such as, for example, Truro, St. Ives and Helston.

At Helston, the residents of two of its streets play against the residents of the other streets, on the 2nd of May, when the boundaries of the town are perambulated. (*Old English Customs extant at the Present Time*, P. H. Ditchfield, 1896, p. 58; see also vol. 1, 1936, pp. 1-2.)

The Day of the Invention of the Holy Cross
3rd May

This day commemorates the Invention of the Cross, in which St. Helena, mother of Constantine the Great, is said to have taken a memorable part. The day is sometimes called St. Helena's day, because of her alleged participation in the search; it should be borne in mind, however, that the day of St. Helen is the 18th of August.

STINGING-NETTLE CUSTOM

[*Devonshire*] A curious and very old custom is celebrated annually by the children of Bovey Tracey. On the 3rd of May this year, 1880, W. B., Esq., was passing through the village and noticed that all the children carried nettles and were flogging one another with them. The custom used to be prevalent at North Tawton. (*Trans. Devon Assoc.*, vol. 12, 1880, p. 105.) At Torquay, Bovey Tracey and other places in Devonshire, the 3rd of May was called " Sting-nettle day."

MAYOR'S MONDAY, BOVEY TRACEY

[*Devonshire*] This, the first Monday after the 3rd of May, was duly celebrated at Bovey Tracey yesterday. Time was when the day was observed with greater enthusiasm than now, when the inhabitants of Bovey, almost to a man, joined in the procession, headed by a band of music, and took part in beating the bounds of the Parish. Yesterday, the mayor-elect and about forty freeholders drove round the outskirts of the Parish, inducing " colts " to kiss the magic stone, pledging allegiance in upholding ancient rights and privileges, and dining together at the Dolphin Hotel. (*Plymouth Daily Mercury*, 9th May, 1882.)

FAIRS

[*Essex*] An annual fair of seven days' duration was granted to the Abbot and monks of Waltham Abbey during the reign of

Henry III. This fair, even in Dr. Fuller's time, had been divided into two fairs of shorter duration, one held on the 3rd of May and the other on the 14th of September. (*The Parish of Waltham Abbey*, John Maynard, 1865, p. 21.)

Old St. George's Day
4th May

[*Devonshire*] The important St. George's Fair held at Modbury is described on p. 182. The fair had all the ceremonies pertaining to fairs, the proclamation, the bush serving as a licence, the court of piepowder, the raising of the glove. For a few years after the change in the calendar, the fair continued to be held on St. George's day but, by common consent, was held on Old St. George's day, the 4th of May.

8th May

HELSTON FURRY DANCE

At Helston, this day is devoted to dancing and pleasure and the chief ceremony of the day is an old Celtic dance called the " Furry." During a long series of years changes have taken place in the proceedings, but the essential features of the Furry remain. The dancing-floor is furnished by the streets of the town and the floors of its houses and, in a full execution of the dance, its performers would traverse a few miles. A procession is formed by a number of couples, *e.g.* thirty, each of a lady and a gentleman, who dance and execute pirouette-like movements, at the same time progressing along the streets and through the houses. The procession is headed by a brass band playing the Furry Dance tune. The traverse ends at the Angel Inn, which is of great renown because a legend relates how the Archangel Michael, Patron of Helston, met the Devil carrying a stone from Hell, and enforced him to drop the stone, which happened to fall in the premises of the Angel Inn.

[*Cornwall*] The 8th of May is called " Furry day," supposed to be Flora's day, not in respect of the goddess but from the garlands commonly worn on that day. Very early in the morning some troublesome rogues go round the streets with drums, disturbing their neighbours and singing parts of a song the whole of which nobody recollects and of which I only know that there is mention in it of the " Grey Goose Quill " and of going to the greenwood to bring home the summer and the May, and, accordingly, hawthorn flowering-branches are worn in the hats. The people make it a general holiday and anyone found working is carried on a pole to a wide part of the river, where he must attempt to leap across the river or pay a fine in money. About 9 a.m., they [the people, including the rogues aforesaid] appear before the school and demand a holiday for the Latin boys; this is always granted; then they collect money from house to house. About noon, they assemble and dance hand in hand round the streets, accompanied by a fiddler, and thus continue till it is dark; this is called a " Faddy." In the afternoon, the local gentry go to some farmhouse and have tea, sillabub and other refreshments, and then return in a Morris dance to the town and dance throughout the streets till it is dark, claiming a right to go through any person's house, in at one door and out at another. Here it used to end, but corruptions have crept in, by degrees, for the gentlemen now conduct their partners, elegantly dressed in white muslins, to the ballroom [at the Angel], where they finish their dance and, after supper, faddy it to their respective homes. (*Gentleman's Magazine*, vol. 60, part 1, 1790, p. 520.)

That " Furry " is a corruption of " Flora " is a vulgar error; I scruple not to deduce " furry " from the old Cornish word " fer " = a fair or jubilee. At Helston,[1] the 8th of May is ushered in, very early in the morning, by the sounds from drums and kettles. It is a general holiday, strictly kept. The morning revellers, after demanding a holiday for the schoolboys and collecting from house to house, fade[2] into the country and, about noon, return with flowers and oak branches in their caps and hats and complete their furry dance. In the afternoon, the local gentry,

---

[1] The Furry of the Lizard was formerly held in May, and in the Isle of Man there are May games on the 12th of May answering to the Furry.

[2] Fade, an old English word = go.

8th May

after their return to the town from some farm-house, danced through the streets in accordance with custom but, at present, a select party only make their progress through the streets very late in the evening and quickly vanish from the view, re-appearing in the ballroom [at the Angel], where they meet their friends and complete the dance. The following are a few lines from the Furry Song :

> " Ro-bin—Hood—and—lit-tle John
> They—both—are—gone—to—Fair—O—
> And we—will to—the merry—green wood
> To see—what they—do—there—O—
> And—for—to—chase—O—
> To chase—the Buck—and—Doe
>   With—Ha—lan—tow
>   Jolly rumble—O.
>
> And we—were up as soon—as a-ny Day—O—
>   And for—to fetch—the Sum-mer—home.
> The Sum-mer—and—the—May—O—
> For Sum-mer—is—a—come—O—
> And Win-ter—is—a—go—O—
>   With—Ha—lan—tow, etc.
>
> Where—are—those—Spani-ards
> That make—so great—a—Boast—O—
> They shall eat—the Grey—Goose—Feather
> And we—will eat—the Roast—O—
>   In—ev-ry—Land—O—
>   The Land—that ere—we—go—
>   With—Ha—lan—tow, etc."

(*The History of Cornwall, Civil, Military, etc.*, Rev. R. Polwhele, 7 vols., vol. 1, 1816, pp. 41-6.)

An interesting description by Mr. Quin appeared in his paper, *The Royal Cornwall Gazette*, 13th May, 1864 : " Major Grylls led off with Miss Charlotte Grylls. In all there were forty-one couples. During the first part of the tune, they tripped on in couples, forming a long string, the gentleman leading his partner with his right hand. At the second part of the tune, the first gentleman turns, with both hands, the lady behind, and her partner turns the same way with the first lady; then each gentleman in the same manner with his own partner; then they trip on as before, each part of the tune being repeated. The other couples pair and turn in the same way and at the same time." The dance terminated in the Assembly Room at the Angel. (*Bygone Days in Devon and Cornwall*, Mrs. Henry Pennell Whitcombe, 1874, pp. 158-64.)

The Furry or Flora day, at Helston, was kept up on Monday, 9th May, 1881, instead of the 8th, which fell on the Sunday. The dancing through the streets was confined this year to one class only, the gentry. In former times, even within living memory, there were four or even five parties of dancers, *e.g.* the gentry, the tradesmen, the servants, etc. At 1 p.m. the dancers left the Market-house. The band played the Furry tune throughout the dance; it is a quaint, lively tune. There were fifteen couples; the band preceded them everywhere but the men carrying flags usually stopped outside the houses. Arriving at the Bowling Green, the couples danced round it, by ancient custom, and then proceeded to the Angel, where the usual ball was held. (*The Antiquary*, vol. 3, 1881, pp. 284-5.)

The tradesmen's procession or faddy used to take place, annually, in the morning, apparently about 11 a.m.

Early in the morning of the 8th of May or Flora day, at Helston, the Volunteer Band goes about the town playing, in slow time, the quaint old hornpipe tune; the Band is followed by a crowd of men and boys. Later in the morning, carriages and brakes arrive in crowds; booths are erected near the footways, and sweets are piled up in quantity large enough to give happy moments to all the boys and girls in western Cornwall. In the meadows, by the river, a circus tent is being erected as fast as the crowds of children will permit and, in due time, the circus procession passes through the town, members of the troupe impersonating a selection of English monarchs. The crowd, a few thousands strong, includes farmers, farm and other labourers, servant girls in new straw-hats and bright pink bodices, countless boys and girls, and a party of sailors from the *Ganges*. The

10*th May*

town is dressed with garlands, strings of flags, and green boughs. At about 1 p.m., preceded by the Band, a procession of gaily dressed ladies, and gentlemen wearing top-hats, leaves the Corn Market and commences the time-honoured dance. The fun and excitement during the proceedings was well supported by the party from the *Ganges*. (*Highways and Byways in Devon and Cornwall*, Arthur H. Norway, 1897, pp. 84-6.)

For the first time since the War broke out, Helston celebrated the ancient custom of the Furry Dance. Couples danced through the streets and, if the doors were open, in and out of the houses. (*The Daily Graphic*, 10th May, 1919.)

10*th May*

[*Cambridgeshire, etc.*] In olden times, dotterels were often killed in falconry. The 10th of May was specially devoted to this sport and was known on the borders of Cambridgeshire and Hertfordshire as " Dotterel's day." (*Trans. Herts. Nat. Hist. Society*, vol. 3, 1884, p. 84.)

12*th May*

The gunners on Breydon water are accustomed to call this day " Godwit day," because then the godwits begin to move southwards. (*Folk-Lore of British Birds*, Rev. Charles Swainson, 1886, p. 199.)

13*th May*

[*Dorset*] At Abbotsbury, on the 13th of May, locally known as " Garland day," the children go round the village with large garlands of flowers. After they have called on all the inhabitants, they proceed to the beach. The garlands are placed in boats, taken out to sea, brought back again, and taken to the church. Of old, the boats, each with a garland, put off from the shore, and every floral offering was placed on the waves, in the firm belief that it would bring luck to the mackerel fishing. (*Sir Benjamin Stone's Pictures*, vol. 1, 1905, pp. 70-1.)

[*Derbyshire*] On the 13th of May, the miners dress their coves or cowes (the places in which they deposit the ore) with oak branches, garlands and other rural decorations. This is called the "miners' holiday." A dinner of beef, pudding and ale is provided on the occasion and, when the weather is favourable, the festivities are conducted in the open air. The Bar-masters preside and music and old songs conclude the proceedings. (*The History and Gazetteer of the County of Derby*, Stephen Glover, 2 vols., vol. 1, Derby, 1831, p. 261.)

14th May

[*Monmouthshire*] There is a fair in Abergavenny, on the 14th of May, and one on the first Monday in May, in Monmouth. These are hiring fairs but very few girls go to them now. The custom seems to be dying out. (Author's cuttings, undated.) A fair on the 14th of May is still held at Abergavenny.

[*Shropshire*] Another ancient "rite of May" was Well-dressing, but I have notes of only one case, in Shropshire, in which the ceremony was observed on a fixed day of the month of May and had not been transferred to some church festival, *viz.* the case of the roadside well at Betchcot. This was dressed with flowers, within the memory of, at any rate, one old man of the place, on the 14th of May, up to about the year 1810. (*Shropshire Folk-Lore*, Charlotte Sophia Burne, 1883, p. 414.)

[*Wiltshire*] A festival used to be held at Poulton, near Marlborough, on the 14th of May, and was attended by people from the town; known as "Jacky John's Fair," formerly "Johnny Jack's," gingerbread was its important commodity. Johnny Jack, a confectioner in Marlborough, used to wear a gilded gingerbread hat, parading the streets and shouting a word which sounded like "Pannamahoi." A crowd would then collect and follow him to Poulton. Arriving there, Johnny Jack proceeded to a sycamore tree that grew near the river, and then threw up his hat, which crashed on the ground and broke into pieces, for which the crowd scrambled. A revel followed; oranges were thrown into the river and were scrambled for by the children, who then threaded the needle into Marlborough. For some years after the fair was discontinued, children went to the old spot near the sycamore tree, on 14th May, and threaded the needle into Marlborough. (*Folk-Lore*, vol. 20, 1909, pp. 81-2.)

16th May

[*Norfolk*] In the Parish of Rockland, on the 16th of May, annually, a country fair is held and called the " Guild," evidently a relic of the Guild of John the Baptist held here in St. Peter's Church before the Reformation. A mock mayor of the Guild is elected and chaired about the three parishes of Rockland to obtain donations to spend on a revel. The occupiers of some of the houses enjoy the privilege of hanging oaken boughs over their doors to indicate that they can supply home-brewed ale during the day of the fair. These houses are called " bough houses," just as similar houses in Pershore are called " bush houses."—Rockland's Rectory. (*N. and Q.*, ii, 7, 1859, p. 450.)

18th May

[*Somerset*] Yeovil Fair always began with the blowing of a horn at 4 a.m. There was no special horn and no special blower, so far as is known now. Brandy snaps were always a great feature. (Miss Mayo, Yeovil, to Miss J. B. Partridge.)

St. Frankin's Days

19th, 20th and 21st May

[*Devonshire*] In the Taw valley, at Eggesford, Burrington and other places, there is a saying that the 19th, 20th and 21st of May, or three days near that time, are Francimass or St. Frankin's days and that then comes on a frost very injurious to the blossom of apple trees. The popular belief is that the occurrence of destructive frosts at this time of year is the result of a conspiracy arranged by the Devil and a certain brewer or brewers. According to one version, a brewer named Frankin, who found that cider was running his ale very hard, vowed his soul to the Devil on condition that the latter would send three frosts in May, annually, and thus cut off the apple blossom. Another version is that the brewers of North Devon agreed to put deleterious matter into their ale provided the Devil would kill the apple blossom year by year.—Told me at Chawleigh and at Burrington,

August 1894, S. Baring-Gould. (*Trans. Devon. Assoc.*, vol. 27, Plymouth, 1895, p. 64.)

27th May

[*Lancashire*] At Chipping, near Clitheroe, a mock mayor used to be and may still be elected. On the 27th of May, 1881, in accordance with an old custom, the villagers put a man, suitably intoxicated, in a chair on a cart and dragged it through the village amid great uproar. Those who formed the procession carried mops, firearms and sticks, decorated in different colours. Two intoxicated men, playing cornopeans, headed the procession. The police intervened and arrested ten of the men, who were tried and acquitted, one of the justices saying that he approved of old customs being celebrated. (*The Antiquary*, vol. 4, 1881, p. 80.)

Oak-apple Day

29th May

This day is the anniversary of Charles II's entry, amid great rejoicings, into Whitehall in the year 1660; on this account, the day is believed by many to commemorate the Restoration but it is probably best-known as Oak-apple day, commemorating Charles's adventure in the famous oak tree at Boscobel, early in September, 1651. The custom of wearing, on the 29th of May, oak branches, twigs and leaves and also oak galls or apples, when these were obtainable, became very popular. Most of this popularity was lost before the year 1880. There were, however, celebrations of the custom during the ensuing forty years, the latest authentic record known to me being dated 1919; *see* p. 260.

THE WEARING OF THE OAK

In the celebration of this distinctive custom, twigs and leaves of the oak and oak apples were worn in button-holes, hats, caps and other articles of personal wear or were carried in the hand. The custom used to be celebrated, annually, in not less than twenty-nine counties, *viz.* Hampshire, Berkshire, Buckinghamshire, Northamptonshire, Lincolnshire and the counties to the west or north of these, and also Suffolk. The inclusion of Buckinghamshire in this list depends on one definite record; *see* below. For Suffolk, there are several records stating that, on the 29th of May, men and boys wore oak apples in their hats.

The duration of the celebration of the custom was regulated by a 12 o'clock rule, similar to the 12 o'clock rule applied on the 1st of April.

The proceedings for obtaining branches, twigs, leaves and oak apples for use on the 29th of May were initiated chiefly as modifications of the May-day custom of Going-a-Maying. There were differences: the most valued find on May day was hawthorn blossom, on the 29th it was an oak apple; the Mayers went into the fields, hedgerows and woods, starting at about 12-30 a.m., the prospective wearers of the oak rarely left their beds before 5 a.m.; the time of the Mayers was spent in revelling, whistling, singing, dancing and blowing cows' horns, but the searchers for the oak spent their time chopping and sawing, ruining many fine trees and also the tempers of the owners.

COUNTY RECORDS

[*Berkshire*] Oak leaves are worn in the button-hole up to twelve noon; afterwards, the oak leaves are discarded and ash leaves are worn until sunset. (*A Glossary of Berkshire Words and Phrases*, Maj. B. Lowsley, Eng. Dial. Soc., 1888, p. 145.)

[*Buckinghamshire*] Eton, 1845. Yesterday being the 29th, we had a whole holiday and every boy who has not a sprig of oak with him has a pinch. These pinches are no common ones; they hurt pretty well and a kick is generally administered with it.—Letter of Alfred Lyall to his mother. (*Life of Sir Alfred Lyall*, Sir Mortimer Durand, 1913, p. 10.)

[*Cheshire*] I was travelling from Crewe to Runcorn on the 29th of May. There were six girls in the carriage with me, all wearing oak leaves and two of them carrying bunches of nettles. On being asked what the nettles were for, they said: "To beat those who have no oak." (*Bye-Gones relating to Wales and the Border Counties*, Oswestry and Wrexham, 1889-90, p. 169.)

[*Cumberland*] The custom of wearing oak leaves on the 29th of May still flourishes among the schoolboys and I saw one little boy being heartily kicked by a schoolfellow, in accordance with the custom. (Oral information from Miss M. Fox, 1916.)

[*Derbyshire*] In Derbyshire, it is still the custom for boys to wear sprigs of oak in their hats or button-holes ; boys not wearing the oak are stung with nettles. (*Old Church Lore*, William Andrews, Hull, 1891, p. 179.)

[*Devonshire*] At Tavistock, the 29th of May is still a holiday much observed, though far less than it used to be some years ago. A notion prevailed that, on that day, any person might cut oak boughs, wherever he pleased, provided it was done before 6 a.m. —8th January, 1833. (*The Borders of the Tamar and the Tavy*, Anna Eliza Stothard, afterwards Bray, vol. 2, 1879, p. 121.)

At Tiverton, in the year 1810, the 29th was as complete a holiday as it could ever have been in any part of England. At early dawn, the town was awakened by the furious clanging of church bells. The people arose, dressed hastily and went forth into the neighbouring woods and hedgerows to cut the oak. Everybody wore twigs of oak and an oak apple. Oak apples had been collected for many days before the 29th and were then gilded. (*Early Associations of Archbishop Temple*, F. J. Snell, 1904, pp. 206-7.)

At Exeter, boys and girls wore gilded oak apples and leaves on the 29th of May. (*Reminiscences of Exeter Fifty Years Since*, James Cossins, 2nd edition, Exeter, 1878, p. 34.)

On taking a seat in a railway carriage at Torre, Torquay, on the 29th of May, 1880, I remarked to my fellow-passengers, all residents of Torquay, " I see there are many people wearing oak leaves to-day." I was informed that this was the custom and that stinging-nettles were carried to sting those who do not wear the oak.—W. Pengelly. (*Trans. Devon. Assoc.*, vol. 12, Plymouth, 1880, p. 108.)

[*Dorset*] The boys of Lyme Regis continue to gild their oak apples and apply an opprobrious epithet to those who do not wear the oak or who continue to do so after twelve noon. (*The History and Antiquities of Lyme Regis and Charmouth*, George Roberts, 1834, p. 257.)

[*Gloucestershire*] Until some thirty years ago, Minchinhampton people used to gather boughs of oak, with oak apples, which they covered with gold leaf. At Randwick, oak leaves or oak apples are worn on Shick-shack day, or May 29th. (*Folk-Lore*, vol. 23, 1912, p. 451.)

[*Hampshire*] In my native village in the south country, the schoolboys and some of the villagers wore oak leaves and, occasionally, oak apples. Anybody who did not wear the oak was bonnetted or pinched and called a Shuck-shack.—West Neon. (*Church Times*, vol. for 1891, p. 223.)

In Hampshire, the wearing of the oak on Shick-shack day, or the 29th of May, is observed and those who do not wear the oak are liable to the drenching which, in Devon, belongs to the 1st of May. (*Folk-Lore*, vol. 22, 1911, p. 298.)

[*Herefordshire*] Formerly, every person, old or young, male or female, wore a sprig of oak and anyone not wearing oak was liable to be pelted with wild birds' eggs, especially the eggs of blackbirds and thrushes. (*The Folk-Lore of Herefordshire*, Ella Mary Leather, Hereford, 1912, p. 193.)

[*Lancashire, etc.*] In my boyhood's days it was considered wicked not to have a bit of oak in one's cap on Royal Oak day, and the neglect of it rendered one liable to be pinched, nettled or sodded. Every child knew that it was worn to show that the oak was in full leaf on that day, so as to hide the King from the men who wished to kill him. (*Folk-Lore: Old Customs and Tales of my Neighbours*, Fletcher Moss, Didsbury and Manchester, March, 1898, p. 45.)

[*Lincolnshire*] At Grantham, on the 29th of May, called "Nettle day," the oak was worn generally; those who did not wear it were liable to be stung by nettles. (*County Folk-Lore*, vol. 5, *Lincolnshire*, Mrs. Gutch and Mabel Peacock, 1908, p. 205.)

[*Northamptonshire*] The Blue Coat boys and the Orange School boys, at Northampton, used to celebrate Oak-apple day by attending church in new clothes, with gilded oak-apples and oak leaves in their button-holes. (*Northamptonshire Notes and Queries*, vol. 4, Northampton, 1892, p. 264.)

[*Northumberland*] On Royal Oak day, at Newcastle and other

towns, it was customary to wear oak leaves on hats. (*A Glossary of North Country Words*, John Trotter Brockett, Newcastle upon Tyne, 1825, p. 178.)

[*Nottinghamshire*] A custom, now dying out, is celebrated in Nottinghamshire on the 29th of May. Children wear twigs of oak and carry nettles for stinging those who do not wear them; then a sprig of oak is given to prevent further molestation. Dog oak (maple) is sometimes worn, but if this is detected the punishment is more severe. In the northern parts of the county, hens' eggs kept for a long time were used for pelting those not wearing the oak, but the eggs of small wild birds have been used lately. (*Nottinghamshire Facts and Fictions*, collected and edited by John Potter Briscoe, Principal Librarian, Nottingham Free Library, 2nd edition, 1876, pp. 10-11.)

[*Oxfordshire*] The Rev. Gascoigne Mackie, who was at Magdalen College School, 1876-82, tells me that Royal Oak day was kept with great vivacity at the school. To wear oak was compulsory and to neglect to comply entailed merciless persecution.—A. R. Bayley, Malvern. (*N. and Q.*, x, 7, 1907, p. 306.)

[*Shropshire*] Until only four or five years ago, men and boys in the Parish of Weston Rhyn wore sprigs of oak in their hats on the 29th of May. (*Bye-Gones relating to Wales and the Border Counties*, Oswestry and Wrexham, 1899-1900, p. 404.)

Among the boys of Oswestry Grammar School, it is a custom to wear oak balls and to carry nettles. I have been stung frequently for not wearing the oak ball, but a boy could not be nettled after twelve noon. To wear oak leaves was not considered to be sufficient protection. (*Bye-Gones relating to Wales and the Border Counties*, 17th July, 1889, pp. 172-3.)

[*Somerset*] Oak-apple day is sometimes called " Oaken-bough day." Farm boys stick sprays of oak, with oak-apples if procurable, in their hats. (*West Somerset Word-Book*, Frederic Thomas Elworthy, Eng. Dial. Soc., 1886, p. 528.)

In this part of Somerset, the village children substitute ash or maple for oak, in the afternoon of the 29th.—Ethelbert Horne, Downside Abbey, Bath. (*N. and Q.*, xi, 10, 1914, p. 7.) Similarly, in Berkshire and Oxfordshire, oak was worn in the morning and ash in the afternoon.

[*Staffordshire*] It is the custom for boys and girls to wear a piece of oak until twelve o'clock; those who omit to do so are stung with nettles.—Stone. (*Notes on the Folk-Lore of North Staffordshire*, [W.] Wells Bladen, p. 29.)

The 29th of May is kept, at Hanbury, by wearing oak balls. Those who have no oak balls are nettled. (Mrs. Copestake, who has lived forty years at Bulls Park, on the Forest Banks, 27th May, 1892.)

[*Suffolk*] In Suffolk, the 29th is called Oaken-apple day, on which boys wear oak apples in their hats in commemoration of Charles's adventure at Boscobel. (*A Dictionary of Archaic and Provincial Words*, James Orchard Halliwell, 2nd edition, 2 vols., vol. 2, 1850, p. 584.)

[*Warwickshire*] In Warwickshire, it is the custom to wear an oak ball in the hat or button-hole on "Oak-ball day." (*A Warwickshire Word Book*, G. F. Northall, 1896, p. 161.)

[*Worcestershire*] Thirty years ago, boys and girls wore sprigs of oak or oak apples on the 29th of May. I have worn it myself many a time. Anyone failing to wear oak was pinched.—Alvechurch. (Miss J. B. Partridge.)

At Worcester, until recent times, oak leaves were religiously taken to school. Woe betide the boy who could not show his oak on the 29th of May. (*The Trans. of the Worcestershire Naturalists' Club*, vol. 5, Worcester, 1913, p. 219.)

Gilded oak apples were in great favour at Upton-on-Severn and the custom of wearing the oak was observed rigidly at Malvern.

At Clent, the 29th of May was a greater festival than May day itself. On that day, everybody wore oak apples. (*A Short History of Clent*, John Amphlett, 1890, p. 165.)

[*Yorkshire*] At Northallerton, on the 29th of May, children who were found to be without sprigs of oak were pelted with eggs. The custom was kept up later than the year 1850. (*Church Times*, 27th April, 1900.)

Royal Oak day is still celebrated at Masham by the boys

decking themselves with leaves of the oak. Formerly, the bells were rung. (*The History and Antiquities of Masham*, John Fisher, 1865, p. 464.)

Towards the end of the nineteenth century, children all wore the oak and obtained a holiday.—Richmond. (Miss J. B. Partridge, from Mrs. Day.)

During the days of spring, boys collect the eggs of wild birds, hens and ducks to be kept for use on the 29th of May, in mobbing or pelting those who do not wear the oak. (*Folk-Lore of East Yorkshire*, John Nicholson, 1890, p. 14.)

I was presented, at breakfast, with a piece of oak branch with leaves on it to wear in honour of Royal Oak day and for fear I should get nettled. Some of the school children ran about with nettles tied on a stick to nettle people who had no oak.—At Carlton in Cleveland. (Letter to Miss C. S. Burne from Miss M. Marwood dated 29th May, 1919.)

There is a custom of patching, on the 29th of May. To patch = to pelt with eggs those who have not a sprig of oak about them. (*County F.-L.*, vol. 6, *East Yorkshire*, Mrs. Gutch, 1912, p. 97.)

Children carrying an oak twig in their hand, on the morning of the 29th or Rump day, repeat :

" Rump a dump day,
Twenty-ninth of May.
Show your rump
Or else I bump."

This threat is carried out by belabouring any other child who is without an oak branch or sprig. (*The History of Honley*, Mary A. Jagger, Huddersfield, 1914, p. 134.)

Royal Oak day was observed by the carrying about of sprigs of oak, generally worn in the hat or cap. (*Morley : Ancient and Modern*, William Smith, 1886, p. 143.)

DECORATING CHURCHES AND HOUSES

The customs of the 29th of May described in the preceding section were dominated by the use of oak apples, oak leaves and twigs, which became, in effect, personal decorations and visible signs of the celebration of a comparatively homogeneous series of

Oak-apple Day

customs. Our ancestors, however, initiated the celebration of a very complicated series of customs for the use of oak, in its various forms, in decorating inanimate objects ranging from church towers to doors, windows and mantelpieces of private houses. In recent times, locomotives and other railway stock have been added to the list. These recent extensions of the custom of decorating inanimate objects on the 29th of May will be considered independently.

COUNTY RECORDS

[*Buckinghamshire*] At Edlesborough, it is the custom to attach an oak bough to the flagstaff on the church tower on Oak-apple day. (*Old English Customs extant at the Present Time*, P. H. Ditchfield, 1896, p. 120.)

[*Cheshire*] In Cheshire, church towers sported their big boughs of oak on the 29th of May. (*Folk-Lore: Old Customs and Tales of my Neighbours*, Fletcher Moss, Didsbury and Manchester, March, 1898, p. 45.)

[*Herefordshire*] At Kingsland, Herefordshire, an octogenarian told me that there used to be great doings there on the 29th, and added " we used to climb up and put a great bough of oak on the church tower." (*The Folk-Lore of Herefordshire*, Ella Mary Leather, Hereford, 1912, p. 102.)

[*Staffordshire*] In Staffordshire, church towers sported their big boughs of oak. (Fletcher Moss, in work and page cited above.)

[*Wiltshire*] The following story is told me about Wishford in Wiltshire. An oak bough is cut, annually, on May the 29th and hauled down into the village. It is then decked with ribbons and hung from the church tower, and the day is kept as a revel. It gives the villagers the right of getting dead wood from Grovely Wood.—1896, John U. Powell. (*Folk-Lore*, vol. 12, 1901, p. 76.)

[*Worcestershire*] At Alvechurch, a big branch of oak was set up on the church tower. This is remembered by old people only. (Miss J. B. Partridge.)

At Clent, it was customary to hoist an exceptionally large oak branch, or several branches, to the top of the church tower, and the marks on the stone caused during the strenuous hauling operations were visible for many years after the cessation of the custom in the later part of last century.

[*Devonshire*] At Tiverton, when Whit Sunday happened to fall on the 29th of May, it was the custom, in decorating churches, to add garlands of oak to the usual birch and floral decorations used for Whit Sunday. (*Early Associations of Archbishop Temple*, F. J. Snell, 1904, p. 206.)

This record for Tiverton suggests that there was a discussion between Cavalier and Puritan, followed by a compromise for settling the form of the custom.

[*Hampshire*] At Upton Grey, Hampshire, the church bells are rung at 6 a.m. and, after this, the ringers place a large branch of oak over the church porch and another large branch over the lych-gate and smaller ones in the gateway of every house in the village. By this means, it is supposed that good luck for the year is assured. (*The Saga Book of the Viking Club*, vol. 3, p. 45.)

[*Northamptonshire*] The statue of Charles II on the portico of All Saints' Church, Northampton, is always enveloped in oak boughs on the 29th of May. (*A Glossary of Northamptonshire Words and Phrases*, Anne Baker, 2 vols., vol. 2, 1854, pp. 68-9.)

We have next to deal with the customs of the 29th of May in which parts of houses and cottages, external and internal, were decorated with oak boughs and leaves and oak apples. The records of these customs are very numerous, but an analysis of the most definite and reliable gives the following results.

[*Essex, etc.*] At Newport, Essex, the church bells are rung at 5-30 a.m., after which the ringers place a branch of oak on every door-step in the village. Later in the day they call for donations. At Basingstoke, Hampshire, working men arise early on the 29th to gather slips of oak and oak apples. Some of these they attach to the knockers, latches or other parts of the doors of the larger houses in view of receiving donations later. At Grantham, Lincolnshire, oak branches were fixed to the hasps which secured the shutters of the cottages to the wall (1878). Branches of oak, with oak apples, were set up in the home at Minchinhampton, Gloucestershire; the oak apples were gilded. In Suffolk, oak leaves and an oak apple, sometimes gilded, were exhibited in the front window and on the mantelpiece. At Exeter, it was customary for tradesmen to decorate their windows and doors with oak. Generally, and in many towns and villages, branches and leaves of the oak and, where they could be procured, oak apples, were attached to or near the doors and windows of houses and cottages, *e.g.* at Bromyard; Shrewsbury; Worcester, Alvechurch and Upton-on-Severn; Gloucester and Bristol; Lyme Regis; Tiverton and Tavistock; Northampton; and also in Derbyshire, Somerset and Warwickshire.

DECORATING HORSES

The custom of decorating horses' harness, especially their bridles, with oak branches, leaves and oak apples, on the 29th of May, used to be very popular in Bromyard, Kingsland, and almost every town and village in Herefordshire. The custom was also popular in Newton; Shrewsbury; Bath and Taunton; Bristol, Worcester and Dudley; Morley, Newcastle and many other places in the north.

DECORATING RAILWAY STOCK

[*Lancashire, etc.*] Five or six years ago, many locomotives running on the Manchester, Sheffield and Lincolnshire Railway, now part of the L. and N. E. Ry., were decorated with branches of oak on the 29th of May. (*Curious Church Customs*, William Andrews, editor, Hull, 1895, p. 34.)

[*Staffordshire*] I travelled by rail through the Staffordshire Black Country on 29th May, 1883, and noticed that all the engines and many of the sheds and signal-boxes were furnished with boughs of oak. (*Shropshire Folk-Lore*, Miss Charlotte Sophia Burne, 1883, p. 365.)

CAVALIER AND ROUNDHEAD PROCESSIONS AND RIVALRIES

These customary events of the 29th of May belong mainly to Devonshire. In their more elaborately staged displays they included an oaken bower adapted to seat and shield a young impersonator of Charles II from attacks by a man impersonating the Protector. Rough play was common.

[*Devonshire*] In the year 1810, at Tiverton, and for many generations previously, the 29th was as complete a holiday as could have been seen since the year 1660. At early dawn, the whole town was awakened by the furious clanging of church bells and soon the townspeople sallied forth to obtain large branches of oak. At about 10 a.m. a procession was formed in which an important character was called King Charles, impersonated by a little boy, about 3 years old, dressed in white, decorated with ribbons and flowers, and with a crown on his head. He sat in a compact bower, made by interlacing oak branches; open in front, it was carried by two men without coats, their shirt sleeves and hats being decorated with ribbons. On each side walked the boy-king's bodyguards, dressed like the carriers and armed with cudgels for repelling the savage charges of the impersonator of the Protector. When the procession halted before a house, the bower was set down and the guards, in broad Devonshire, struck up a song known by every schoolboy:

" It was in the year of forty an wan,
When the meadows an vealds war all in their bloom."

The impersonator of Cromwell joined up about 11 a.m.: he was the biggest ruffian that Tiverton could produce; his face was covered with a mixture of oil and lamp-black, and round his waist was tied a bag containing a similar mixture, with which he treated the face of anyone who was caught by him and refused to pay the ransom demanded from him. Influenced by the jeers of the crowd and the nature of his rôle, he was liable to lose his temper and, consequently, a long, stout rope was tied round his waist, the free end being held by his " Cabinet Council," half a dozen ruffians something like himself. The Rev. Caleb Colton of Tiverton was once caught by the " Protector," suffered hideously from his grip, and escaped from a dive into the grease bag by the prompt payment of a guinea.—From an account of one who came, saw, and recorded his impressions long after to readers of the *Leisure Hour* in 1853. (*Early Associations of Archbishop Temple*, F. J. Snell, 1904, pp. 206-8.) This custom, apparently discontinued before the middle of last century, has been said (*Brand*, i, 1848, p. 276) to be as old as 1660.

I remember seeing in Devonport on Oak-apple day, some thirty years ago, the procession of " King Charles II in the oak," *i.e.* a boy, with tinsel crown, sitting amid evergreens, in a cart preceded by a drum and fife band.—W. S. L. S. (*Western Antiquary*, vol. 1, Plymouth, 1882, p. 57.)

At Tavistock, in the afternoon of the 29th of May, there used to be a mock battle, Cavaliers *v.* Roundheads, the former drenching their opponents, who attempted to tear down the oak decorations from the windows and doors.—Jan. 8th, 1833. (*The Borders of the Tamar and the Tavy*, Anna Eliza Stothard, afterwards Bray, vol. 2, 1879, p. 121.)

[*Staffordshire*] In Staffordshire, on the 29th of May, schoolboys with oak in their hats were opposed by an equal number of schoolboys without oak. According to custom, the proceedings were supervised by the master and others and were arranged so that the wearers of the oak were victorious. (*Midland Weekly News*, 13th May, 1893.)

CHURCH-BELL RINGING

[*Warwickshire, etc.*] On the 29th of May, 1660, the church bells rang merrily and a new bell-ringing custom was initiated. This new custom enjoyed a marked popularity. It seems now to have been discontinued, but at Ansley, Hampton and Middleton in Warwickshire, Swineshead in Lincolnshire, Great Missenden in Buckinghamshire and Newport in Essex, the custom was long maintained.

GARLAND CUSTOMS

After occupying a prominent position amongst the means for celebrating May day, the garland was introduced also into the series of proceedings devised for celebrating the 29th of May. It might be expected that there would be a conspicuous display of oak among the flowers of the garland for the 29th, but, except occasionally, oak does not seem to have been used in this way. In the case of the children's garland custom, *e.g.* in parts of western and southern Worcestershire, their May-day garland simply became their garland for the 29th of May. At Tavistock and many

266   *Calendar Customs*

other places, birds' egg festoons were introduced among the flowers. Finally, the remarkable garland custom of Castleton, Derbyshire, presents features having little relation to other garland customs but citable in support of a view that many customs of the 29th were the results of controversy followed by compromise.

THE CASTLETON GARLAND CUSTOM

The garland is of bell form and large enough to envelope the head and most of the body of a powerfully-built man; it is constructed on a wooden framework which is entirely covered by all kinds of wild flowers and formed with a socket at its top to receive " the queen," a large bunch of tulips and other choice flowers. When complete, the garland weighs about 120 lbs. Those taking an official part in the ceremonies include the bell-ringers, the king or man who, on horseback, carries the garland and wears a red jacket, the queen or lady, a man in female attire who also rides a horse, a troupe of morris dancers and a number of musicians. The starting-place for the proceedings is the inn at which, in due sequence, the garland is made. At 6 p.m., after a preliminary ride round by the king and queen, in fancy dress, the ringers put the garland over the king's head and the procession starts from the inn, in the following order: the musicians; the king; the morris dancers; and the queen: there are also the leaders of the king and queen's horses. During its progress round the town, the procession stops at all the public-houses and the morris dancers entertain the spectators. Finally, the king rides with the leader of his horse to the south side of the church tower, church officials remove the " queen " from its socket and, by means of a strong rope in the hands of not less than six men on the top of the tower, the garland is raised and secured to the nearest pinnacle. Branches of oak are placed on the three remaining pinnacles. (*Folk-Lore*, vol. 12, 1901, pp. 408-9; *Old Church Lore*, William Andrews, editor, Hull, 1891, p. 180.)

At Castleton, we have the garland ceremony of the May King on 29th May—an ancient rite which seems to have survived in

Oak-apple Day

no other part of Great Britain. (*Memorials of Old Derbyshire*, Rev. J. Charles Cox, editor, 1907, p. 347.)

After obtaining first-hand information during a visit to Castleton in the summer of 1909, Miss C. S. Burne concluded that the custom was due to the efforts of the Rev. Samuel Cryer, Vicar of Castleton from 1644 to 1697, who worked harmoniously with his parishioners, the result being that a floral crown was hoisted to the tower on the new authorized holiday. (*Folk-Lore*, vol. 21, 1910, pp. 20-6.)

TAVISTOCK GARLAND CUSTOM

[*Devonshire*] At Tavistock, boys call the 29th of May " Garland day " and, in parties, carry their garlands about the town to obtain donations. The boys are artistically dressed, and some oak leaves are included in their decorations. Before the day arrives, the boys go about halfing, *i.e.* collecting eggs of all kinds, except those of the redbreast, for the garland. The garland has two crossed hoops entwined with flowers and in the middle are the eggs, but any garland found with a redbreast's egg is at once destroyed.—8th January, 1833. (*The Borders of the Tamar and the Tavy*, Anna Eliza Stothard, afterwards Bray, vol. 2, 1879, p. 122.)

HEREFORDSHIRE GARLAND CUSTOM

[*Herefordshire*] In many parts of the county, early in the morning of the 29th of May, ropes were stretched across the village streets and garlands of all the flowers in bloom at the time, and also large boughs of oaks and numerous gaily-coloured ribbons, were suspended from the ropes. (*The Folk-Lore of Herefordshire*, Ella Mary Leather, Hereford, 1912, p. 102.)

GAINSBOROUGH GARLAND CUSTOM

[*Lincolnshire*] For some days before Royal Oak day, the boys collect as many birds' eggs as possible and, in the morning of the 29th of May, obtain a supply of oak and a large quantity of flowers, with which they make a crown-shaped garland having gilded oak apples and festoons of birds' eggs. This garland is suspended across the street and every youngster enjoys himself for the rest of the day by blowing a cow's horn or a tin horn.—T. Dyson. (*N. and Q.*, i, 5, 1852, p. 307.)

UPTON-ON-SEVERN GARLAND CUSTOM

[*Worcestershire*] At Upton-on-Severn, Oak-apple day is anxiously anticipated by old and young. Early in the morning, ropes are stretched across the street, upon which are hung garlands composed of all the flowers in bloom. The garlands are also adorned with coloured ribbons and handkerchiefs, and all the teaspoons which can be collected are hung in the middle. Maypoles, though less common, are used as well as large boughs of oak, and many gilded oak apples are worn in button-holes. (*The Illustrated London News*, 30th May, 1857.)

MAY DOLLS

[*Devonshire*] At Starcross and other villages in the Exmouth district, children celebrate the 29th of May, annually, by carrying about what they call a " May baby," *i.e.* a doll, neatly dressed, adorned by flowers, and laid in a box covered by a cloth. (*N. and Q.*, ii, 2, 1856, p. 405.)

MAYPOLES

In this section on Oak-apple day, nothing has been said about the maypole, but in a number of counties, such as, for example, Herefordshire, Leicestershire, Shropshire and Worcestershire, maypole ceremonies were kept up on this day.

[*Herefordshire*] At Kingsland, Bosbury, and Bromyard, the folk speak of the 29th of May as a more important festival than May day itself. " The 29th was our real May day in Bromyard," said one. " You'd see maypoles all the way down Sheep Street decorated with oak boughs and flowers, and people dancing round them, all wearing oak leaves." (*The Folk-Lore of Herefordshire*, Ella Mary Leather, Hereford, 1912, p. 102.)

[*Shropshire*] At Ashford Carbonel, Shropshire, dancing round the maypole and other May games are kept up on " The Maypole Piece " on the 29th of May. The maypole, decorated with garlands, is erected on the " tump " or hillock which is a feature of the field. Generally a few farmers and others arrange for a barrel or two of cider to be installed on the Green, and the merry proceedings terminate near midnight. (*Bye-Gones relating to Wales and the Border Counties*, Oswestry and Wrexham, 1905-6, pp. 100-1.) As a result of litigation the Ludlow County Court decided that the custom was valid and this decision was upheld by the Court of Exchequer in 1875.

[*Worcestershire*] At Clent, Hartleybury, Malvern, Offenham, Upton-on-Severn and Worcester, the 29th of May was more popular than May day and, at Clent, Offenham and Upton-on-Severn especially, dancing round the maypole was popular until about the year 1870.

At Offenham, the period of rustic festivity seems to have been transferred from May day to the 29th of May but, instead of the maypole being decked with fresh flowers and boughs, the custom is to hang it with ribbons and crowns of artificial flowers. On the night previous to my visit, made on the 30th of May [1851, apparently], the villagers had danced round the maypole and then had tea in a neighbouring barn, where they had a merry time till a late hour. (*The Rambler in Worcestershire*, John Noake, 2 vols., 1851-4, vol. 2, p. 88.)

On May-pole day, the 29th of May, the children, assisted by their parents, decorate a pole with may-blossom and with flowers liberally contributed by all the neighbours possessing flower gardens. The May-pole is carried from house to house by two or three strong lads and, at intervals, is set up and held in an upright position by the lads, while the children join hands and dance round it, singing :

> " All around the May-pole we will trot,
> See what a May-pole we have got ;
> Garlands above and garlands below,
> See what a pretty May-pole we can show."

(*A Glossary of Words and Phrases used in South-East Worcestershire*, Jesse Salisbury, 1893, p. 65.) This custom was celebrated annually in 1927-32 at Evesham and neighbouring villages.

SHICK-SHACK DAY

The 29th of May was often called Shick-shack day in Berkshire, Devonshire and some other southern counties. In Gloucestershire and Oxfordshire, shick-shack was a name for an oak branch or twig for wear on the 29th. Anyone found without oak on the 29th was called a shig-shag or a shuck-shack in Hampshire, a shit-shag in Wiltshire and a jit-jack in Somerset, all variants of shick-shack. Shig-shag was commonly a term of abuse; in Hampshire, a person who refused a donation for small presents of oak on the 29th was abused by means of the lines:

" Shig-shag, penny a rag,
Bang his head in Cromwell's bag,
All up in a bundle."

I have not found the term "shick-shack" in any dictionary consulted. Shack occurs in the term " common of shack "=a right of pasture over certain arable lands during the winter half of the year.

CHIMNEY-SWEEP'S CUSTOM

[*Devonshire*] The chimney-sweeps of Plymouth used to go about dressed up and dance about a large coop covered with evergreens, a man being inside. They used to carry their brushes and other implements and rattle them to the accompaniment of a band which went with them.—S. V. Bird. (*Western Antiquary*, vol. I, Plymouth, 1882, p. 71.)

DURHAM CATHEDRAL TOWER CUSTOM

[*Durham*] Immediately after evensong on the 29th of May, the lay clerks and choristers of Durham Cathedral still ascend the central tower and sing three anthems on the south, east and north sides of the tower, in due order. The western side is excepted, it is said, because a chorister fell from that side and received fatal injuries. A custom of singing from the top of the tower was initiated, it is said, when the monks sang the *Te Deum* after the battle of Neville's Cross, October 1346; that such custom fell into disuse but was revived to commemorate the Restoration.—J. T. F., Doncaster. (*N. and Q.*, x, 8, Aug. 3rd, 1907, p. 96.)

May

POPULAR SAYINGS AND BELIEFS

" Marriages in May are unlucky."

This belief has been recorded definitely for Cheshire, Derbyshire, Devonshire, Herefordshire, Lancashire, Lincolnshire, Norfolk, Northumberland, Staffordshire, Suffolk, Yorkshire. In Worcestershire, Easter is the favourite time for marriages and Whitsuntide is next in order.

[*Yorkshire*] It so happened that yesterday I had both a Colonial Bishop and a Home Archdeacon taking part in the services of my church and visiting at my house. By a singular coincidence, both had been solicited by friends to perform the marriage ceremony not later than to-morrow because in neither case would the bride-elect submit to be married in the month of May. —Alfred Gatty, Ecclesfield, 29th April, 1850. (*N. and Q.*, i, 1, 1850, pp. 467-8.)

" Kittens born in May are unlucky."

The meaning of this is emphasized by the following county records :

[*Cheshire, etc.*] " May kittens should all be drowned."—Cheshire.

" Our old cat chatted yesterday and we are going to drown them all."—Devonshire.

" We always kill May kittens."—Hampshire.

" It is the common practice to drown May kittens."—Northumberland.

Even the milder forms of the belief imputed to May kittens and cats a habit of carrying vermin into the house and of lying over babies to suffocate them or " suck their breath."

[*Devonshire*]

" If you buy [or use] new brushes in May,
You sweep one of the family away."

From inquiries I have made, I find that, in consequence of this belief, very few brushes are sold by tradesmen here [Great Torrington in the month of May]. Even when they are so sold, the buyers, although paying for them at the time, do not take the brushes away till May is past.—G. M. Doe. (*Trans. Devon. Assoc.*, vol. 37, 1905, p. 115.)

[*Suffolk*]
> "Sweep with a broom that is cut in May,
> And you will sweep the head of the house away."

(*County F.-L.*, vol. 1 (2), *Suffolk*, The Lady Eveline Camilla Gurdon, 1893, p. 129.) This saying is also well-known in Sussex.

"To sleep in a room with hawthorn bloom in it, during the month of May, will be followed by some great misfortune." (*County F.-L.*, vol. 1 (2), *Suffolk*, The Lady Eveline Camilla Gurdon, 1893, p. 129.)

A native of the neighbourhood of Oswestry said:
> "Dōn put off your winter clothes
> Till you see the June rose."

It was the first time I had heard this variant of the old saying: "Cast not a clout till May be out." (*Bye-Gones relating to Wales and the Border Counties*, Oswestry and Wrexham, 1893-4, p. 322.)

> "A wet and windy May
> Fills the barns with corn and hay."

—Cheshire and Staffordshire.

"A May wet was never kind yet."—Worcestershire.

"In the month of May, the cuckoo sings all day."

> "May come early or May come late
> Is sure to make the old cow quake."

"Shear your sheep in May and shear them all away."

[*Hertfordshire*] Our country people say:
> "A swarm of bees in May
> Is worth a cow and her calf and a load of hay,"

this being a local [Great Gaddesden] variation of the well-known proverb:
> "A swarm of bees in May is worth a load of hay,
> But a swarm in July is not worth a fly."

(*The Modern Husbandman*, William Ellis, vol. 3, part 1, 1750, p. 167, in the part of the vol. headed *Agriculture Improved*.)